D0579521

The Renaissance

AN ENCYCLOPEDIA FOR STUDENTS

The Renaissance

An Encyclopedia for Students

Paul F. Grendler, Editor in Chief

PUBLISHED IN ASSOCIATION WITH THE RENAISSANCE SOCIETY OF AMERICA

Volume 1

ACADEMIES—CROMWELL

CHARLES SCRIBNER'S SONS®

THOMSON

New York • Detroit • San Diego • San Francisco • Cleveland • New Haven, Conn. • Waterville, Maine • London • Munich

The Renaissance An Encyclopedia for Students

Paul F. Grendler, Editor in Chief

Developed for Charles Scribner's Sons by Visual Education Corporation, Princeton, N.J.

For Scribners

Publisher:
Frank Menchaca

Editors:
John Fitzpatrick, Sharon Malinowski

Cover and Interior Design:
Jennifer Wahi

Imaging and Multimedia:
Lezlie Light, Robyn Young, Mary Grimes, Dave Oblender, Leitha Etheridge-Sims, Dan Newell, Christine O'Bryan

Composition:
Evi Seoud

Manufacturing:
Rhonda Williams

For Visual Education Corporation

Project Directors:
Darryl Kestler, Amy Livingston

Writers:
John Haley, Mark Mussari, Charles Roebuck, Rebecca Stefoff

Editors:
Tobey Cloyd, Cindy George, John Kennedy

Associate Editor:
Sarah Miller

Copyediting Supervisor:
Helen Castro

Electronic Preparation:
Fiona Shapiro

For more information, contact
Charles Scribner's Sons
300 Park Avenue South
New York, NY 10010
Or visit our Internet site at
http://www.gale.com/scribners

LIBRARY OF CONGRESS CATALOG-IN-PUBLICATION DATA

The Renaissance : an encyclopedia for students / Paul F. Grendler.
p. cm
Summary: An encyclopedia of the Renaissance with articles on various aspects of social, cultural, and political history such as literature, government, warfare, and technology, plus maps, charts, definitions, and chronology.
Includes bibliographical references and index.
ISBN 0-684-31281-6 (set hardcover : alk. paper) — ISBN 0-684-31282-4 (v. 1) — ISBN 0-684-31283-2 (v. 2) — ISBN 0-684-31285-9 (v. 3) — ISBN 0-684-31284-0 (v. 4) — ISBN 0-684-31424-X (e-book)
1. Renaissance—Encyclopedias, Juvenile. [1. Renaissance—Encyclopedias.] I. Grendler, Paul F. II. Encyclopedia of the Renaissance. III. Title.

CB361.R25 2003
940.2'1'03—dc22

This title is also available as an e-book
ISBN 0-684-31424-X (set)

Contact your Gale sale representative for ordering information

Printed in the United States of America
10 9 8 7 6 5 4 3 2 1

Table of Contents

Maps

Genealogical Charts

Color Plates

Volume 1

Volume 2

Volume 3

Volume 4

Preface

In the middle of the fourteenth century, the Italian scholar and poet Petrarch looked at his world with fresh and critical eyes and had new ideas. In place of medieval values and methods of learning, he looked back to the literature and philosophy of the ancient world for inspiration and advice on how to live. By the time of his death in 1374, other Europeans had begun to share his vision. By about 1400 a group of Italians, scholars as well as men and women from many walks of life, had created a new intellectual movement called humanism that combined ethics, rhetoric, and education. Their ideas began to transform Italian and European civilization.

The intellectual, artistic, political, and social initiatives that began in Italy about 1350 spread to the rest of Europe and to the wider world over the next three centuries. The men and women of those times believed that they were giving birth to a new age. They called it a Renaissance because they saw their era as a rebirth of the best of the ancient world and as a departure from the world of the Middle Ages. By the late fifteenth century, their actions, concerns, writings, and artistry had spread to the rest of Europe. In the sixteenth century few doubted that a new age had dawned. The changes affected every area of life and knowledge, from art to zoology, from commerce to science. The Renaissance was one of the most innovative periods in the history of mankind. It transformed Europe and then the rest of the world, even into the twenty-first century.

The influence of the Renaissance is still remarkably strong. Everyone recognizes the paintings of Leonardo da Vinci and Michelangelo. Students at many levels read the plays of Shakespeare, which have probably been performed more frequently than those of any other playwright in history. His *Romeo and Juliet* has been retold so many times in prose and poetry, screen and music, that everyone knows the tragic story. At the other extreme, the word "Machiavellian still refers to the use of deceit to reach political goals and the notion that the end justifies the means, even though Niccolò Machiavelli set down these ideas nearly five hundred years ago. In addition, the writers and artists of the Renaissance have inspired authors, artists, and musicians in every century."

In 1999 Charles Scribner's Sons, in collaboration with the Renaissance Society of America, produced the six-volume *Encyclopedia of the Renaissance* (ER), with Paul F. Grendler as editor in chief. It was the first comprehensive encyclopedia in any language devoted to the Renaissance. Librarians and scholars hailed it as the essential reference work on this period. It received the Dartmouth Medal of the American Library Association, the Roland H. Bainton Reference Prize of the Society for Sixteenth Century Studies, and many other honors.

Now Charles Scribner's Sons presents *The Renaissance: An Encyclopedia for Students,* a condensed version of ER written especially for students. Like ER, it covers people and events beginning in Italy about 1350, then broadens geographically to embrace the rest of Europe in the middle to late fifteenth century. The coverage ends around 1620, when Europe once again moved into a new age with different values and events. Between these dates the encyclopedia discusses important political events, concepts, ideas, works of art and literature, and scientific achievements across Europe. It incorporates the most recent scholarship on these subjects. In particular, it addresses the three most important developments in the study of the Renaissance in the second half of the twentieth century: the numerous studies of humanism throughout Europe, the increased concentration on the social history of the Renaissance, and the study of the many roles of women. *The Renaissance: An Encyclopedia for Students* provides comprehensive discussions of all aspects of the European Renaissance. Coverage of the rest of the world is limited to how Europeans influenced other continents, and discussion of the Protestant and Catholic Reformations is limited to the way they affected the Renaissance and vice versa.

The work contains 461 entries organized alphabetically. These discuss the important themes, events, ideas, and individuals of the Renaissance on a level

suitable for a young audience. Each page consists of a major column containing the article text plus a minor column. The latter contains many special features designed for students: entry titles, brief definitions of unfamiliar terms, small illustrations, lists of rulers, and sidebars that expand the main text. Cross-references appear at the end of articles. The encyclopedia also contains 60 color plates, which are organized into four visual essays that illustrate various aspects of Renaissance society: "Art and Architecture," "Daily Life," "The Renaissance City, and" New Frontiers."

More than 160 black-and-white illustrations of people, places, artifacts, and events enhance the text. The work also contains 18 maps and 5 genealogical charts. A chronology of the most important events of the Renaissance can be found at the beginning of each volume.

Many talented people made this work possible. Frank Menchaca, publisher of Charles Scribner's Sons, launched *The Renaissance: An Encyclopedia for Students.* John Fitzpatrick oversaw the project from the vantage point of Scribner's. The staff at Visual Education Corporation did the essential work of organizing the table of contents, rewriting the articles, and editing the volumes. Darryl Kestler and Amy Livingston managed the project, assisted in the editorial work by Tobey Cloyd, Cindy George, and Sarah Miller. The work is the product of all these able and dedicated people.

It is our hope that *The Renaissance: An Encyclopedia for Students* will encourage students everywhere to appreciate, understand, and learn more about a fascinating part of our past.

Paul F. Grendler

Chapel Hill, N.C.

Timeline of the Renaissance

Date	*Historical Events*	*People Events*
		Giotto di Bondone *(1267/75–1337)*
1337	*Hundred Years' War between France and England (to 1453)*	
		Petrarch *(1304–1374)*
1348	*Black Death devastates population of Europe (to 1350)*	
		Giovanni Boccaccio *(1313–1375)*
	Giovanni Boccaccio writes the Decameron *(to 1351)*	
		Christine de Pizan *(1364–ca. 1430)*
1378	*Great Western Schism within Roman Catholic Church (to 1417)*	
		Leonardo Bruni *(ca. 1370–1444)*
		Filippo Brunelleschi *(1377–1446)*
1397	*Manuel Chrysoloras begins teaching Greek in Florence*	
		Donatello *(ca. 1386–1466)*
1401	*City of Florence hires Lorenzo Ghiberti to design bronze doors for Baptistery*	
		Cosimo de' Medici *(1389–1464)*
		Jan van Eyck *(before 1395–1441)*
1408	*Donatello sculpts* David	
		Rogier van der Weyden *(ca. 1399–1464)*
		Fra Angelico *(ca. 1400–1455)*
1420	*Filippo Brunelleschi constructs dome for Cathedral of Santa Maria del Fiore in Florence (to 1436)*	
		Lorenzo Valla *(1407–1457)*

1436 *Leon Battista Alberti publishes* On Painting

Piero della Francesca *(ca. 1412–1492)*

1450 *Pope Nicholas V founds Vatican Library*

Andrea Mantegna *(ca. 1430–1506)*

1453 *Turkish invaders capture Constantinople*

Marsilio Ficino *(1433–1499)*

ca. 1454 *Johann Gutenberg prints Bible*

Sandro Botticelli *(ca. 1444–1510)*

1464 *First printing press in Italy*

1469 *Marriage of Ferdinand of Aragon to Isabella of Castile unites two Spanish kingdoms*

Donato Bramante *(ca. 1444–1514)*

1476 *First printing press in England*

1478 *Inquisition established in Spain*

Pope Julius II *(ca. 1445 1513)*

Sandro Botticelli paints Primavera

1484 *Marsilio Ficino publishes translation of Plato's complete works*

1485 *Henry VII founds Tudor Dynasty in England*

Lorenzo de' Medici *(1449–1492)*

1486 *Giovanni Pico della Mirandola publishes* Conclusions, *including the introduction now known as* Oration on the Dignity of Man

1487 *Bartolomeu Dias sails around southern tip of Africa*

Isabella of Castile *(1451–1504)*

Girolamo Savonarola *(1452–1498)*

1492 *Spanish expel Moors from Granada, completing unification of Spain*

Leonardo da Vinci *(1452–1519)*

Christopher Columbus sails to Americas

Holy Roman Emperor Maximilian I *(1459–1519)*

1494 *Charles VIII of France invades Italy, beginning Wars of Italy*

***Hans Holbein the Elder** (ca. 1460–1534)*

Uprising in Florence drives out Medici family

***Giovanni Pico della Mirandola** (1463–1494)*

Treaty of Tordesillas divides New World territories between Spain and Portugal

***Desiderius Erasmus** (ca. 1466–1536)*

Aldine Press established in Venice

***Niccolò Machiavelli** (1469–1527)*

1497 *Vasco da Gama sails to India (to 1499)*

***Albrecht Dürer** (1471–1528)*

1500 *Álvares Cabral claims Portugal for Brazil*

1502 *Spain establishes first European colony in the Americas on island of Hispaniola*

***Thomas Wolsey** (ca. 1472–1530)*

1503 *Spanish take control of Naples*

***Ludovico Ariosto** (1474–1533)*

1504 *Michelangelo Buonarroti sculpts David*

1506 *Leonardo da Vinci paints* Mona Lisa

1508 *Michelangelo Buonarroti paints ceiling of Sistine Chapel in Rome (to 1512)*

1511 *Desiderius Erasmus publishes* Praise of Folly

1512 *Council of Lateran V (to 1517)*

***Pope Leo X** (1475–1521)*

1514 *Raphael paints* Sistine Madonna

***Michelangelo Buonarroti** (1475–1564)*

Albrecht Dürer engraves St. Jerome in His Study

1517 *Thomas More publishes Utopia*

1517 *Martin Luther attacks the Roman Catholic Church in his 95 Theses*

***Baldassare Castiglione** (1478–1529)*

1518 *Titian paints* Assumption of the Virgin

Thomas More *(ca. 1478–1535)*

1519 *Charles V elected Holy Roman Emperor, making him ruler of much of central Europe in addition to Spain*

Raphael *(1483–1520)*

1521 *Spanish forces conquer Mexico*

1522 *Ships under the command of Ferdinand Magellan complete first voyage around the world*

Martin Luther *(1483–1546)*

Thomas Cromwell *(ca. 1485–1540)*

1524 *Peasants' War in Germany (to 1526)*

Heinrich Agrippa of Nettesheim *(1486–1535)*

1525 *Forces from Holy Roman Empire take French king Francis I prisoner at Battle of Pavia*

1527 *Imperial troops capture and loot Rome and take Pope Clement VII prisoner*

Titian *(ca. 1488–1576)*

1528 *Baldassare Castiglione publishes* The Book of the Courtier

Francis I of France begins expansion and renovation of château of Fontainebleau

1529 *Turkish forces gain control of Hungary*

Correggio *(1489–1534)*

1531 *Franáois Rabelais publishes Pantagruel*

Henry VIII of England *(1491–1547)*

1532 *Niccolò Machiavelli publishes* The Prince

Francis I of France *(1494–1547)*

Ludovico Ariosto publishes Orlando Furioso

1533 *England breaks away from Roman Catholic Church*

François Rabelais *(ca. 1494–1553)*

1540 *Pope Paul III approves Society of Jesus*

Philipp Melanchthon *(1497–1560)*

1542 *Francis Xavier performs missionary work in India and Japan (to 1552)*

***Holy Roman Emperor Charles V** (1500–1558)*

***Benvenuto Cellini** (1500–1571)*

***Parmigianino** (1503–1540)*

1543 *Nicolaus Copernicus publishes heliocentric theory of the universe*

***Andrea Palladio** (1508–1580)*

Andreas Vesalius publishes On the Structure of the Human Body

***John Calvin** (1509–1564)*

***Andreas Vesalius** (1514–1564)*

***Petrus Ramus** (1515–1572)*

***Mary I of England** (1516–1558)*

1545 *Council of Trent (to 1563)*

***Pierre de Ronsard** (1524–1585)*

1550 *Giorgio Vasari publishes* Lives of the Artists

***Pieter Brueghel the Elder** (ca. 1525–1569)*

***Philip II of Spain** (1527–1598)*

1554 *Mary I of England marries Spanish prince who later becomes King Philip II of Spain*

***Paolo Veronese**(1528–1588)*

1556 *Charles V abdicates, dividing Spain and the Holy Roman Empire*

1559 *Pieter Brueghel the Elder paints* Carnival and Lent

***Michel de Montaigne** (1533–1592)*

Wars of Italy end with Treaty of Cateau-Cambrésis

***Elizabeth I of England** (1533–1603)*

1562 *Wars of Religion in France (to 1598)*

***El Greco** (ca. 1541–1614)*

1563 *Construction of El Escorial palace begins*

***Mary Stuart** (1542–1587)*

1569 *Gerhard Mercator publishes new world map*

***Torquato Tasso** (1544–1595)*

1570 *Andrea Palladio publishes* Four Books on Architecture

1571 *Christian forces defeat Turkish fleet at Battle of Lepanto*

***Tycho Brahe** (1546–1601)*

1572 *St. Bartholomew's Day massacre in France*

***Miguel de Cevantes Saavedra** (1547–1616)*

1579 *Netherlands splits into Spanish Netherlands and Dutch Republic*

1580 *Sir Francis Drake completes voyage around world*

***Giordano Bruno** (1548–1600)*

Union of Spain and Portugal under Philip II

***Edmund Spenser** (ca. 1552–1599)*

Michel de Montaigne's Essays *published*

1581 *Torquato Tasso publishes* Jerusalem Delivered

1582 *Catholic nations adopt Gregorian calendar*

***Henry IV of France** (1553–1610)*

1583 *Matteo Ricci becomes first Catholic missionary in China*

***Philip Sidney** (1554–1586)*

1588 *England defeats the Spanish Armada*

***Francis Bacon** (1561–1626)*

1590 *Edmund Spenser publishes* The Faerie Queene

***Christopher Marlowe** (1564–1593)*

1592 *First performance of Christopher Marlowe's The Jew of Malta*

***William Shakespeare** (1564–1616)*

1595 *William Shakespeare writes* A Midsummer Night's Dream

1598 *Edict of Nantes allows practice of Protestant faith in France*

***Galileo Galilei** (1564–1642)*

Daphne, *the first known opera, performed in Florence*

***James I of England** (1566–1625)*

1599 *Globe Theater opens in London*

***Tommaso Campanella** (1568–1639)*

1600 *William Shakespeare writes* Hamlet

***Michelangelo Merisi da Caravaggio** (1571–1610)*

1608 *Zacharias Jansen invents telescope*

***Johannes Kepler** (1571–1630)*

1609 *Twelve Years' Truce in Netherlands (to 1621)*

1611 *Peter Paul Rubens paints* Descent from the Cross

***Ben Jonson** (1572–1637)*

1618 *Thirty Years' War within Holy Roman Empire (ended with Peace of Westphalia in 1648)*

***Peter Paul Rubens** (1577–1640)*

1628 *William Harvey publishes theory on circulation of blood*

1633 *Roman Catholic Church condemns Galileo for publishing defense of the Copernican system*

***Charles I of Britain** (1600–1649)*

1642 *English Civil War (to 1648)*

***John Milton** (1608–1674)*

1667 *John Milton publishes* Paradise Lost

Absolutism

See *Government, Forms of.*

Academies

* **humanist** Renaissance expert in the humanities (the languages, literature, history, and speech and writing techniques of ancient Greece and Rome)

* **patron** supporter or financial sponsor of an artist or writer

In the 1400s, humanists* in Italy formed casual gatherings to discuss scholarly topics. They saw these groups, which they called academies, as a way to revivethe ideas and values of ancient cultures. The most famous academy was the Platonic Academy, established in FLORENCE in the 1460s. The philosopher Marsilio FICINO was its leader, and Cosimo de' MEDICI acted as its patron*. This academy helped spread ancient Greek ideas, particularly those of the philosopher PLATO. Many members of the Platonic Academy were aristocrats. Their association with the academy helped make the pursuit of knowledge an upper-class occupation.

Most early academies were very informal. Many never even gave themselves an official name. In the 1540s academies became more visible and widespread. By 1600, 377 academies existed in Italy, and another 870 appeared during the next century. Most of these academies were in major cities. Although most towns had at least one or two academies, a large city might have dozens. Many of them arose in cities with universities (such as Bologna) or with royal or noble courts (such as Milan). Rome had more academies than any other city, with over 130.

Most Italian academies promoted all kinds of learning, but a few focused on particular arts or sciences. Italian academies tended to be local groups, attracting scholars and artists from the surrounding area. Many of them had humorous names, such as "the Passionate," "the Confused," or "the Sleepy." A city's level of academy activity rose and fell with its cultural and political importance. This fact helps explain why most Italian academies were short-lived. Some closed within a year or two of their founding. Many that lasted longer were inactive for much of their life span.

During the 1600s, scholars founded academies in several major cities outside of Italy. The French crown established the Académie Française in Paris in 1634. Its goal was to promote French language and literature. The Royal Society of London, founded in 1662, focused on scientific knowledge. These academies were national rather than local organizations. As a result, they lasted longer than their Italian models. (*See also* **Art, Education and Training.**)

Accounting

Accounting and bookkeeping practices introduced during the Renaissance made it easier for merchants to keep track of their profits and losses. The most significant of these new techniques was double-entry bookkeeping.

The Double-Entry System. During the Middle Ages, merchants and landowners used single-entry bookkeeping to track the money they spent and received. With this system, also called "charge and discharge,"

the merchant recorded each day's receipts and expenses in an account book. The book showed how much money the merchant took in or paid out on each individual transaction. However, it did not enable tradespeople to see at a glance which customers owed them money or which accounts were most profitable over time.

Double-entry bookkeeping involved recording each transaction twice, often in two separate columns in the account book. In the left-hand column, the merchant listed the amount of money spent for goods, along with other information such as the date of the sale. When the merchant received payment for a sale, this information went in the right-hand column. This double-entry system allowed merchants to keep a running total of profits and losses. When the total in the right column was greater than that in the left column, it showed that the merchant had made money on a transaction.

Merchants often kept separate books for each account. Someone who dealt in grain, cloth, and sugar might have an account book for each product. Each transaction noted in the account books was later transferred to the ledger, a book that included transactions for all accounts. The totals for both columns in the ledger were supposed to be the same. The merchant would list any money made or lost on a sale in another category, "profit and loss," to make the books balance.

Spread of Double-Entry Bookkeeping. Italian merchants were the first to adopt double-entry bookkeeping, and by the 1400s the system had spread throughout Italy. It took some time for merchants in other countries to begin using the double-entry system. Records from France, Holland, and Germany indicate that the single-entry system was still common in the mid-1400s. Only after 1500 did double-entry bookkeeping become widespread throughout Europe.

Some scholars believe that double-entry bookkeeping was a major factor in Europe's move from feudalism* to capitalism* because it enabled merchants to calculate profits and losses. Others disagree, saying that merchants could have done this using single entry. A third view is that the two developments influenced each other. Expanding trade produced the need for more efficient bookkeeping systems. At the same time, the double-entry system encouraged the growth of commerce by making it easier to keep track of increased trade activity. (*See also* **Economy and Trade; Money and Banking.**)

* **feudalism** economic and political system in which individuals gave services to a lord in return for protection and use of the land

* **capitalism** economic system in which individuals own property and businesses

Europeans of the Renaissance had some knowledge of northern Africa, part of the Islamic world. Spain had been closely involved with the region since the A.D. 700s. However, the relationship between the Spanish and the North Africans included considerable warfare, and during the Renaissance the Spanish attempted to cut all ties. By contrast, before the 1300s Europeans knew little of sub-Saharan Africa (the region south of the Sahara desert). Contact with this area really began in the Renaissance when Europeans explored the coastal areas of Africa.

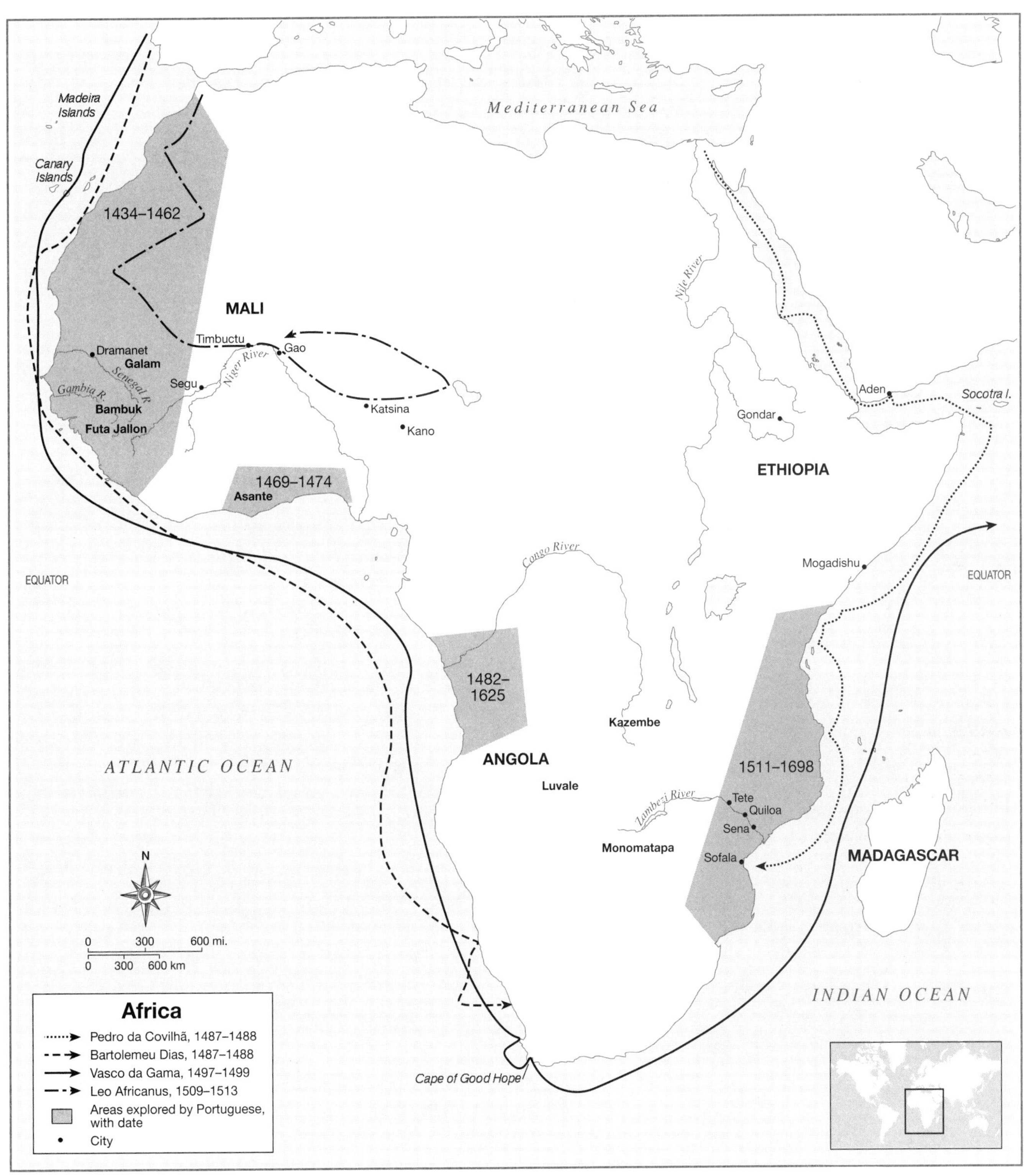

* **Iberian Peninsula** part of western Europe occupied by present-day Spain and Portugal

Northern Africa. During the Middle Ages, Muslim invaders from North Africa had conquered most of the Iberian Peninsula*. Under their rule, people from many different cultures—Islamic, Christian, and Jewish—met and exchanged ideas, and a rich blend of civilizations resulted.

However, the Christian monarchs of Iberian lands struggled to regain control of their lost territory. Between the 700s and the 1400s, they gradually recaptured these lands from the Muslims. The last section of Spain returned to Christian control in 1492. The new rulers forced everyone within their realms to convert to Christianity or leave. The remaining Muslims and Jews were forced out of the region in the 1600s.

These events created a barrier between the Muslim and Christian worlds. After the 1400s, there was little interaction between the Spanish and Portuguese and the peoples of North Africa. As a result, the cultural and technological developments of the European Renaissance did not extend into North Africa. European thinkers were challenging established ideas about politics, religion, and society. The Islamic cultures of northern Africa, however, remained committed to their old ways of thinking.

While Europeans were exploring Asia and the Americas, the rulers of the Muslim world concentrated on expanding their power in the Middle East and Africa. During the 1500s, the OTTOMAN EMPIRE gained control of all of North Africa except Morocco. In 1580 the Ottoman Turks and the Spanish established a truce, agreeing not to attack each other's lands. But the two civilizations had little contact. Even in the early 1600s, when European sailors and merchants arrived in North Africa with the latest ships and weapons, the Ottomans showed little interest in copying the new technologies.

The Renaissance marked the beginning of a dramatic shift in power between Europe and the Islamic world. Europe was expanding in many ways—developing new colonies, trade routes, scientific theories, and cultural viewpoints. For the most part, Muslims did not share in these discoveries because of limited communication with Europeans and because they did not welcome new ideas. Europe came to dominate the globe, and the power of Muslim empires diminished.

West African Kingdoms

Several powerful empires flourished in west Africa during the Renaissance. They established vast trading networks, exchanging goods such as gold and salt between southern and northern Africa. Mali, founded on the remnants of the earlier kingdom of Ghana, included the great city of Timbuktu. By the 1300s Mali extended from the Atlantic coast to the southern reaches of the Sahara desert. In the 1400s the Songhai took over the eastern portion of the kingdom of Mali. They built an empire centered on the middle Niger River. It remained a major power until it was conquered by Morocco in 1591.

Sub-Saharan Africa. Until the 1300s, Europeans knew little about Africa south of the Sahara. When the king of Ethiopia sent messengers to Spain in 1306, the Spanish believed the message had come from "Prester John"—a legendary Christian monarch thought to control distant kingdoms. For many years afterward, most Europeans assumed that Prester John was the ruler of Ethiopia. Christian nations sought alliances with Ethiopia as a way of controlling the Muslim empires in Africa.

Ethiopia remained in contact with Europe. Monks of the Ethiopian Orthodox Church, which had split off from the Roman Catholic Church many centuries earlier, traveled to Italy and the Mediterranean

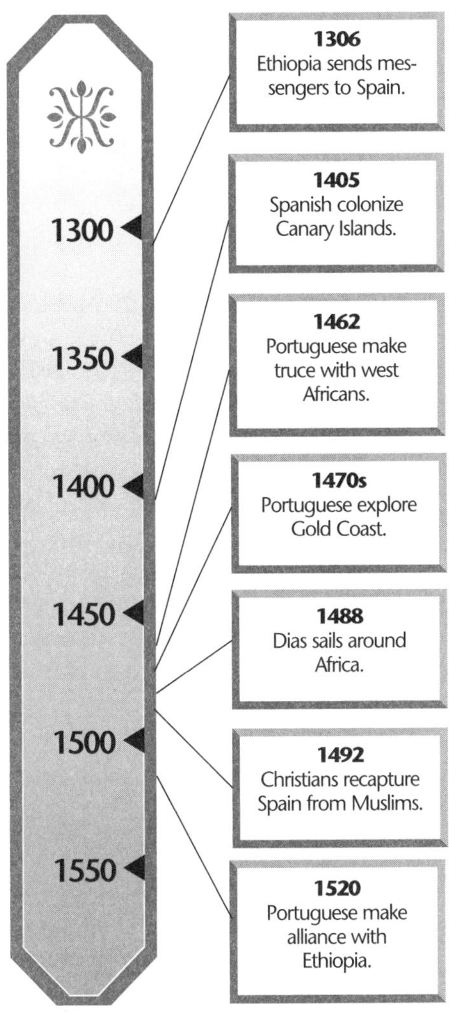

island of Cyprus. In 1414 Ethiopian monks attended the Council of Florence, a meeting to discuss the possibility of reuniting the Ethiopian Orthodox Church and the Roman Catholic Church. Europeans studied the language of Ethiopia, and merchants from Italy and the Catalan region of Spain explored the region. During the Renaissance, European maps of Ethiopia became progressively more accurate.

Meanwhile, European mariners were exploring the islands off Africa's Atlantic shores. In 1312 a sailor from GENOA discovered a sea route to the Canary Islands, just off the northwest coast of Africa. Merchants and raiders from several western European countries visited the Canaries throughout the 1300s. In 1405 the Spanish established a colony there. European sailors also discovered and colonized the islands of the Azores and Madeira to the northwest. These new colonies helped them solve a navigational problem. Ocean currents made sailing to west Africa easy, but returning was difficult. By stopping at Madeira and the Azores on the way home, sailors could avoid the troublesome currents.

Europeans had a special interest in Senegal, a region on Africa's west coast known for gold. By the mid-1400s Portuguese sailors had become regular visitors there. Traveling farther south along the African coast, Portuguese merchants reached present-day Ghana in the late 1400s. They called it the Gold Coast because of its rich gold deposits. The merchants also entered the Kingdom of Benin in what is now Nigeria.

The Portuguese who visited Benin met ambassadors from an unknown land carrying items marked with a cross-shaped symbol. They assumed that these ambassadors came from Prester John's kingdom. In 1482 the Portuguese sent two explorers to seek out Prester John's lands. The first, Diogo Cão, traveled by sea. He found no signs of the mythical Christian kingdom, but he did discover that the African coast stretched southward much farther than Europeans had realized. The second explorer, Pero da Covilhã, traveled by land and eventually reached Ethiopia. In 1488 explorer Bartholomeu Dias became the first European to sail around the southern tip of Africa.

When the Portuguese first visited west Africa, they raided the area for slaves. However, after a series of attacks by African ships, the Portuguese negotiated a truce with the west African nations in 1462. This opened up the area to trade in such valuable goods as gold, pepper, ivory—and slaves, mostly prisoners of African wars. The Portuguese also entertained visitors from many African countries. Several African monarchs considered converting to Christianity, and the king of Kongo actually became a Christian. The Portuguese also established relations with Ethiopia through the explorer Pero da Covilhã, who helped the two kingdoms form an alliance in 1520. (*See also* **Councils; Exploration; Islam; Portugal; Spain.**)

Africanus, Leo

See *Geography and Cartography.*

Agricola, Rudolf

1444–1485
Humanist and author

Rudolf Agricola was an early supporter of humanist* learning in northern Europe. He also made important contributions to the fields of education and RHETORIC*. The son of a church official, Agricola was born near Groningen in the Netherlands. He studied the arts and law at three universities. He then moved to Italy and began to explore the new field of HUMANISM. During his ten years in Italy, Agricola studied Latin, ancient literature, history, and philosophy. He also became a skilled public speaker.

* **humanist** referring to a Renaissance cultural movement promoting the study of the humanities (the languages, literature, and history of ancient Greece and Rome) as a guide to living

* **rhetoric** art of speaking or writing effectively

* **treatise** long, detailed essay

Agricola returned to Germany in 1479. That summer, he completed his most important work, *Three Books on Dialectical Invention.* Although the word *dialectic* in the title refers to a method of reasoning, the work is really a treatise* on rhetoric. Its three parts cover such subjects as how to structure an argument, how to influence an audience, and the importance of constant training in writing. Agricola used many examples from ancient authors to illustrate his principles. This work had enormous influence on both teaching practices and research.

Agricola wrote many other works during his lifetime. These included speeches, Latin translations of ancient Greek texts, and a biography of the poet PETRARCH. Most of his works were not published until the 1500s. However, they had a major impact on humanism in Northern Europe. Agricola's writings were used as textbooks and encouraged the study of ancient learning. Agricola spent the last few years of his life giving lectures in the city of Heidelberg. (*See also* **Education.**)

Agriculture

The Renaissance saw several new developments in the field of agriculture. Farmers and horticulturists* experimented with new crops and growing techniques. Two major changes during this time were improvements in irrigation and the planting of forage crops, which were used as food for livestock. Other new crops entered Europe from distant parts of the world. These changes marked the beginning of an agricultural revolution in which modern techniques replaced more traditional practices.

* **horticulturist** person involved in horticulture, the science of growing flowers, fruits, vegetables, and other plants

Renaissance Approaches to Agriculture. New ideas about farming began to emerge in Europe during the 1300s. Around 1320 the Italian writer Pietro de Crescenzi published his *Book of Estate Cultivation.* He recommended rotating grain crops—that is, growing a different crop each year in the same field—without allowing the field to lie fallow (unused) in between. He also suggested the use of turnips as a forage crop.

Another influential Renaissance text was *Writers on Rural Subjects* (1472). This volume contained agricultural writings by four ancient Roman authors: Cato, Columella, Palladius, and Varro. The book made the ideas of the ancients easily available to Renaissance estate owners. It sparked an interest in reviving classical* knowledge about farming techniques.

* **classical** in the tradition of ancient Greece and Rome

During the 1500s, authors created new texts on agriculture for wealthy farmers. In his *Book on Agriculture* (1513), Spanish horticulturist Gabriel Alonso de Herrera used his own observations to confirm the the-

European agriculture changed a great deal during the Renaissance. New crops and techniques enabled farmers to become more productive at working the land.

ories of ancient writers. He emphasized the importance of water in maintaining soil quality. Another influential author was Italian scientist Camillo Tarello. In the 1560s he recommended rotating crops of wheat and clover.

These authors were at the leading edge of a new scientific approach to farming. Farmers in southern France also took part in this trend. They used their gardens to test wild plants and to collect their seeds for future use. Many of their discoveries were later transferred to northern Europe.

See color plate 5, vol. 2

New Crops. One of the key agricultural advances of the Renaissance was the planting of forage crops. These crops helped farmers maintain livestock during the winter months. Some forage crops, such as alfalfa and clover, also helped restore fertility to the soil. This feature enabled farmers to reduce or eliminate the practice of leaving fields fallow to replenish the soil.

Alfalfa had been cultivated as a forage crop in ancient times, but it fell out of use in Italy during the Middle Ages. However, Arabs in Spain continued to grow it. Alfalfa reappeared in Italy around 1540, after the rediscovery of Columella's writings on this valuable plant. At the same time, newly printed books on botany provided detailed descriptions of wild alfalfa. The wild form of the plant served as a useful source of seed. Over the next 50 years, alfalfa growing spread through northern Italy. Some farmers grew alfalfa along with rice.

The discovery of the AMERICAS in 1492 brought many new food plants to Europe. Scientists studied these plants and identified those suitable for Europe's soil and climate conditions. The first American crop to spread widely throughout Europe was maize, or corn. By 1498 it was abundant in parts of Spain. Maize spread so quickly that some Europeans forgot its origin and called it "Turkish wheat."

Sweet potatoes were another American plant that took hold rapidly, particularly in Spain. Most mentions of potatoes during this period refer to sweet potatoes. Europeans grew some white potatoes in the 1500s because they believed they had useful medicinal purposes. Tobacco was grown for the same reason until around 1600, when it became a com-

Agriculture and Population

Advances in agriculture during the Renaissance rearranged the population of Europe. During the Middle Ages, farmers had to leave large plots of land fallow each year. New methods of cultivation enabled the farmers to use their lands more fully, increasing the food supply. This, in turn, caused the population to expand. Because the new techniques took hold more quickly in northwestern Europe, the population of the continent shifted. In the year 1200, just over 25 percent of the population lived in northern Europe. By 1750, the number was over 40 percent.

mercial crop. Other plants from the Americas became valuable crops during the 1600s.

New Techniques. European farming methods changed gradually throughout the Renaissance. The quality of the soil was a major concern. Early in the period, farmers focused on fertilizing their fields better so that they would not have to leave them fallow. Later farmers developed cross-plowing, a technique of plowing each field twice—once lengthwise and once crosswise—to turn the soil more fully.

Farmers also took a different approach to seeding. In the Middle Ages, farmers had sowen seeds thickly on all types of soil. During the Renaissance, they returned to the ancient principle that it was wasteful to sow thickly on poor soil. They also developed new methods of crop rotation to use their agricultural resources as efficiently as possible. Continuing a trend that had begun in the Middle Ages, farmers began to plant each field three times a year instead of only twice. The third crop was usually oats, which they used to feed their horses. The use of horses for plowing, rather than oxen, was another development that began in the Middle Ages and continued throughout the Renaissance.

One major change during the Renaissance was enclosure. Farmers put fences around their fields to separate them from common pasture or open areas. Enclosure may have helped farmers increase their yields by allowing them to decide which crops to grow in each field. New methods of surveying land produced more accurate boundaries for estates and farms. Landowners abandoned traditional measures, such as how far a team of oxen could plow in a day, and adopted standard units of measurement.

The use of irrigation expanded greatly during the Renaissance. Between 1400 and 1600, farmers in southern Europe built extensive networks of dams and canals to irrigate their fields. Farther north, irrigation projects made it possible to plant forage crops in meadows. In other areas, agriculture depended on draining water away from the land. In the 1400s, the Dutch used power from windmills to drain inland seas and form new areas of farmland called polders. A regional water court oversaw the drainage system and resolved disputes. (*See also* **Science; Technology; Weights and Measures.**)

Agrippa of Nettesheim, Heinrich

1486–1535
Philosopher

* **astrology** study of the supposed influences of the stars and planets on earthly events

* **treatise** long, detailed essay

Heinrich Agrippa of Nettesheim was one of the most controversial thinkers of his time. He devoted most of his career to the study of the occult, or supernatural. His most famous work, *Occult Philosophy* (1533), deals with topics such as magic and astrology*. His other works discuss ideas that were controversial for his time. He attacked the clergy and proclaimed the natural superiority of women in a 1509 treatise*. Agrippa counted among his friends other prominent Renaissance figures who shared his interests in the occult arts.

Born in Cologne, in what is now Germany, Agrippa spent most of his life traveling. He lived in Italy from 1512 to 1518. There he became

familiar with the philosophers Marsilio FICINO and Giovanni Pico della Mirandola. These thinkers believed in a secret body of ancient wisdom handed down through sources such as the Jewish Kabbalists*, the Greek philosopher PLATO, and the ancient mathematician Pythagoras. Their works had a strong influence on Agrippa's ideas.

* **Kabbalist** believer in a mystical Jewish religious system that involves reading encoded messages in the Hebrew Scriptures

Agrippa spent a year in Switzerland as the city physician in the city of Fribourg. He also served as the personal physician to Louise of Savoy, mother of the king of France. However, Louise dismissed Agrippa when he refused to cast a horoscope for her son. At this low point in his career, Agrippa wrote his most pessimistic work, *On the Vanity and Uncertainty of Arts and Sciences* (1530). This text attacked all forms of human learning, from law and medicine to the occult sciences that had been the focus of his own studies.

In 1528 Agrippa moved to ANTWERP, where he served as a historian to the governor, MARGARET OF AUSTRIA. However, his unusual ideas and attacks on the clergy got him into trouble with his employer and other city leaders. In 1533 Agrippa left Antwerp for Bonn. Two years later he returned to Lyon, where he was promptly arrested because of his public criticisms of the French king's mother. Friends managed to have him released, and he died that year in Grenoble, France.

After Agrippa's death, his works were translated and reprinted in several languages of his day. He developed a reputation as an expert in strange, possibly dangerous forms of learning. Legends even arose about his dealings with the devil. Agrippa's life influenced later legends about Dr. Faust, a black magician featured in a play by Christopher MARLOWE. Agrippa's writings paint a picture of a man who mastered many fields of learning, but who ultimately found all of them worthless. (*See also* **Magic and Astrology; Philosophy.**)

Alberti, Leon Battista

1404–1472
Italian author and architect

* **humanist** Renaissance expert in the humanities (the languages, literature, history, and speech and writing techniques of ancient Greece and Rome)

Leon Battista Alberti was an Italian author, architect, and humanist* of the 1400s. His works embody the Renaissance ideal of combining ancient and modern ideas. He wrote in both Latin and Italian on a great variety of subjects. As an architect, he incorporated forms used by the ancient Greeks and Romans into modern structures. In the 1800s, historian Jakob BURCKHARDT described Alberti as the "universal man of the Renaissance," meaning a man who could do many things well.

Early Life. Alberti was born in Genoa, Italy. He entered the University of Bologna to study law but preferred literary activities to legal studies. During his ten years at the university, he produced many works in Latin, including a comedy and several pieces on moral themes that were based on the works of Lucian, an ancient Greek writer.

After finishing his law degree in 1428, Alberti joined the Roman Catholic clergy. He sought employment in the papal Curia, the organization that assisted the pope in governing the church. Meanwhile he continued to write, producing two works in Italian on the subject of love. These pieces were very popular, both in their original form and in

The Malatesta Temple was Leon Battista Alberti's first major project as an architect. He converted an existing church in the Italian town of Rimini, adding elements of ancient Roman design.

translation. In fact, they were the only works of Alberti's to be printed during his lifetime.

In 1432 Alberti received a post in Florence. The city was home to many humanists, but they gave Alberti a cool welcome. In response, he wrote a Latin essay protesting the low social status of students and teachers.

Literary Works. While in Florence, Alberti wrote *The Family,* a three-part work in Italian. It contained a series of dialogues on the principles of running a household, covering such topics as education, marriage, and the management of an estate. Alberti later added a fourth section on friendship.

Alberti originally wrote *The Family* in the dialect of Tuscany, the region surrounding Florence. However, the language did not come naturally to him, and he revised the piece in a style that blended formal discourse with everyday speech. Alberti went on to become a leading supporter of the use of the vernacular* in writing. He later created the first Italian grammar book and composed poetry in Italian.

Alberti also continued to write in Latin. His 1436 work, *On Painting,* discussed the principles of perspective* and the use of stories as subjects for paintings. It also stressed the importance of humanist learning in the visual arts. Alberti translated this work into Italian to make it available to artists who did not speak Latin.

Alberti's other Latin writings included a treatise* on law, a dialogue on church duties, and a book of fables. He also produced an autobiography in 1437. Alberti's most ambitious Latin work was *Momus, or On the*

* **vernacular** native language or dialect of a region or country

* **perspective** artistic technique for creating the illusion of three-dimensional space on a flat surface

* **treatise** long, detailed essay

* **satire** literary or artistic work ridiculing human wickedness and foolishness

Ruler, published in 1450. This four-part novel was a satire* on the foolish ambitions and political schemes of both gods and men.

Architecture. Alberti received his first job as an architect in 1438. The ESTE family, which ruled the city of Ferrara, hired Alberti to design an arch to support a statue of Nicolò III, the head of the family. In 1443 Alberti went to Rome with the Curia. While there, he produced an elaborate map of the city. He also participated in various projects involving restoration and city planning.

After 1450, Alberti devoted more time to architecture. His first major project involved converting a church in the town of Rimini into a new structure called the Malatesta Temple. He created an outer shell around the old building with a front based on a Roman arch. In 1452 Alberti completed a work on architecture called *On the Art of Building.* It addressed every aspect of architecture, from symmetry* and proportion to urban planning.

* **symmetry** balance created by matching forms on opposite sides of a structure

In the 1460s and 1470s, Alberti worked on several projects for Giovanni Rucellai, a wealthy merchant in Florence. His plan for the Rucellai palace successfully adapted elements of ancient Greek and Roman architecture. Alberti also undertook several projects for the GONZAGA family, which ruled the city of Mantua. One of these, the church of Sant' Andrea, is widely viewed as his masterpiece. Begun in the 1470s, the building was not completed until after Alberti's death. The huge arched vaults of Sant' Andrea, based on ancient Roman architecture, had an influence on the design of St. Peter's and of many other churches in Rome.

Alberti's Influence. Alberti's accomplishments were largely overlooked for a generation after his death. This was due, in part, to Alberti's own secretive nature. He often wrote under assumed names, and he supervised many of his architectural projects from a distance. Moreover, he failed to finish many of his more ambitious literary efforts. Alberti's works began to attract interest in the 1520s with the publication of *Momus* and the translation of several of his other works.

Alberti was a true Renaissance thinker. In his translations of Latin works and his monuments based on ancient models, he smoothly blended old and new ideas. At the same time, his treatises on grammar, painting, and architecture provided a basis for new literary and artistic creation. (*See also* **Architecture; Florence; Humanism; Italian Language and Literature; Literature; Rome.**)

Alchemy

Alchemy was an early science based on a particular view about the nature of matter. Alchemists believed that they could bring about physical changes in matter, such as turning lead into gold. Some historians see Renaissance alchemy as the forerunner of modern experimental chemistry. However, alchemy was also a philosophical system that was concerned with the idea of perfection.

Origins and Influences of Alchemy. Renaissance alchemy rested on a combination of ancient, Islamic, and Christian ideas. Its foundation was a set of ancient ideas about how matter forms and changes. During the Middle Ages, Arab philosophers studied these ideas and built on them. For example, they developed the concept that sulfur and mercury were involved in the creation of matter. They believed that sulfur and mercury interacted with air, earth, fire, and water to give various types of matter unique properties.

Alchemy came to Europe in the 1200s when Christian scholars translated Arabic texts into Latin. As Christians embraced alchemy, they changed it to reflect their own beliefs. Renaissance Christians believed that God had ranked every creature, plant, and mineral in a great chain of being. Lead, for example, was a low-ranking mineral; gold was the highest-ranking. Changing lead to gold changed its position in God's order. The idea of changing lead to gold was a little bit like the religious idea of transubstantiation. According to this belief, during the Roman Catholic Mass, a miracle changes bread and wine into the body and blood of Christ.

The ideas, images, and symbols of alchemy appeared throughout Renaissance culture. They influenced art, music, medicine, and the early sciences. Alchemy was a respected profession. Many members of noble and royal families sponsored alchemists in their studies. Alchemists tried to keep their ideas and techniques secret by using obscure symbols in their writings.

*** literacy** ability to read

Alchemy changed significantly during the 1500s. As printed books and LITERACY* became more common, more people became familiar with the basic ideas of alchemy. People claiming to be alchemists began offering their wares and services to the public at fairs and markets. Meanwhile, a German alchemist named PARACELSUS was developing new theories and challenging old ones. Followers of Paracelsus kept alchemy alive in Europe well into the 1600s.

Alchemical Ideas and Practices. Renaissance alchemy relied on the idea that metals "grew" in the earth just as plants and animals grow. Their growth followed an ordered process, changing low metals into high ones. Metals continued to grow and change until they reached the perfect state of pure gold.

Alchemists tried to speed up this natural process through the use of heat and chemicals. They mixed materials over fires and carefully noted their changes in color and other properties, trying to nurture their metals to higher states of perfection. Alchemists risked fire, explosion, and exposure to toxic substances.

The goal of many alchemists was wealth, but none ever succeeded in turning other metals into gold. Some alchemists, however, sought not gold but a substance called the philosopher's stone. They believed that the stone could heal the sick and make human beings immortal. Alchemists tried refining metals to obtain this precious substance. No alchemist ever found the philosopher's stone, but alchemy did sharpen Europeans' scientific skills. (*See also* **Magic and Astrology; Mining and Metallurgy; Philosophy; Science.**)

Aldine Press

See *Printing and Publishing.*

Alexander VI

1431–1503
Pope

* **illegitimate** refers to a child born outside of marriage

As pope, Alexander VI became a symbol of corruption within the Roman Catholic Church. He was born Rodrigo BORGIA, a member of a powerful family in Spain. In 1456 his uncle Pope Calixtus III made him a cardinal. A year later he received the high position of vice-chancellor of the Catholic Church. While he was a cardinal, Rodrigo had seven illegitimate* children. However, his behavior was not particularly shocking for the times.

Rodrigo became pope on August 11, 1492. He used his position of power to gain land and wealth for his children. He made his son Cesare duke of Romagna. He also took land from nobles in central Italy for his other children, including his daughter Lucrezia, the Duchess of Ferrara. These actions earned him the ill will of many cardinals. He threatened those who opposed him, and some died suspiciously. He also made no secret of his affairs with women. His mistress Giulia Farnese bore him a son in 1498, while he was pope.

However, some of Alexander's actions were positive. He struggled to keep the French king Charles VIII from invading Italy in the 1490s. He also added to the beauty of the Vatican. He hired artists to create new buildings and paintings in his living quarters. Perhaps his most important act as pope was dividing up the lands of the New World between Spain and Portugal in 1493. (*See also* **Americas; Farnese, House of; Popes and Papacy.**)

Allegory

See *Literature.*

Americas

The discovery of the Americas by Christopher COLUMBUS in 1492 had a profound influence on the Renaissance and on later history. Searching for a route from Europe to Asia, Columbus arrived in the West Indies, a part of the world unknown to Europeans. European nations began establishing colonies in North and South America, a venture that forever changed life on both sides of the Atlantic Ocean.

EUROPEAN EXPLORATION

When reports of the Americas reached Europe, they transformed the Renaissance view of the world. Europeans saw the New World as a land of untapped opportunity and fresh ideas. However, exploring the vast continents was a challenging task.

By the time European explorers arrived in the Americas, the region was already inhabited by hundreds of distinct peoples. The newcomers fanned out across the landscape, learning about the geography, resources, and people. Eventually they began staking claims to territory.

The Americas in 1492. Historians estimate that the population of the Americas was 57.3 million in the 1490s, at the beginning of European contact. Mexico, the most populous region, had roughly 21.4

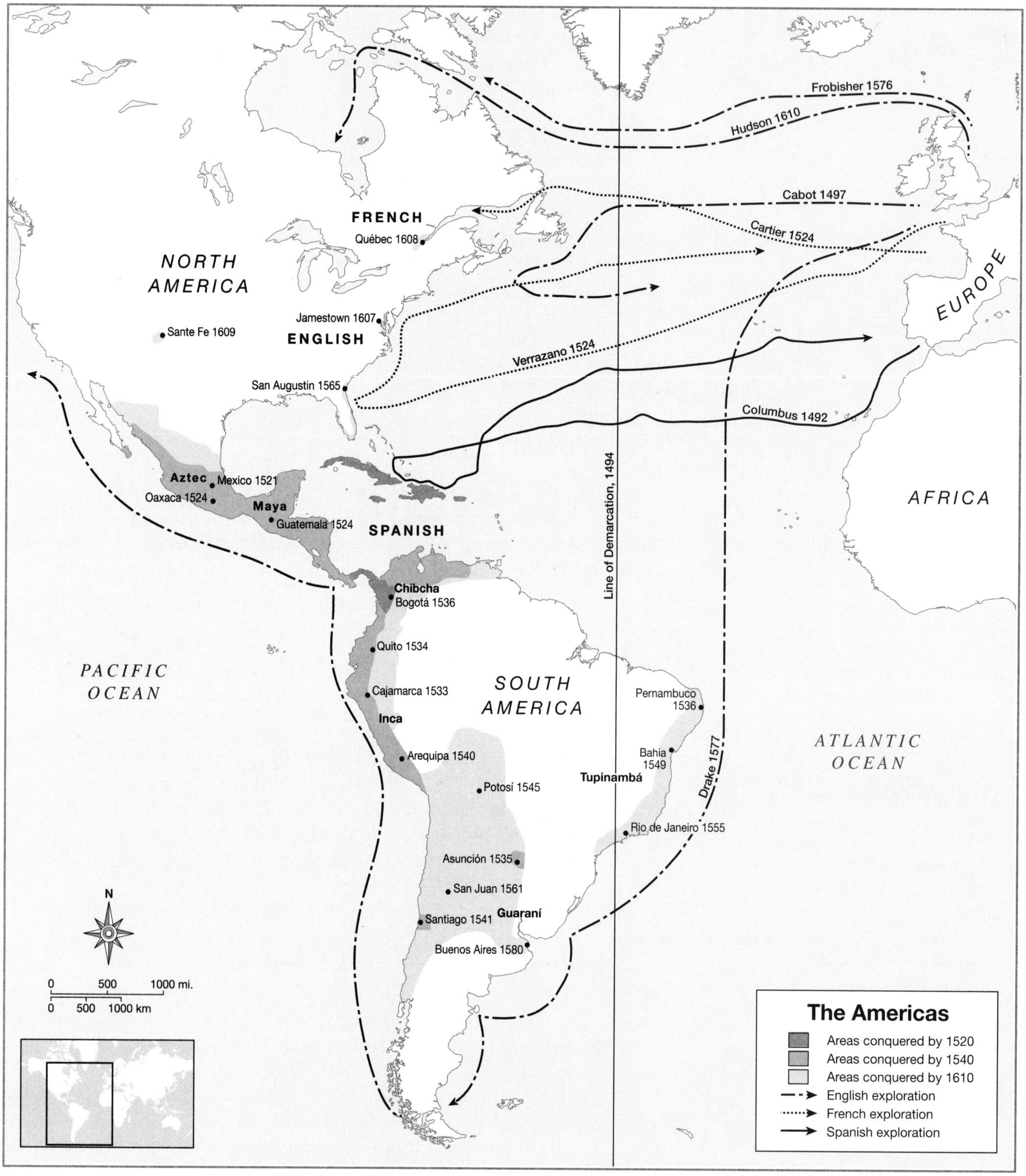

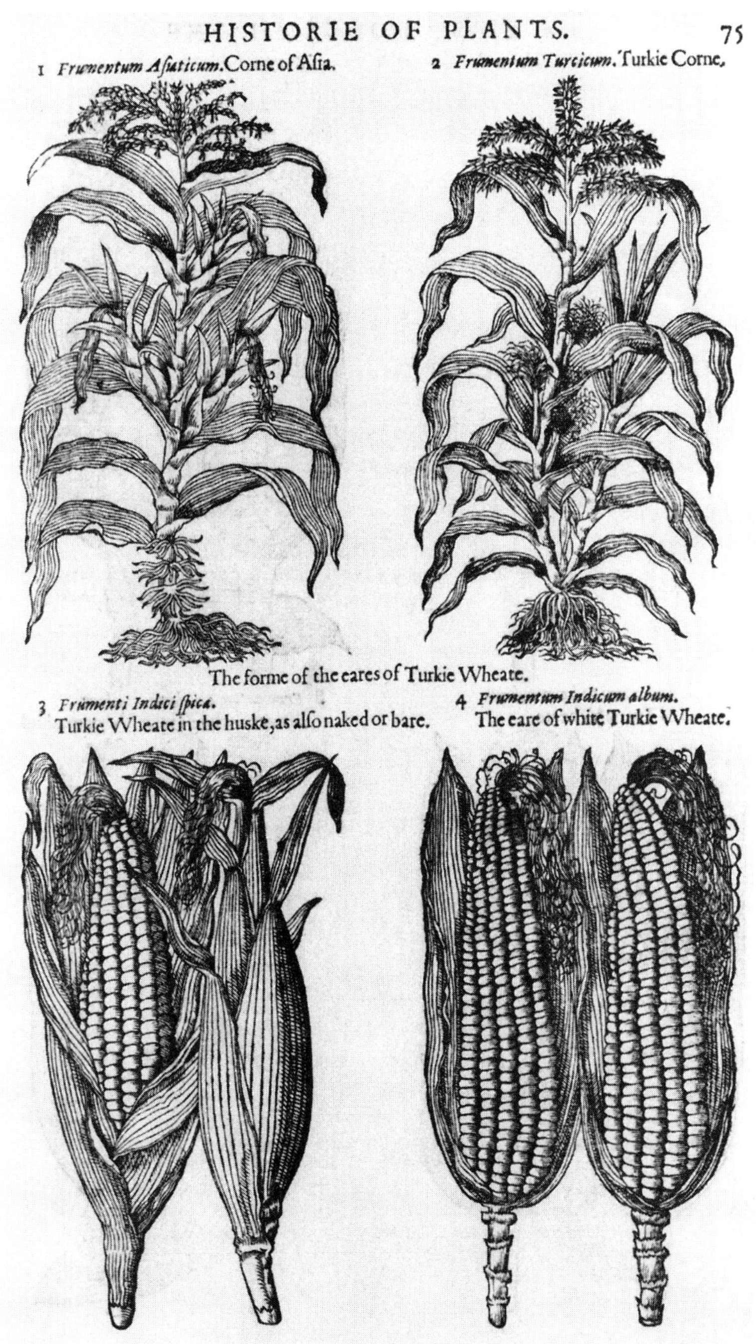

European explorers brought many crops from the New World back across the Atlantic Ocean. Some of the new foods, such as corn, became very popular in Europe.

million inhabitants; the Andes Mountains (in present-day Ecuador, Peru, and Chile) had about 11.5 million; while the rest of North America (excluding Mexico) had only about 4.4 million. These indigenous* peoples occupied a wide range of environments, from deserts and open plains to mountains, woodlands, and rain forests.

*** indigenous** native to a certain place

Some areas, especially those suitable for intensive agriculture, were home to major civilizations. The Aztec and Mayan peoples lived in Mexico and Central America, and the Incas occupied the Andes

Mountains of South America. Other flourishing cultures included the Chibcha in Colombia and the Iroquois Confederation, an association of several groups in eastern North America. Many of these peoples excelled at crafts such as weaving, pottery making, wood carving, and metalworking.

Native American societies had developed highly varied and productive systems of agriculture. They practiced terrace farming and irrigation, and raised crops of corn, cassava (a starchy root), and other staple foods. However, unlike societies in Europe, Africa, and Asia, the Native Americans had few domesticated* animals. The peoples of the Andes raised llamas, alpacas, and vicuñas, but most others fished and hunted for game. In the North American plains, for example, herds of wild bison supplied food as well as materials for shelter and clothing.

* **domesticated** raised by humans as farm animals or pets

Native American peoples had close spiritual ties with the land and with the plants and animals that flourished there. Most groups considered the land central to their history and identity. By contrast, the Europeans viewed the land in the Americas and its inhabitants as a source of economic gain. This clash in values led to tragic conflicts as the Europeans sought control over both the indigenous peoples and their territory.

Early European Contact. The first Americans whom Europeans met were not members of the larger civilizations that had developed complex societies and cities. Instead, they were generally farmers, fishers, and hunters from small villages. These early encounters led Europeans to conclude that their own culture was superior to those of the indigenous peoples (whom they called Indians because Columbus thought that he had reached the Indies, or Asia). Belief in their own superiority helped the Europeans justify their attempts to conquer the Americas.

Most of the Europeans who came to the New World believed that the Indians should be converted to Christianity. They also thought that they had the right to make the Indians work for them. Even Bartolomé de LAS CASAS, a priest who protested against the settlers' harsh treatment and exploitation* of the Indians, felt that the Native Americans should become Christian subjects of the Spanish government.

* **exploitation** relationship in which one side benefits at the other's expense

The first wave of Europeans depended on the indigenous peoples to help them survive in unfamiliar lands. The explorers rarely found themselves in empty wilderness. Even the most thinly inhabited regions contained villages or camps. Some Indian groups offered the newcomers food and shelter and guided them from place to place. They also provided information about the local culture and geography. However, other groups were more wary, or even hostile, toward Europeans who arrived in their territory.

Most Europeans did not attempt to establish long-term relationships with Native Americans. Instead, they often seized food and other supplies and took captives to serve as guides and interpreters. They also captured and sometimes killed Indian leaders and waged all-out wars against certain groups. In time the Europeans managed to overpower most of their indigenous rivals.

Reluctant Guests

Occasionally, Europeans in the Americas became isolated from their own people. In the 1530s Álvar Núñez Cabeza de Vaca was stranded when his expedition to Florida collapsed. He lived with Native Americans for several years and came to appreciate their culture. But he still believed that the indigenous peoples should become Christian subjects of Spain. Most Europeans who lived in Indian societies for a while were overjoyed to be "rescued" by other explorers. However, Gonzalo Guerrero, shipwrecked on the Mexican coast in the 1510s, refused to rejoin the Spanish and even led the Maya against them.

COLONIZATION

Spain—the sponsor of Columbus's historic trip—dominated European activity in the Americas in the 1500s. Portugal, France, and England also launched voyages of exploration, but the Spanish were the first to establish outposts in American territory. Spanish settlers began in the Caribbean and then moved on to Mexico, Florida, and mainland Central and South America. In the process, they encountered and conquered some highly developed civilizations, including those of the Aztecs and the Incas.

The Caribbean. For almost 20 years after Columbus's voyage, Spain concentrated on the island of Hispaniola (now the site of Haiti and the Dominican Republic). The Spanish conquered the tribes in the interior of the island and killed many of the caciques, or local chiefs. In 1502 Spain sent a governor and 2,500 colonists to Hispaniola. But the government was weak, and conflict broke out frequently, not only between colonists and Indians but also among groups of colonists. Many of the Spaniards went to live in Indian villages to survive.

Eventually the Spanish established a system for colonization. In most cases they gained firm control over an area and then used it as a base to take over another region. By 1511 Spanish forces operating from Hispaniola had conquered Cuba, Puerto Rico, and Jamaica.

The Spanish developed a colonial economy based on agriculture. They set up the *encomienda,* a system that gave certain Spaniards control over a piece of land and the indigenous people who lived on it. Most of the land grants went to conquistadors* and colonists with important social and political connections. The Spanish forced the Native Americans to work in their plantations and mines and eventually came to depend on local labor.

* **conquistador** military explorer and conqueror

Gold mining enjoyed a brief period of success, and the Spanish used the profits to import supplies from Europe and to explore the mainland. However, by 1515 the gold deposits had dwindled, and the Native American population had declined due to hardships and disease. Settlers who stayed on the islands turned to raising sugarcane and cattle and began importing African slaves for labor.

The Mainland. Spain's activities on the mainland followed the same pattern as in the Caribbean. After locating precious metals or other valuable goods, the settlers established towns and captured or killed Native American leaders to gain control. Then the government granted *encomiendas* to prominent Spaniards, and more colonists arrived from Spain to settle in the territory.

Spain's conquistadors gained control of Mexico in 1521 with the capture of the Aztec capital of Tenochtitlán. Their next goal was the Inca empire of Peru. In 1532 conquistadors captured and executed the Inca emperor Atahualpa and divided his enormous treasure among themselves. Because Spain's mainland colonies were larger and wealthier than the Caribbean islands, they developed on a new and impressive scale.

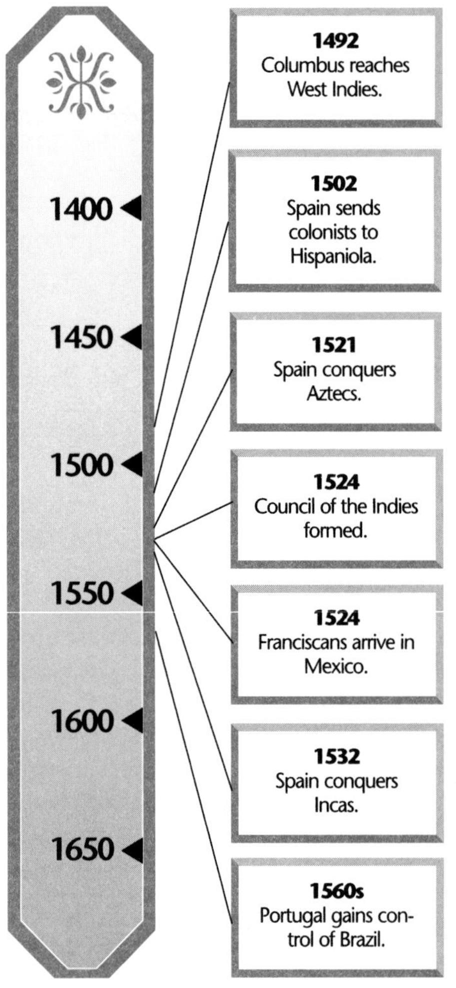

The Spanish established two vast colonies, New Spain (including Mexico and some of the surrounding territory) and Peru (incorporating much of South America). High-ranking Spanish officials called viceroys governed these colonies. Towns and cities multiplied. Many—including Mexico City, the capital of New Spain—grew up on Indian sites. A flood of immigrants arrived from Spain, including many women and children. The Spanish imported large numbers of African slaves, who became an essential element in the colonies' economic success.

The Spanish government closely regulated activities in its American colonies. A department called the Casa de Contratación (House of Trade) oversaw the movement of people, ships, goods, and precious metals between Spain and the colonies. In 1524 the crown set up the Consejo de Indias (Council of the Indies), the highest governing body for the Americas.

Religion and Economy in Spanish America. Early in the 1500s, the Roman Catholic Church gave the Spanish monarchs broad powers over the church in the Americas. The crown could appoint candidates to church offices and construct new churches and other religious institutions. Two forces shaped the activities of the church in the American colonies: the drive to convert the Indians to Christianity and the need to serve two societies, Spanish and Indian.

The RELIGIOUS ORDERS, groups of priests and monks such as the Dominicans and Franciscans, played the most important role in the Spanish American church. Dominicans sailed to Hispaniola in 1510, and Franciscans followed. Missionary activity became even more focused with the arrival of 12 Franciscans in Mexico in 1524. At first the missionaries viewed their role in the Americas in terms of converting the Indians to Christianity. However, their early efforts at large-scale conversion soon gave way to a more gradual approach based on education. The Spanish built impressive monasteries where they provided religious instruction to the Indians. As a result the Roman Catholic Church had a lasting influence in the Americas.

The economy of Spanish America depended mostly on mining and agriculture. The colonists exported silver from mines in Mexico and Peru and imported cloth, clothing, iron, and other goods. They also operated farms with the help of Indian and African laborers. The farms produced enough food to support the growing population.

Other European Settlements. Compared with Spanish America, the colonial ventures of other European countries during the Renaissance were minor. Europeans who tried to settle in North America and on the eastern shores of South America made slow progress.

Some settlements faced hostility from groups of Native Americans. The first English colonists in North America, for example, were unable to maintain friendly relations with local Indians. Other settlements failed because of competition among European nations. France and Portugal both attempted to establish colonies in Brazil, but the Portuguese gained control of the region in the 1560s. The French were

also active in Florida until the Spanish established their authority there. In general, Spain's land claims and strong navy limited the success of other European powers in the New World until the early 1600s. (*See also* **Economy and Trade; Exploration; Geography and Cartography; Slavery.**)

Amsterdam

See color plate 11, vol. 3

The Dutch city of Amsterdam was the leading commercial center of Northern Europe from the late 1500s to the late 1600s. Located at the point where the Ij and Amstel Rivers meet, Amsterdam dominated shipping between ports of the Baltic Sea and northeastern Europe. A network of dikes and dams, built in the 1200s, controlled the rivers' flow. A meeting place for people of many different cultures, the city attracted a large number of thinkers and artists.

Founded around 1300, Amsterdam was a fairly young city at the beginning of the Renaissance. Its population rose from about 3,000 in 1400 to 30,000 in 1580, making it the largest city in the province of Holland. Like other provinces in the NETHERLANDS, Holland was controlled by the Roman Catholic monarchs of Spain. In 1568 Dutch Protestants rebelled against Spanish rule and took over large parts of Holland. However, Amsterdam's leaders were Catholic, so the city remained loyal to Spain. As a result, it became cut off from the rest of the province, seriously hurting its trade.

Amsterdam surrendered to the rebels in 1578. A new city government took over that included both Protestants and Catholics. Throughout the 1600s, the city encouraged religious tolerance. Although it declared the Dutch Reformed Church the official religion, people were free to practice other faiths privately. In 1650 about one in every five Amsterdamers was Catholic, even though the Catholic Church was officially banned.

From about 1620 to 1700 the Dutch Republic basked in a "golden age." The Netherlands had become the most important economic power in Europe, and Amsterdam was its leading city. Amsterdam's merchants dominated trade with Asia and the AMERICAS. Two large companies, the Dutch East India Company and the Dutch West India Company, controlled trade in these regions. Dutch commercial power made Amsterdam one of Europe's leading financial centers.

By 1700 the city had a population of about 205,000, but its influence in European affairs was declining. Rivalry with other countries was wearing down the Dutch Republic. The English harassed the country by sea, while the French attacked it by land. After 1700 the Netherlands was no longer a major European power, and Amsterdam lost its position as the continent's economic center.

Although known mainly as a commercial city, Amsterdam emerged as a major cultural center during the 1600s. It was particularly famous for its painters, led by the great master Rembrandt von Rijn. Rembrandt and his pupils developed the art form known as still life, which featured inanimate objects such as flowers or fruit. Amsterdam was also a literary city. While it produced few important writers of its own, it was home to many thinkers and writers from other countries. The city's publishing

houses produced more than 1,400 titles between 1639 and 1650. (*See also* **Art in the Netherlands; Asia, East; Economy and Trade; Printing and Publishing.**)

Anatomy

During the Renaissance, medical scholars made great advances in understanding the structure of the human body. Throughout the Middle Ages, physicians had relied on the theories of ancient thinkers to explain how the body worked. Renaissance students of anatomy took a new approach, focusing on firsthand observation. Still, their work was not completely revolutionary. Although they made new discoveries, they did not challenge the basic theories of the ancient Greeks.

Changing Views of Anatomy. During the Middle Ages, there was a sharp distinction between the fields of medicine and surgery. Doctors treated disease, while surgeons tended to wounds and broken bones. Most people saw medicine, which required book learning, as a more advanced skill than surgery. Anatomy was held in low regard because it was the responsibility of surgeons. This view changed during the Renaissance. New methods and discoveries led to a belief that anatomy was essential to the study of medicine.

The practice of dissection—cutting open bodies to examine their inner parts—plays a key role in anatomy. In the 1100s and 1200s, medical scholars studied anatomy by dissecting pigs. By the end of the 1200s, they were dissecting human bodies. In 1316 Mondino dei Liuzzi, a professor of medicine at the University of Bologna, wrote the first complete study of human anatomy. His book, *Anatomy,* became the basis for anatomical studies in European universities in the 1300s and 1400s.

During the Middle Ages, the study of anatomy was a matter of learning the different parts of the body. In the 1500s, however, students of anatomy began to perform their own studies of the body. By seeking firsthand knowledge, they followed in the footsteps of the ancient Greek physician GALEN. Galen's view of anatomical research was based on *autopsia,* a Greek word meaning "seeing for oneself." Galen's treatise* *On Anatomical Procedures* was discovered and translated from the Greek in 1531.

* **treatise** long, detailed essay

Renaissance medical scholars also linked anatomy with philosophy and theology*. They pointed to the human body as an example of God's marvelous workmanship. The new view of anatomy had a great impact on medicine. By the late 1500s, students at the University of Padua were claiming that anatomy was the very foundation of medicine.

* **theology** study of the nature of God and of religion

Anatomy also came to play an important role in art. Renaissance artists emphasized a natural, lifelike style, similar to that of ancient Greek and Roman sculpture. They turned to anatomy to help them portray the human form more accurately. The paintings and drawings of RAPHAEL, Albrecht DÜRER, and MICHELANGELO BUONARROTI show these artists' understanding of anatomy. LEONARDO DA VINCI even sought out corpses to dissect. His knowledge of anatomy enabled him to draw specific body parts, such as the hand and shoulder, in very realistic detail.

Renaissance medical scholars relied on observation as well as on ancient theories to explain how the body worked. Their approach led to major discoveries in the field of human anatomy.

See color plate 9, vol. 4

Major Discoveries. The most important anatomist of the Renaissance was Andreas VESALIUS. In the 1530s he began to find fault with Galen's theories of anatomy because Galen had dissected animals rather than humans. Vesalius decided to recheck Galen's work using human corpses. He ended up completely rewriting human anatomy in a massive and brilliantly illustrated work, *On the Structure of the Human Body* (1543). Vesalius and later anatomists contradicted Galen on a number of details, such as the structure of the liver. However, they did not challenge Galen's ideas about how the body worked.

Some anatomists tried to outdo Vesalius by creating even more precise anatomies of the body. Others made detailed studies of specific parts of the body, such as the ear and the kidney. Some parts of the body take their names from the Italian anatomists of the 1500s who discovered them. For example, the eustachian tube, between the nose and the ear, is named for Bartolomeo Eustachi.

However, the most important new development after Vesalius was comparative anatomy. This discipline involved studying the anatomy of various life-forms, including humans, and comparing their body structures. Girolamo Fabrici da Aquapendente, an anatomist at the University of Padua, was the first to study comparative anatomy in detail. He hoped to publish a complete comparison of all animal life-forms. He never finished this work, but he did publish parts of it in the early 1600s.

The last great achievement of Renaissance anatomy was the discovery of the circulation of the blood. Galen had believed that the body produced new blood in the liver and used it up as it was needed. In the early 1600s, English anatomist William HARVEY concluded that the heart cir-

culates blood continuously throughout the body. He reached this conclusion by calculating how much blood the heart pumped in a given time. He realized that if the blood did not move in a circle, the body would burst. Harvey published his findings in 1628. Although he made his medical discoveries through observation and logic, he continued to believe that there must be philosophical explanations behind them. (*See also* **Medicine; Science.**)

Angelico, Fra

ca. 1400–1455
Painter

* **illumination** hand-painted color decorations and illustrations on the pages of a manuscript

* **Dominican** religious order of brothers and priests founded by St. Dominic

* **patron** supporter or financial sponsor of an artist or writer

The painter known as Fra Angelico was born Guido di Pietro in FLORENCE. Guido and his brother Benedetto were trained in the production of manuscripts. Benedetto was a scribe, or professional copyist, and Guido created illuminations*. By 1425 the two brothers had entered a Dominican* order. Guido changed his name to Fra Giovanni when he became a monk. After his death, the Dominicans renamed him Fra Angelico, "the angelic friar."

From the early 1420s until Benedetto's death in 1448, the two brothers ran a large and successful workshop, producing manuscripts and paintings. They created most of their works for Dominican houses throughout Tuscany (the region around Florence). However, Fra Angelico's beautiful illustrations also attracted the attention of wealthy patrons* in Florence. Eventually his fame spread to Rome, where he worked for Pope Eugenius IV and Pope Nicholas V.

Fra Angelico's style was different from that of many other artists of his time. He did not embrace new techniques such as chiaroscuro, the alternation of areas of light and shadow. Instead he adopted a natural style. He used old-fashioned techniques such as gilding (applying a thin layer of gold to a surface), punch work (creating small, repeating patterns with a steel punch), and vivid use of color. These methods were part of the tradition of sacred art from the early 1300s.

* **fresco** mural painted on a plaster wall

By the mid-1430s Fra Angelico was operating the largest painter's workshop in Florence. Like most Tuscan artists of his time, he was best known for his frescoes*. His largest fresco project was at the Dominican convent of San Marco in Florence. Aided by artists from his shop, Fra Angelico painted the walls of more than 48 rooms and 3 corridors in the convent. Many of these frescoes show scenes from the life of Christ. They include two of his finest achievements, the *Annunciation* and the *Transfiguration.*

* **cloister** covered passageway around a courtyard in a convent or monastery

In Rome, Fra Angelico painted in more public spaces, including St. Peter's, the Vatican Palace, and the cloister* of Santa Maria sopra Minerva. Many of these works have disappeared, but Fra Angelico's frescoes depicting the lives of St. Stephen and St. Lawrence still exist in the private chapel of Pope Nicholas V in the Vatican Palace. (*See also* **Art in Italy; Books and Manuscripts; Illumination; Patronage.**)

Anguissola, Sofonisba

1532–1625
Italian painter

Sofonisba Anguissola was one of the first internationally known female artists. Despite limitations faced by women in the Renaissance art world, she became an accomplished painter and produced an impressive body of work.

Born in Cremona, Italy, Anguissola received a humanist* education and studied painting with local artists. She began her career in Italy and then spent 14 years as court painter in Madrid. In 1573 she married a Sicilian nobleman and returned to Italy. A second marriage, after the Sicilian's death, took her to Genoa for the next four decades.

* **humanist** referring to a Renaissance cultural movement promoting the study of the humanities (the languages, literature, and history of ancient Greece and Rome) as a guide to living

Anguissola specialized in painting portraits rather than historical scenes because women were not allowed to study anatomy or male models. She used her portraits to challenge traditional images of women. In *The Chess Game* (1555), she shows her sisters engaged in a competitive intellectual activity. She also painted herself several times, perhaps to emphasize her position as a female artist in a masculine profession. MICHELANGELO encouraged her, and a Roman nobleman praised her creativity in spite of the common belief that only men could be creative. Anguissola developed a distinctive style in which the faces of the subjects stand out vividly against muted backgrounds. Her portraits, which often suggest a situation or story, influenced later genre* painters. (*See also* **Art in Italy.**)

* **genre** type of painting that portrays scenes from everyday life

Anne of Brittany

1477–1514
Duchess of Brittany

Anne of Brittany led the duchy* of BRITTANY after her father, the duke, died in 1488. As the wife of two French kings, she also played a significant role in the political and cultural life of France during the early years of the Renaissance.

* **duchy** territory ruled by a duke or duchess

Located on the western edge of France, Brittany was considered a desirable property. As a result Anne, its ruler, attracted numerous suitors from the royal families of Europe. Fearing that Brittany might end up in the hands of a foreign power, the French king Charles VIII attacked. He took control of the region and married Anne in 1491. This led in time to the union of Brittany with France.

Charles died in 1498, and the following year Anne married his successor, Louis XII. During Louis's reign, Anne made great efforts to encourage the arts. She brought poets, painters, decorators, and translators to the court to enhance the image of the king. Her support for the artist Jean Bourdichon resulted in the famous 1508 illustrated manuscript *Book of Hours.*

Anne's daughter Claude became the wife of one French king, Francis I, and the mother of another, Henry II. Anne always remained loyal to Brittany and tried to preserve its autonomy*. (*See also* **France.**)

* **autonomy** independent self-government

Antiquarianism

See *Classical Antiquity.*

Anti-Semitism

Anti-Semitism, or prejudice against Jews, was widespread during the Renaissance. Libels, damaging lies about Jews and Judaism, persisted from the Middle Ages. For example, the blood libel held that Jews killed Christians—especially children—to use their blood in rituals. The earlier crucifixion libel accused Jews of crucifying Christian children. Christian religious leaders and even humanists* promoted such views. Their teachings led to the persecution of Jews throughout Europe.

* **humanist** Renaissance expert in the humanities (the languages, literature, history, and speech and writing techniques of ancient Greece and Rome)

Many Renaissance Christians felt that Jewish people, beliefs, and culture polluted Christian society. They particularly scorned the Jewish practice of lending money for interest. One Italian preacher taught that moneylenders infected society as a disease infected the body. An Italian historian blamed Jews for an outbreak of syphilis, a sexually transmitted disease. German Christians believed that the presence of Jews damaged the fabric of their society.

European countries took a variety of steps to rid themselves of this Jewish "pollution." England barred all Jews from the country between 1290 and about 1655, although it did not enforce this ban strictly. Other nations, such as Portugal, forced Jews to convert to Christianity. Italian religious and legal scholars argued that baptism should be forced on Jewish children to save their souls. In some places, prejudice against Jews led to deadly violence. In 1391 riots in Spain destroyed most of the country's Jewish communities. The Spanish massacred some Jews and forced others to convert. In Trent, a city in the Holy Roman Empire*, the claim that Jews had murdered a Christian boy led to the destruction of the entire Jewish community in 1475. Hostility toward Jews was also violent in Protestant lands, such as Germany. In 1543 Protestant leader Martin LUTHER published an attack called *The Jews and Their Lies.*

* **Holy Roman Empire** political body in central Europe composed of several states; existed until 1806

Jews who converted to Christianity, called CONVERSOS or New Christians, also faced discrimination. Many of their cultural traditions seemed strange to other Christians. In Spain, many people mistook these traditions for Jewish religious practices. As a result, most of the people accused of heresy* by the Spanish Inquisition* were *conversos.* Two thousand or more New Christians died during the Inquisition. Spain also passed laws to prohibit New Christians from intermarrying with other Christians.

* **heresy** belief that is contrary to the doctrine of an established church

* **Spanish Inquisition** court established by the Spanish monarchs that investigated Christians accused of straying from the official doctrine of the Roman Catholic Church, particularly during the period 1480–1530

In 1516 the government of Venice decreed that Jews should not live alongside Christians. It restricted them to a separate part of the city, called a GHETTO. In the mid-1550s the pope announced his support for ghettos, which were often separated by walls from the rest of the city. Jews could work elsewhere in the city but had to return to the ghetto in the evening. Jews who hoped to escape the ghetto by conversion had to give up their social and cultural ties to Judaism. This requirement hints at the more modern anti-Semitic idea that Jews could never fully integrate into society. (*See also* **Inquisition; Jews; Religious Thought.**)

Antwerp

Antwerp, a city in present-day Belgium, was a major European trade center during the Renaissance. Goods such as spices, silver, and cloth flowed into its port, making Antwerp (then part of the Netherlands) the central market of Europe. Between 1500 and 1560, the city experienced dramatic growth, with the population soaring from 40,000 to 100,000.

Antwerp's new wealth was not evenly spread. Tension between rich and poor increased as a small group of major merchants and business owners became enormously wealthy. However, the city's large middle class of artisans* and small-scale merchants also prospered during this period of economic expansion.

* **artisan** skilled worker or craftsperson

Antwerp's growth had a profound impact on its culture. Its commercial activities required trained workers, encouraging the development of public education. By the mid-1500s the city had a well-developed school system, with five religious schools and over 150 schoolteachers. More than 40 percent of these teachers were women.

See color plate 12, vol. 3

The expanding upper and middle classes increased the size of the market for artistic products and luxury goods. The arts developed into a thriving industry, and Antwerp became a leading exporter of artwork. The city's art and ARCHITECTURE reflected the new styles of the Italian Renaissance. A striking example is the city hall that was built in the 1560s. Antwerp also exported luxury items, especially diamonds. Book production was another major industry. The city's literary culture made it an international meeting place for humanist* authors and scholars.

The Roman Catholic Church dominated Antwerp until the 1520s. At that time, various Protestant groups gained ground. By 1585 Calvinists* controlled the city. However, that same year Spanish troops attacked, causing thousands of Protestants to flee. After that, Antwerp became a major force in the Counter-Reformation, a movement to bring new life to Catholicism. (*See also* **Art in the Netherlands; Catholic Reformation and Counter-Reformation; Economy and Trade; Printing and Publishing; Social Status.**)

* **humanist** referring to a Renaissance cultural movement promoting the study of the humanities (the languages, literature, and history of ancient Greece and Rome) as a guide to living
* **Calvinist** member of a Protestant church founded by John Calvin

Architecture

Like other art forms in the Renaissance, architecture drew increasingly on the traditions of ancient Greece and Rome. The revival of classical* forms was strongest in Italy, where the Renaissance began. Several Italian architects produced important treatises* on the principles of architectural design that provided models for others to follow. Northern Europe, by contrast, never completely abandoned the Gothic* styles of the Middle Ages. These survived in modified forms well into the 1600s.

* **classical** in the tradition of ancient Greece and Rome
* **treatise** long, detailed essay
* **Gothic** style of architecture characterized by pointed arches and high, thin walls supported by flying buttresses

DEVELOPMENT OF THE RENAISSANCE STYLE

The Renaissance style of architecture first emerged in FLORENCE in the early 1400s. It marked a rejection of medieval* styles and a celebration of ancient forms. One pioneer of the new style was Filippo BRUNELLESCHI, who designed the magnificent dome of Florence's cathedral, Santa Maria del Fiore.

* **medieval** referring to the Middle Ages, a period that began around A.D. 400 and ended around 1400 in Italy and 1500 in the rest of Europe

Renaissance architecture took many different forms throughout Europe. Other parts of Italy combined the Renaissance styles that developed in and around Florence with their own local traditions, creating a variety of distinct architectural styles. Italian Renaissance architecture also spread to other areas of Europe, but slowly and unevenly. It took 100 years or more for classical styles to take hold in France, Spain, Portugal, and Northern Europe. In these areas, the Italian styles blended with local traditions and Gothic forms to produce new and original designs. Architects adapted Renaissance styles based on their areas' landscape, climate, building materials, and customs.

Although Renaissance architects copied ancient forms, they had little opportunity to observe the designs firsthand. Few examples of ancient Roman architecture remained intact. Many structures had been destroyed or badly damaged, while others had been rebuilt and modified in later periods. Architects outside Italy had even less access to ancient buildings. Only a privileged few could actually visit the Roman ruins in Italy. Most had to depend on drawings, sketches, and books handed down from master to student.

In 1416 Italians rediscovered *On Architecture,* a treatise written by the ancient Roman architect Vitruvius around 27 B.C. This work offered a great deal of insight into the theory and practice of architecture in ancient Rome. However, Vitruvius had lived before the time of the Roman Empire, when many of the surviving ruins were built. Therefore, the structures that could be studied in Italy were quite different from those described by Vitruvius. Renaissance architects had to rely on imagination to fill in the gaps in their knowledge.

BUILDING STYLES

Although Renaissance buildings varied a great deal from region to region, they shared various common features. This was particularly true of churches because the form of the religious service imposed certain requirements on the shape of the building. Palaces and villas*, by contrast, took on distinct forms that reflected the social and cultural traditions of an area.

* **villa** luxurious country home and the land surrounding it

Church Layouts. A typical European church of the Middle Ages featured a long, narrow central hall, or nave. During the Renaissance architects began to explore the idea of creating churches with a central plan, laid out symmetrically* around a central point. Such a church might take the form of a circle or a Greek cross, with vertical and horizontal arms of equal length. However, such designs did not provide a clear separation between the priest and the congregation. They also did not hold enough people.

* **symmetrical** balanced with matching forms on opposite sides of a structure or piece of art

The tension between these two types of forms is visible in the layout of the church of St. Peter's in Rome. The Italian architect Donato BRAMANTE originally designed the church in the form of a Greek cross topped by a huge dome. However, later architects who worked on the church, including RAPHAEL and MICHELANGELO, altered the plan many

The church of St. Peter in Rome combines traditional forms with elements of classical architecture. This aerial view shows the church's large dome and long central hall, called a nave.

times over the course of construction. By the time the church was completed in the early 1600s, it had stretched to contain a longer nave while still including Bramante's original cross shape. In this way, St. Peter's combined traditional forms with the ideal shapes—circle and square—inspired by classical architecture.

See color plate 10, vol. 1

In France, most architects continued to follow Gothic styles, although they sometimes used classical forms to decorate the outsides of buildings. Spanish architects designed few major churches in the classical style, but they used some new forms to modify old Gothic buildings. During the reign of PHILIP II (1556–1598), Spanish architecture moved toward a simple, classical style quite unlike the elaborate forms then popular in Italy. In the Protestant countries of northern Europe, churches gradually took on a functional auditorium shape. This design reflected the Protestant churches' emphasis on preaching.

Residential Buildings. The designs of homes—particularly large and luxurious ones, such as palaces and villas—also changed during the Renaissance. In Italy during the 1300s, a typical palace had looked like it was carved out of one rough block of stone. Over time, ancient Roman styles crept into the design of palaces. Buildings such as the Farnese palace in Rome had rooms with elegant frescoes*, courtyards surrounded by columns, and ornamentation both inside and out. Architects developed precise guidelines for how much decoration a dwelling should have based on its owner's social status.

* **fresco** mural painted on a plaster wall

Villas, even more than urban palaces, reflected the goal of re-creating the lifestyles of ancient Rome. Pliny the Younger and other writers from that time had described the magnificent villas of wealthy Romans. The

structures that survived inspired Renaissance architects, who let their imaginations run free. Their villas often contained beautiful gardens, artificial caves, courtyards filled with sculpture, and private theaters.

In France, these Roman styles never took hold. The wealthy continued to prefer traditional castles, or châteaus, in the styles of the Middle Ages. One notable architectural feature of French châteaus involved using a combination of brick and stone. This practice, which became popular in the late 1500s, helped blend large new building complexes into existing cities.

Urban Planning. During the Renaissance, architects developed theories about city design. The ruins of ancient Roman buildings provided few clues to the city's overall layout, so architects relied largely on some written sources, such as Vitruvius. However, the limited information left much to the imagination, leading architects to propose new ideas on urban design.

Two notable examples of Renaissance town planning are the Italian cities of Pienza and Palmanova. These cities use simple geometry and central planning to create a sense of order. Architects tried to apply the same ideas to existing cities, but they had few opportunities to redesign cities on a grand scale. Instead, they focused on the layout of squares and streets, placing major buildings in these areas. In the late 1500s a large-scale urban renewal in Rome transformed the city into a network of public squares and major roads.

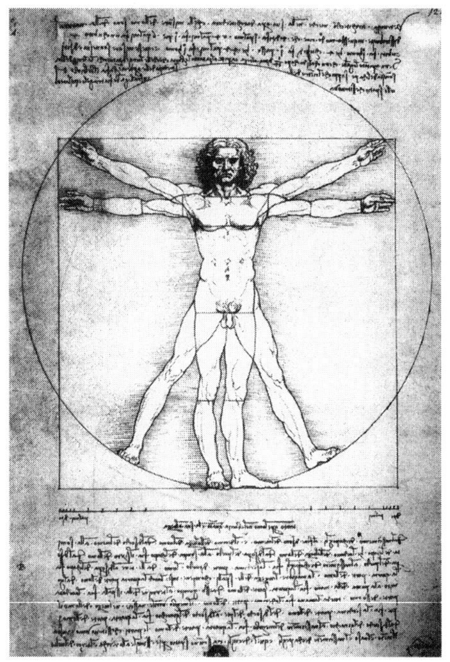

Artist Leonardo da Vinci created his famous drawing of the "Vitruvian Man" around 1490. It illustrates the idea of the ancient Roman architect Vitruvius that the human body with outstretched limbs forms a perfect circle and square.

ARCHITECTURAL THEORY

In the 1500s and 1600s, various Italian architects attempted to establish the basic principles governing architecture. They explained their ideas in treatises. Some architects looked to the natural world for ideas about the ideal proportions of objects. This approach helped to link architecture to painting, sculpture, and literature, which often tried to imitate nature. Architectural treatises helped raise the status of architecture from a technical skill to an art. They also helped spread ideas about architecture throughout Europe.

The first manuscripts on architecture appeared in the mid-1400s. Many early writers, such as Leon Battista ALBERTI, modeled their works on Vitruvius's *On Architecture.* Alberti's *On the Art of Building,* published in Florence in 1486, presented the basic principles of ancient architecture. Alberti copied Vitruvius in using the human body as the model for good design. He defined architectural beauty in terms of the "reasoned harmony of all the parts within a body."

Most of the early architectural treatises were aimed at scholars rather than practicing architects. One of the first authors to focus on the practical needs of architects was Sebastiano Serlio (1475–1554). He wrote seven easy-to-understand volumes in Italian, illustrated with woodcuts*, that provided a complete program of instruction for architects. The final book dealt with practical problems an architect might face, such as building on a slope.

* **woodcut** print made from a block of wood with an image carved into it

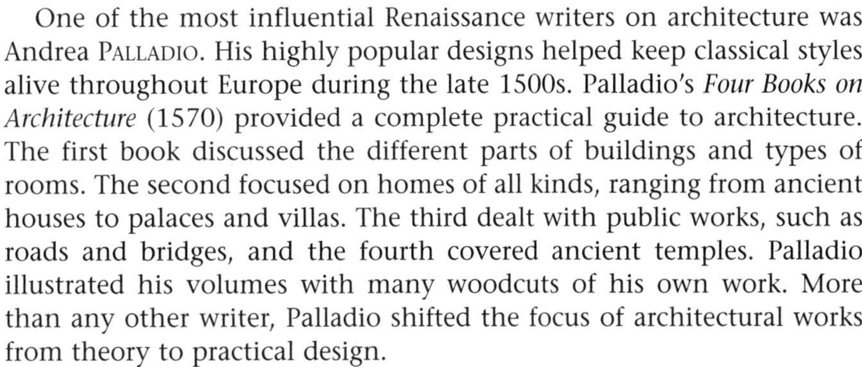

One of the most influential Renaissance writers on architecture was Andrea Palladio. His highly popular designs helped keep classical styles alive throughout Europe during the late 1500s. Palladio's *Four Books on Architecture* (1570) provided a complete practical guide to architecture. The first book discussed the different parts of buildings and types of rooms. The second focused on homes of all kinds, ranging from ancient houses to palaces and villas. The third dealt with public works, such as roads and bridges, and the fourth covered ancient temples. Palladio illustrated his volumes with many woodcuts of his own work. More than any other writer, Palladio shifted the focus of architectural works from theory to practical design.

During the 1500s, architects formed academies of design, modeled on the literary academies that had recently appeared throughout Italy. The Accademia del Disegno in Florence, founded in 1563, provided architects with a professional identity and a place to discuss and teach architecture. The use of *design* rather than *architecture* in the name suggests that its founders were trying to link architecture to other art forms. Later architects explored their craft's connections to the sciences. (*See also* **Art; Cities and Urban Life; Classical Antiquity; Classical Scholarship; Luxury; Palaces and Townhouses.**)

Human Geometry

The ancient Roman architect Vitruvius saw the human body as the source of ideal geometric forms. He observed that a human with outstretched limbs fit precisely within the shapes of a circle and a square. Renaissance artist Leonardo da Vinci illustrated this idea in a drawing that became very famous. The artist saw in this drawing an image of the human body as a small-scale model of the entire universe.

Ariosto, Ludovico

1474–1533
Italian poet

Ludovico Ariosto was a Renaissance poet and playwright, best known for his poem *Orlando Furioso* (Mad Roland). The poem was wildly successful in Ariosto's lifetime and inspired artists and musical composers well into the 1700s. Ariosto also gained recognition for his critical view of humanism*.

* **humanism** Renaissance cultural movement promoting the study of the humanities (the languages, literature, and history of ancient Greece and Rome) as a guide to living

Education and Career. Ariosto called Ferrara, Italy, his home for much of his life. He received a humanist education as a child and studied Latin literature and philosophy at the University of Ferrara. His father, an officer in service to the ruling Este family, wanted Ariosto to have a career in government. Therefore, at his father's insistence, Ariosto reluctantly enrolled in law school.

When Ariosto's father died in 1500, the young man dropped out of school to support his family. He worked for many years as an administrator and diplomat for a church official who was part of the Este family. In 1517 the duke of Ferrara, another Este leader, accepted Ariosto into his court. The duke later gave Ariosto a post as the government officer in charge of a mountainous Italian province. During his years of service to the Este, Ariosto wrote poetry, including *Orlando Furioso.* He completed the work in 1516 and revised in 1521.

In 1525, Ariosto returned from the mountain province and turned to supervising the construction and operation of the duke's theater. This gave him the opportunity to work with set designers on several of his own plays. Ariosto devoted his final years to plays and other literary projects, including the third and final revision of *Orlando Furioso,* which came out in 1532.

Ariosto and Humanism. Although Ariosto received a humanist education, he had doubts about its value. Several of Ariosto's works criticize humanist education through satire*. In *Orlando Furioso,* the character Ruggiero appears unable to learn ancient texts, suggesting that Ariosto believed some people were not suited to this type of education. In another piece, Ariosto mocked the humanist view that education in the classics was a cure-all for society's problems. He also attacked humanists as being immoral and suggested that their teachings were incomplete and sterile.

* **satire** literary or artistic work ridiculing human wickedness and foolishness

Important Works. Ariosto's most important and influential work, *Orlando Furioso,* is a long narrative* poem. In it, Ariosto used a medieval* war as a backdrop to explore many Renaissance themes, including love and insanity. He also expressed his views on such topics as the growing knowledge on geography, political and military alliances of the time, and the place of women in society.

* **narrative** storytelling
* **medieval** referring to the Middle Ages, a period that began around A.D. 400 and ended around 1400 in Italy and 1500 in the rest of Europe

The work drew on two different literary traditions: the ancient epic and the romances of the Middle Ages. Both describe the adventures of a hero, but in different ways. In an epic, the hero moves unfailingly toward a grand destiny. In a romance, by contrast, events tend to sidetrack the hero and distract him from his goals. Ariosto's central character, Roland, is a Christian knight fighting against the Saracens (Muslims) according to the rules of chivalry*. In this respect, he resembles an epic hero. He falls in love with the heroine Angelica and sets out to find her, encountering many adventures along the way, much like a hero of romance. However, in the middle of the story Roland becomes mad, losing his ability to function as a proper hero. The poem becomes more and more complex, as various characters appear and behave in unexpected ways that often do not fall within the traditions of epic and romance. In the confusing world of the story, the right course of action is not always clear.

* **chivalry** rules and customs of medieval knighthood

Orlando Furioso was a best-seller in the 1500s, and its popularity lasted well into the next century. The poem inspired many later works of art and music. A number of European painters, including Peter Paul Rubens, painted scenes from the poem. Other famous artists illustrated editions of the work. One reason the poem appealed to artists was that it reflected Ariosto's own interest in art. It contained numerous descriptions of popular works of art as well as praises for several artists of his day. *Orlando Furioso* also inspired musical composers such as Claudio Monteverdi. A century later, Antonio Vivaldi and George Frideric Handel each used the poem as the basis of an opera.

In addition to his narrative poem, Ariosto wrote lyric poetry* and plays. He modeled his lyric poetry, written in Italian and Latin, on the works of earlier Roman and Greek poets. Ariosto produced his first two plays around 1490. Both were comedies based on Roman models but adapted to Italian life in the 1400s. Ariosto produced what many critics think is his best play, *Lena,* in the late 1520s, just a few years before his death. (*See also* **Chivalry; Humanism; Italian Language and Literature; Poetry.**)

* **lyric poetry** verse that expresses feelings and thoughts rather than telling a story

Aristocracy

Social inequality was an accepted part of Renaissance society. Every European culture awarded special powers and privileges to the aristocracy, or nobility. However, societies had different ways of defining what it meant to be noble. The role of the aristocracy varied throughout Europe and changed over the course of the Renaissance.

Definitions of Aristocracy. The men and women of the Renaissance based their ideas about aristocracy on concepts inherited from the ancient world. In Greek philosophy, an aristocracy was a state or community ruled by the best men. Eventually, the term came to refer to the ruling class in such a society.

Societies used three different concepts to identify the "best" individuals. According to the political definition, aristocrats were those who held political power—usually the wealthiest members of society. The hereditary definition, by contrast, depended on birth. The idea behind this view was that great people passed on their qualities to their descendants. By the 1000s and 1100s, many cultures had developed a military definition. According to this view, a nobleman was a man who fought. This idea presented the aristocracy as one of three main segments of society, along with the clergy (those who prayed) and the commoners (those who worked).

All three definitions of aristocracy relied on the notion that some people were better than others. In other ways, however, the three definitions were quite different. The political and military visions allowed individuals to rise from one class to a higher one, while the hereditary view fixed a person's social class at birth. The hereditary and military models recognized the idea that poor people could be noble, but the political view usually defined nobles as wealthy.

These three contrasting views all remained powerful between the 1400s and 1600s. Europeans admired individuals who combined all three ideals—men from old families who fought in battles and governed. However, new ideas about nobility began to gain ground during the Renaissance. Humanists* such as Dutch scholar Desiderius ERASMUS and English statesman Thomas MORE mocked ignorant and violent noblemen. They suggested that to be truly noble, people needed education. Aristocrats across Europe responded to this message. During the 1500s, they attended universities in large numbers. Learning became a requirement for high positions in society and government. This shift in values improved the position of aristocratic women. Women could not compete in battle, but they could interact with men on more equal terms in the field of learning.

* **humanist** Renaissance expert in the humanities (the languages, literature, history, and speech and writing techniques of ancient Greece and Rome)

Beatrice d'Este belonged to two powerful noble families. The daughter of the duke of Ferrara, she married Ludovico Sforza, the duke of Milan. This portrait by a student of Leonardo da Vinci shows Beatrice wearing the jewelry of the upper class.

Varying Roles. The aristocracy's role in society varied from region to region. Wars in Poland, Hungary, and Spain created a large class of noble warriors. About 10 percent of the people in these regions were members of the aristocracy. Although many of these nobles were poor, a few held vast estates. In France and central Germany, by contrast, nobles made up about 2 percent of the population in 1500 and perhaps as little as 1 percent by 1650.

The position of the nobility also differed between northern and southern areas of Europe. Aristocrats in the Mediterranean region, especially northern Italy, had close ties to urban life. The governments of many Italian city-states made nobles live in the cities as a way of controlling them. Italian aristocrats also tended to be involved in the business of the cities, such as trade and banking. In northern Europe, by contrast, most aristocrats lived on country estates and avoided any involvement with banking or trade. However, these differences faded during the 1400s and 1500s. Urban Italian aristocrats began building country houses, and nobles in England and France spent more time in the cities.

The 1300s and 1400s were a time of crisis for nobles throughout Europe. Many died in wars and in civil conflicts within nations. They also faced economic problems. Wars and the plague* kept Europe's population low between 1348 and 1500, making labor more costly and lowering the value of crops. Aristocratic income, which depended heavily on land, shrank. At the same time, Europe's lower classes grew more dissatisfied with aristocratic power and privilege. They began to question the nobility's value to society. A series of rebellions broke out among peasants in England, France, Germany, and Spain. The wave of discontent climaxed in the great PEASANTS' WAR of 1525, which involved hundreds of thousands of villagers in Germany.

* **plague** highly contagious and often fatal disease that wiped out much of Europe's population in the mid-1300s and reappeared periodically over the next three centuries; also known as the Black Death

Nobles' fortunes improved after 1500, as the population rose and the economy grew stronger. However, inflation had lowered the value of the rents that lords typically received from villagers. To profit from the growing economy, aristocrats took direct control of lands and forests. Some nobles managed their own farms, but most found ways to profit from other people's work. Nobles in England leased land to tenant farmers. In Italy and southern France, aristocrats drew huge incomes from sharecropping. In this arrangement, they allowed farmers to work their land in exchange for half or more of the harvest it produced. In eastern Europe, some nobles forced villagers to work the land without any form of pay.

The Perils of Power

Being a Renaissance aristocrat was not always an advantage. Nearly half of all English dukes in the 1300s and 1400s died violent deaths. Many perished in the Wars of the Roses, a struggle for the English crown that lasted from 1455 to 1485. Civil wars elsewhere in Europe also made nobles' lives risky. Kings acted quickly against aristocrats whose loyalty they doubted, leading to more deaths and the complete disappearance of some noble families.

Aristocracy and the State. The growing power of governments in western Europe helped to transform aristocracies after 1500. The most significant change was government's more active role in defining the nobility. In the past, social status had depended on informal understanding within a society. By 1600, a person required a formal letter from the government to be considered noble. Governments also established elaborate systems for ranking members of the aristocracy.

Governments also took steps to control the aristocracy in other ways. They stepped in to end the tradition of private wars between aristocratic families. Governments encouraged aristocrats to spend more time at court, under the eyes of their rulers. In addition, nobles faced new social competition from the growing ranks of state administrators. These government officials, who were often commoners or minor nobles, gained power and wealth during the 1500s.

Although aristocrats lost some independence, they gained other benefits. In many countries, nobles no longer had to pay taxes. In addition, many gained wealth through direct gifts from monarchs and high-paying government and military positions. By the end of the Renaissance, the aristocracy had survived social, economic, and political change and remained a central part of European society. In fact, many writers and artists of the 1600s focused on aristocrats as useful examples for all social classes. (*See also* **Biography and Autobiography; Chivalry; Court; Plague; Social Status.**)

Aristotle and Aristotelianism

Aristotle was one of the chief philosophers of ancient Greece. His system of thought, known as Aristotelianism, had a great influence on Renaissance scholarship. Aristotle sought to explain what knowledge was, what fields it included, and how to develop it. Renaissance Aristotelianism influenced many areas of study and provided a foundation for modern science and philosophy in the 1600s.

ARISTOTLE'S WORKS AND TEACHINGS

Aristotle (384–322 B.C.) was a student of PLATO, another famous Greek thinker. After attending Plato's Academy for 20 years, Aristotle founded his own school of philosophy, the Lyceum. Although his works were copied and recopied many times during antiquity*, many were later lost.

* **antiquity** era of the ancient Mediterranean cultures of Greece and Rome, ending around A.D. 400

Aristotle's works fall into three categories. Some were notes to aid memory and prepare for further work. None of these works still exist. Others were texts for the general reading public, such as *On Philosophy* and *On Justice*. Only fragments of these survive, but comments made by later Greek and Roman scholars give some idea of their contents. The third category included works that Aristotle intended for school use. For these, he used a terse, concise style. All of Aristotle's surviving writings belong to this category. Because Aristotle may have changed these texts throughout his teaching career, modern scholars cannot be certain of exactly when he wrote them or in what order.

Philosophy and Logic. Philosophy had a much wider range in ancient Greece than it has now. Aristotle dealt with several topics that are still a part of philosophy today, such as logic, metaphysics*, and ethics*. However, he also discussed subjects that are now independent fields, such as mathematics, natural and political science, poetics (the formal discussion of poetry), and rhetoric (the art of speaking or writing effectively). Within each area, he sought to identify the universal truths that were essential to understanding the subject.

* **metaphysics** branch of philosophy concerned with the nature of reality and existence

* **ethics** branch of philosophy concerned with questions of right and wrong

Aristotle referred to logic as a science, but he did not regard it as a specific field. Rather, he saw it as tool used in other sciences. Its basic function was "analytics," an untangling of the complicated processes of human thought. Aristotle invented several elements of logic that are still in use today, such as the proposition (a statement to be proven true or false) and the syllogism (a method of formal argument).

The Sciences. Aristotle classified thought and activity into three realms. The first was the theoretical sciences, which aimed at knowledge alone. He called natural philosophy the first theoretical science. This field was concerned with nature—the world of physical objects that the senses could observe. Aristotle investigated topics such as motion, time, living things, and even the human soul in his study of natural philosophy. The second theoretical science was mathematics. Related to mathematics were the "mixed sciences," such as astronomy and optics, which applied mathematics to the study of natural things. The third theoretical science was metaphysics, which Aristotle regarded as the study of the divine.

Aristotle used the term *practical sciences* for fields related to human conduct. The practical sciences were ethics and politics, which together made up moral philosophy. The goal of these sciences was to achieve what is good for people and for society. Aristotle viewed the good as an ever-changing midpoint, or mean, between extremes. To locate that midpoint, a person had to possess the moral virtues of moderation*, courage, and justice. Aristotle believed that these virtues enabled a person to live a life of contemplation, or reflective thought, which he saw as the sole source of happiness. He taught that true forms of government helped their citizens to achieve happiness in two ways: by promoting the moral virtues and by working for the common good, rather than that of a particular class.

* **moderation** an attitude of avoiding extremes

The productive sciences, in Aristotle's view, were concerned with creating things. He developed his ideas about productive science in *Poetics,* focusing on tragic drama, and *Rhetoric,* exploring the persuasive use of language.

RENAISSANCE ARISTOTELIANISM

The Aristotle familiar to Renaissance scholars was different from the Aristotle known in late antiquity. Over the centuries, scholars and philosophers had preserved and commented on Aristotle's writings. Often they tried to unite his ideas with those of Plato. In the 1000s and 1100s, Aristotelian studies expanded to include the writings of Arabic scholars.

Scholars first began to create Latin translations of nearly all of Aristotle's works in the mid-1100s. Then, after the eastern city of CONSTANTINOPLE fell to the Turks in 1453, Greek scholars from this region moved to the West. The shared their rich knowledge of Greek texts with Latin humanists*, expanding the study of both Plato and Aristotle. New translations and interpretations of Aristotle's thought reshaped Aristotelianism in the Renaissance.

* **humanist** referring to a Renaissance cultural movement promoting the study of the humanities (the languages, literature, and history of ancient Greece and Rome) as a guide to living

Renaissance Views of Aristotle. Aristotle's logical and theoretical works made up the core of university teaching during the Middle Ages and the Renaissance. Scholars took a variety of different approaches to Aristotle's works. Some humanists focused on the historical and cultural references in Aristotle's works. Others used Aristotle to help them find

answers to difficult philosophical questions. Aristotle's thought also strongly influenced the work of some natural scientists who laid the groundwork for modern science, including Galileo GALILEI and William HARVEY.

Two Aristotelians who taught in Padua, Italy, show the variety in Renaissance approaches to Aristotle. Jacopo Zabarella (1533–1589) used observation to determine the truth about nature. His colleague Cesare Cremonini (1550–1631) was content to find truth in the text of Aristotle alone.

Plato Versus Aristotle

Both Aristotle and his teacher Plato have been extremely influential in the Western world. Early Christian thinkers favored Plato because of his teachings on the soul and creation. Aristotle gained importance when his long-lost teachings on arts and sciences became available in the 1100s and 1200s. Then, in the early Renaissance, interest in Plato increased. Historians once considered Plato the major philosopher of the Renaissance, but modern scholars realize that Aristotle had a greater influence on Renaissance thinkers.

The End of Renaissance Aristotelianism. Early historians of the Renaissance believed that humanism had replaced Aristotelianism in the 1400s and 1500s. Scholars today, however, believe that humanism did not have a particular philosophical framework. Instead, its main elements were Greek and Latin grammar, history, rhetoric, and literature. Some humanists were Aristotelians, just as some were followers of Plato or other ancient thinkers. Nonetheless, Aristotelianism ceased to develop after the end of the 1500s. Aristotle's complex system of thought fell out of favor, and its influence steadily declined over the next two centuries. (*See also* **Drama; Humanism; Logic; Philosophy; Political Thought; Rhetoric; Science.**)

Armada, Spanish

In 1588 the king of Spain, PHILIP II, attacked England with a war fleet called the Spanish Armada. The naval battle was a crushing defeat for Spain. Although this battle did not end the conflict between the two nations, both the Spanish and the English came to see it as a turning point in history.

On Course for War. Politics and religion both contributed to the conflict between Spain and England. In the early 1580s, Spain had used its naval forces to take over Portugal and its overseas empire. Both England and France opposed Spain's expansion. France responded by sending ships and troops to support Portuguese rebels. After the Spanish navy smashed a combined French and Portuguese fleet, the victorious Spanish commander suggested to Philip that the navy might settle matters with England, too.

England and Spain stood on opposite sides of a religious divide. Spain was a Roman Catholic nation, but England had become Protestant. The English queen ELIZABETH I had aided Protestant rebels in the Netherlands, which was then a territory of Spain. She also allowed English seafarers such as Francis DRAKE to make piratical attacks on Spanish ships and ports. Philip, in turn, supported Catholic plots against Elizabeth.

By mid-1585 Philip's army seemed close to crushing the Protestant revolt in the Netherlands. England declared its support for the rebels, setting the stage for war with Spain. Philip sought advice from his naval commander, the marquis of Santa Cruz, and his governor-general in the Netherlands, the duke of Parma. They planned to send a massive fleet into English waters to take on the English navy, considered the best in

Europe. Meanwhile, 30,000 of Parma's troops would cross the English Channel for a surprise attack on England. Such plans, however, could not remain secret. Drake learned of the plot and decided to strike first. In 1587 he attacked the Spanish port of Cádiz, destroying several dozen ships and slowing Spain's preparations.

The Battle. Before the fleet could sail, Santa Cruz died. His replacement, the duke of Medina Sidonia, lacked experience in naval combat. Storms then delayed the fleet's departure. In July of 1588 the Armada finally sailed for the English Channel with 125 vessels and 28,000 men.

Some of the Armada's sailors wanted to attack the English port of Plymouth. However, on Philip's orders, Medina Sidonia bypassed Plymouth and directed the Armada toward the planned meeting with Parma's force. The English fleet, which was stationed at Plymouth, slipped out of port at night and worked its way to the Armada's rear. It attacked the Armada on July 31, doing little damage. However, the Spanish lost two ships to accidents. The battle that followed centered on about 30 ships from each side.

The English tested the Spanish defenses for two days. On the third day the Armada lashed back. Knowing that the English had better shipboard guns, the Spanish planned to get close to English ships and then board them for hand-to-hand fighting. But the English kept their distance, peppering the Spanish fleet with cannon fire. The Armada anchored off Calais, France, to await Parma's force, but Parma was not quite ready to sail. The English did not wait. They attacked at night with fire ships—launching empty vessels toward the Spanish fleet and setting them on fire. The Armada fled from its anchorage and out into the North Sea. The Spanish officers decided to retreat to Spain by going north around Scotland and Ireland. They lost more than two dozen ships to storms on the return voyage. Barely half the Armada returned to Spain.

After the Armada. The defeat of the Armada brought joy to England and to Dutch Protestants. The war, however, raged on, with successes and failures on both sides, until James I of England and Philip III of Spain made peace in 1604.

To the English, the victory over the Armada came to represent the dawn of a heroic age of empire. The English also tended to see the battle as the defeat of a large force by a smaller but braver one, forgetting that their navy had had bigger guns and better ships. For the Spanish, the defeat of the Armada became a sign of the long decline that ended in the loss of their empire. (*See also* **England; Ships and Shipbuilding; Spain; Warfare.**)

Arms and Armor

Arms and armor changed significantly during the Renaissance, with improvements in one of them often leading to modifications in the other. New military tactics and techniques triggered some developments, while others were based on fashion. Armor and weapons were

not simply tools of war; they also served important social and artistic functions.

Renaissance armor was not just a means of protection, but also a work of art. Some armor, like the suit shown here, had simple borders cut into the metal. Other pieces displayed elaborate images of saints or ancient heroes. The most expensive armor included designs in silver or gold.

Development of Armor. The most popular form of armor during the Middle Ages was mail—sheets of interlocking iron rings. Though flexible and strong, mail did not protect as well as solid plates. In the 1200s armorers began making plate armor out of materials such as leather and, eventually, steel. The earliest plate armor protected the lower legs and knees, the areas that a foot soldier could easily attack on a mounted knight. Over time, armor expanded to cover more and more of the body.

By the early 1400s, knights were encased in complete suits of overlapping steel plates. A full suit of armor might weigh as much as 60 pounds, but its weight was distributed over the entire body. A knight accustomed to wearing armor could mount and dismount a horse fairly easily and even lie down and rise again without difficulty. A foot soldier wore less armor than a knight. He might have an open-faced helmet and a shirt of mail with solid plates covering his back and chest.

Armor changed again as firearms became more common. Rigid armor would crack when hit by a shot from a pistol or musket. Some armorers responded by making their armor harder, while others produced plates that would dent rather than breaking. However, the only really effective technique was to thicken the armor, which made it too heavy to wear in battle. As armor became less useful, soldiers tended to wear less of it. By 1650 most mounted fighters wore only an open-faced helmet, a heavy breastplate, and a backplate. By 1700 armor had all but disappeared from the battlefield.

Tournaments called for special armor. Since participants did not have to carry the armor's weight as long as they would in battle, they wore heavier armor that offered them greater protection. Each specific event in a tournament required its own type of armor. Some contests involved battles between mounted knights, while others featured hand-to-hand combat on foot.

Most armor, even that worn in battle, was decorated in some way. The decoration ranged from etched borders around the edges of plates to detailed images of saints or ancient heroes. Some very expensive armor was inlaid with patterns in silver or gold. Highly decorated weapons and suits of armor were status symbols, worn only at court or on special social occasions.

Development of Arms. Renaissance weapons fell into three basic categories: edged weapons, staff weapons, and projectile weapons. Edged weapons included swords and daggers. Renaissance swords often had thin, stiff blades to pierce the gaps between the plates in a suit of armor. The blades were usually straight and had two sharpened edges, although some swords featured curved or single-edged blades. Large swords swung with two hands were common among foot soldiers in Germany and Switzerland.

A staff weapon, a pole with a steel head, was used to cut, stab, or strike an opponent. Heavily armored mounted knights favored the lance, a

wooden shaft 10 to 12 feet long with a steel tip. Foot soldiers, especially in Switzerland, often used the halberd, a 5- to 7-foot shaft with a head that had both a cutting edge and a point for stabbing.

Projectile weapons were designed to hurl objects at great speeds. The simplest of these, the sling, threw stones or lead pellets. Most archers in the 1300s and 1400s used the longbow. Both it and the mechanical crossbow could shoot arrows capable of penetrating plate armor at certain ranges. In the 1500s, firearms gradually took the place of bows.

The first pistols, called "hand cannons," appeared in the early 1300s. They were little more than a barrel with a handle, or stock. The barrel had a chamber, or breech, that held shot and powder. The soldier loaded powder into the open end of the barrel (the muzzle) and packed it tight with a rod. The bullet went in after the powder. The gunner touched a lighted fuse to a small hole in the barrel to ignite the powder and fire the shot.

Over the next few hundred years, various improvements made firearms more reliable and easier to fire. The most important development was the invention of firing mechanisms, known as locks, in the 1400s. The simplest kind was the matchlock. It had an arm that held the lighted fuse. Pulling a trigger turned the arm, touching the fuse to the powder. Even easier to use was the wheel lock, which removed the need for a fuse. It ignited the powder by striking a spark from a piece of iron pyrite when the trigger was pulled. A variation of this, the flintlock, relied on flint to produce a spark.

* **siege** prolonged effort to force a surrender by surrounding a fortress or town with armed troops, cutting the area off from aid

* **coat of arms** set of symbols used to represent a noble family

Heavy cannons, or artillery, appeared about the same time as firearms. Artillery pieces were loaded and fired in much the same way as firearms, but they fired much larger stones and iron balls. The biggest artillery pieces were used for castle sieges*. The largest gun ever built could hurl a 300-pound stone ball up to two miles. However, siege cannons weighed thousands of pounds and could not be moved easily. By the late 1400s, field artillery had been developed that could be mounted on wheels and transported. Cannons also became common aboard ships. Like armor, many cannons were highly decorated with designs or the owners' coats of arms*. (*See also* **Warfare.**)

Art

* **guild** association of craft and trade owners and workers that set standards for and represented the interests of its members

The Renaissance was a time of great artistic achievement, during which people gradually began to think of art as a means of expression rather than a craft. Similarly, artists came to be seen as individuals, rather than unknown members of guilds* or workshops. Various factors contributed to this transformation in the nature of art, particularly economic growth and prosperity, new social and intellectual developments, and a revival of interest in ancient Greek and Roman culture. In addition, the intense level of artistic activity from about 1300 to the early 1600s led to advances in theory and technique.

PATRONAGE AND HUMANISM

By the 1200s profits from trade and other commercial ventures had produced a concentration of wealth in cities such as FLORENCE, Italy, and

Antoniazzo Romano's *The Annunciation,* painted sometime between 1475 and 1485, provides an example of the use of perspective in Renaissance art. Artists adopted this new technique to create the illusion of depth in a painting. As artists gained a better understanding of perspective, their work appeared more true to life.

ANTWERP, in present-day Belgium. This prosperity enabled many people—not only rulers and church leaders but also private individuals—to become patrons* of the arts. Familiar with the masterpieces of the ancient world, patrons sought out promising painters and sculptors and commissioned pieces from them. Moreover, support for the arts did not come only from the wealthy and powerful. Even members of the middle class purchased paintings, prints, and figurines.

* **patron** supporter or financial sponsor of an artist or writer

The riches of the Renaissance were only one factor involved in changing attitudes about art. Just as important was the rise of humanism, a cultural movement promoting the study of ancient Greek and Roman literature and ideas. Following the fall of the Roman Empire in the 400s, most of the learning of these ancient societies had been lost to Europeans. During the late Middle Ages, however, Europeans began to rediscover Greek and Roman literary works. They took note of the value ancient writers placed on balance, harmony, and style in public speaking, writing, and the visual arts. These ideals of the ancient civilizations became the central principles of humanism. The artists of the Renaissance eagerly accepted the new movement. As humanism spread across Europe, art based on a revival of classical* traditions found a ready audience.

* **classical** in the tradition of ancient Greece and Rome

Renaissance artists studied many ancient texts on art and design. Among the most influential was the *Ten Books on Architecture* by Roman writer Vitruvius. In this work the author lays out a systematic approach to architecture. He emphasizes composition*; attention to detail; and proportion, including designing buildings to suit the dimensions of the

* **composition** arrangement of objects in a work of art

human body. Vitruvius also identifies various categories of artistic forms and styles, such as the different types of columns used in classical buildings. Although Vitruvius wrote about architecture, Renaissance artists applied his ideas on composition and design to painting and drawing.

THEORIES OF ART

Classical concepts of orderly design gave Renaissance artists a set of rules to follow in the creation of their works. However, other ideas helped shape artistic theory and practice in the Renaissance.

Ancient writers taught that the object of art is to imitate nature as perfectly as possible. However, a work of art can never be more than an image of an actual object. For this reason, artistic imitation involves creating a convincing illusion of reality, to make the work appear as lifelike as possible.

To create realistic images, Renaissance artists returned to the ancient practice of carefully examining nature. Art teachers encouraged their students to study classical statues, live human models, and objects in the everyday world. Artists attempted to master fine details of form, structure, and movement to create the most lifelike images. Workshops provided model drawings called *exempla* for students to copy, to help them master the challenges involved in creating the illusion of reality. For example, the studio of the Italian master Michelangelo Buonarroti produced an entire sheet of paper covered with drawings of eyes. As a result of this close study of nature, Renaissance artists achieved a high level of realism. The figures in their paintings seem to have weight and substance and one can almost feel the texture of the fabrics and solid objects.

ARTISTIC DEVELOPMENTS OF THE RENAISSANCE

Renaissance art evolved from a common set of principles, but it took many directions and changed considerably over time. Moreover, despite the emphasis on following classical ideals, some Renaissance artists did not hesitate to break the rules to create new styles of their own.

Early Renaissance Art. The artists of the 1300s and early 1400s created their works before the rediscovery of most of the classical writings on art and design. They attempted to imitate nature and to follow the examples of classical sculpture and art found in ancient ruins, but they did not work according to the formal rules of classical art. As a result, early Renaissance art combines elements of classical and medieval* styles as well as other influences. Compared to later work it is highly experimental and shows great freedom of expression.

One of the first Renaissance artists was the Italian fresco* painter Giotto di Bondone, who worked during the late 1200s and early 1300s. His ability to create lifelike images displaying brilliant color, dramatic

* **medieval** referring to the Middle Ages, a period that began around A.D. 400 and ended around 1400 in Italy and 1500 in the rest of Europe

* **fresco** mural painted on a plaster wall

Not Just a Man's World

During the Renaissance, women worked in almost every art form except architecture. They usually focused on small projects such as illuminated books, but some created paintings, prints, and sculpture. Sofonisba ANGUISSOLA painted portraits for members of the Spanish court, and Artemisia Gentileschi produced biblical and mythological scenes for Italian patrons. Women sculptors tended to work in clay; only one, Properzia de' Rossi, carved stone. Most female artists were nuns, who often trained other nuns in the arts. Other women in the field included the daughters or wives of artists and women from minor noble families.

poses, deep emotion, and a sense of weight and depth made his work immensely popular. While Giotto's style spread throughout Italy, artists in northern Europe were developing their own form of realistic painting. They focused on mastering light, shadow, and color to imitate closely the textures of the physical world.

By the 1400s the growing number of art collectors led to a steady commerce in paintings and illustrated books. This trade helped spread Italian style to northern Europe while making the work of northern artists popular in Italy. Florence became a center of artistic activity, where painters such as Sandro BOTTICELLI produced works for members of the MEDICI family and other wealthy patrons.

Rome in the 1500s. Following the rediscovery of classical learning in the mid-1400s, the center of artistic activity shifted to Rome. The city contained the world's greatest concentration of ancient paintings, statues, monuments, and buildings. It was also the seat of the Roman Catholic Church, a major source of patronage for the arts in the form of commissions from the popes and other church leaders.

By 1500 two of the most important Renaissance artists—MICHELANGELO and Donato BRAMANTE—had moved to Rome. Michelangelo polished his sculptural skills there and created the *Pietà,* a masterpiece portraying Mary holding the body of Christ. Meanwhile Bramante studied the techniques of classical architecture. Both artists made major contributions to buildings at the Vatican, the headquarters of the church in Rome. Bramante redesigned St. Peter's Basilica, the main church at the Vatican, while Michelangelo painted a majestic series of biblical scenes on the ceiling of the Sistine Chapel in the Vatican palace.

See color plate 2, vol. 1

During the 1500s classical principles made a greater impact on art. The painter RAPHAEL, who arrived in Rome in 1508, developed a complete philosophy of art in which he applied the classical rules of architecture to painting. Raphael explained his theory in a letter addressed to Pope LEO X, for whom he completed a number of projects at the Vatican. Based on the imitation of nature, respect for order, and the use of accepted artistic forms, Raphael's views echoed the work of Vitruvius. Yet in his own work, Raphael often moved beyond the classical ideals, breaking rules to create designs that were unique but still balanced and orderly.

Mannerism. While the most creative artists, such as Raphael, played freely with the rules of classical art, less talented artists tended to follow the guidelines rigidly. Renaissance art had begun as a revolutionary movement, but by the early 1500s many artists felt it was becoming too bound up in rules. A new generation of artists launched a movement known as Mannerism, in which they broke free of theory and explored different forms of expression.

Mannerists stretched the rules by using dramatic colors, experimenting with perspective* and form, and creating elegant, vivid, and expressive images. Examples of Mannerist work include religious paintings by PARMIGIANINO, Rosso Fiorentino, and Jacopo da Pontormo, and elongat-

* **perspective** artistic technique for creating the illusion of three-dimensional space on a flat surface

See color plate 8, vol. 1

ed portraits by EL GRECO. Michelangelo's use of nontraditional colors such as purple, orange, and teal blue in the Sistine Chapel also shows the influence of Mannerism.

Mannerism appeared in sculpture and architecture as well. Mannerist sculptors explored the use of colored marble and began to work in harder types of stone that challenged their skills. Architects deliberately broke the rules set down by Vitruvius and Raphael, varying the standard elements and playing with proportion and scale in their building designs. Mannerism gradually gained popularity throughout Europe. Meanwhile, the 1500s saw a surge of interest in art forms other than painting, sculpture, and architecture. Metalwork, jewelry, tapestry, and even weapons and armor gained attention as significant works of art.

ARTISTIC TECHNIQUES AND PRACTICES

During the Renaissance artists adopted the latest technical advances to achieve the effects they were seeking. New materials, such as oil-based paints and inexpensive paper, enabled artists to explore different directions in painting and drawing. Meanwhile, a growing understanding of perspective revolutionized the ways in which artists could make objects appear real.

See color plate 14, vol. 4

Perspective. The main tool that Renaissance artists used to create the illusion of three-dimensional space was linear perspective. This technique draws the viewer's eye to a point called the "vanishing point," and all lines in the picture seem to lead to this point. For example, roads in the scene will seem to run toward the vanishing point and disappear into the distance. Also, objects that are supposed to be farther away are shown at a smaller scale than those that are supposed to be closer, just as they would appear if a person were looking at them in real life.

To make the illusion of depth realistic, the objects in a picture using linear perspective must be drawn according to a very precise scale. If objects in the background are too small or too large compared to those in the foreground, the illusion will not work. The use of perspective thus depends on working out the exact mathematical proportions of objects and distances in the picture. Artists made the illusion of depth even more realistic through the technique of atmospheric perspective. This involves making the shape and color of objects in the foreground clearer and more distinct than those in the distance.

When early Renaissance painters such as Giotto first introduced perspective into their work, they applied it mostly to objects in the foreground and not throughout the scene. In the early 1400s the Italian artist Filippo BRUNELLESCHI made the first systematic use of perspective in two panel paintings of buildings in Florence. In the 1430s Leon Battista ALBERTI presented a thorough explanation of the principles of perspective in a book about painting. Thereafter, the use of the technique became common.

Later artists turned their attention to solving specific problems of perspective, such as creating the illusion of depth on a circular panel or on

The Magic of Images

One of the ideas that Renaissance culture inherited from ancient Greece and Rome and from the Middle Ages was a belief in the power of images. In 1357 the people of Siena, Italy, suspected that a statue of Venus in the central square was bringing misfortune to the city. To solve the problem, they chopped the sculpture to bits, carried the pieces across the border with Florence, and buried them. Such beliefs continued throughout the Renaissance. In the early 1500s, people in Rome flocked to a statue of Mary thought to cure plague. Much like ancient sculptures depicting motherly figures, the statue was also said to combat infertility.

the curved surfaces of ceiling vaults and domes. Some used perspective to draw the viewer into the painting, by incorporating elements that seem to enter the picture from the front. Others used it to emphasize some aspect of the scene, such as placing the vanishing point at the head of Christ in a religious picture.

Drawing. During the Renaissance, drawing emerged as a major art form. Before this time, artists limited the amount of drawing they did because paper, the most suitable material for drawing, was not readily available. However, after the invention of the printing press in the mid-1450s, paper manufacturing improved to meet the demand for printed texts. As a result, paper became less expensive and easier for artists to obtain.

Renaissance artists employed a variety of techniques to produce drawings. In silverpoint, the artist used a pointed tool to scratch lines on the surface of a paper covered with calcium. Each stroke left behind fine particles of silver that tarnished and turned gray. Over time, many artists began to work in charcoal and in pen and ink. Both of these techniques were more flexible than silverpoint and allowed the artist to show textures, shadowing, and changes in tone more effectively.

Art students made copies of drawings by their teachers to study solutions to common artistic challenges and to learn the master's style. This was especially important in workshops that attempted to create a uniform style in their projects. After about 1450 the idea of exploring the natural world by observing and sketching became fairly widespread. Many artists, particularly those eager to move beyond formulas in their designs, used drawing as a problem-solving tool, working out ideas and searching for original solutions on paper. These drawings have a more experimental and rapidly executed look than the carefully finished models intended for students to copy.

During the Renaissance, one of the most popular subjects for drawing was the human body. Artists studied both ancient sculptures and live models as they sought to represent human emotions and movement as realistically as possible. The demand for portraits led many artists to produce numerous studies of heads. In these drawings they worked on mastering the proportions, types, and expressions of human faces.

Drawing was often used in preparation for a painting. By the late 1400s, artists were drawing small-scale models before starting work on a painting. They enlarged these models into full-scale images called cartoons, and then transferred the design to the surface they intended to paint.

Painting. Renaissance artists painted on a variety of surfaces ranging from wood to canvas to walls. The process generally involved multiple steps, beginning with the design and composition stage and moving on to preparation of the surface, mixing pigments (colored powders), and transferring and completing the image.

Artists working on wood panels or canvas coated the surface with several layers of gesso, a mixture of materials such as plaster and glue. Then

they smoothed and polished the surface. Early Renaissance painters reproduced gold tones by gilding, applying a thin layer of gold over a layer of soft red clay. The clay prevented the delicate sheets of gold from breaking. After the mid-1400s, gilding became less popular and artists began to use gold paint, which allowed them to vary the tone more effectively.

Artists painted on damp plaster to create frescoes. First, they applied several layers of plaster until the wall was smooth. Then they transferred a sketch of the painting to the wall and applied a final layer of plaster. Because plaster dries quickly, they only coated the area that they could paint in one day. After the plaster dried, the only way to make changes was by chiseling out the previous work or painting over it. But the new paint tended to flake off.

Each workshop mixed its own pigments from various materials. About 18 standard pigments were commonly used in the Renaissance. Many of these, particularly the most brilliant, were not suitable for frescoes. Painters made ultramarine—a bright blue—by crushing the semiprecious blue stone lapis lazuli. Because lapis was extremely expensive, painters rarely used ultramarine on large pieces. One exception is the scene of the *Last Judgment* by Michelangelo, part of the monumental series in Rome's Sistine Chapel. The pope, who commissioned the work, paid for the ultramarine used in the vivid blue background.

For painting on other surfaces, such as wood or canvas, artists mixed dry pigments with either egg or oil. Oil-based paints dry much more slowly than those made with egg. Developed in the Netherlands in the early 1400s, oil painting did not reach Italy until the 1460s but eventually became common there. Using slow-drying paints, artists could blend and build up layers of color to achieve the richness and depth that distinguish many great works of Renaissance art. (*See also* **Academies; Architecture; Art, Education and Training; Art in Britain; Art in Central Europe; Art in France; Art in Germany; Art in Italy; Art in the Netherlands; Art in Spain and Portugal; Baroque; Decorative Arts; Museums; Patronage; Sculpture; also see entries on individual artists.**)

Art, Education and Training

The methods and materials used to educate artists changed considerably during the Renaissance. Throughout the period, most young artists received their early training as apprentices*. However, during the 1400s learning about art theory gradually became as important as mastering practical skills. By the 1600s, art had evolved from a craft to a course of academic study.

* **apprentice** person bound by legal agreement to work for another for a specified period of time in return for instruction in a trade or craft

Apprenticeship. During the Renaissance, art apprentices studied under the guidance of a master artist. They usually began their training between the ages of 12 and 14, and served for a period of between 1 and 8 years. Parents of apprentices signed a contract with the master that set out the terms of the training. A typical contract required the master to provide food, housing, and clothing as well as instruction. In some cases

the parents paid the master a fee, while in others the apprentice received a salary from the master.

At first, local craft unions, or GUILDS, set standards for apprenticeship. The guilds decided matters such the length of contracts and the number of students a master could train. Some guilds would not allow pupils to switch masters during their apprenticeship or to sell their works independently. At the end of the apprenticeship students often had to show a piece of work to the guild to demonstrate that they had mastered their craft. This is the origin of the term *masterpiece.*

Artistic training varied from one master to another. In Italy, drawing was emphasized. A pupil might start by copying or tracing drawings and paintings before moving on to sketching live models. Students also learned to mix paints and to prepare walls and panels for painting. In addition, many apprentices studied techniques such as perspective* and proportion.

* **perspective** artistic technique for creating the illusion of three-dimensional space on a flat surface

Art Texts. The first art textbooks appeared in the 1400s. They differed from the practical handbooks about painting that artists had used during the Middle Ages. The early Renaissance texts discussed the theory of art and basic principles for art instruction. In *On Painting* (1435), the architect Leon Battista ALBERTI explained the use of geometry and optics (the study of the properties of light) in painting. He also discussed composition* and the qualities of the ideal painter. Books such as Alberti's instructed amateurs as well as professional artists, signaling a change in the public image of art. By the 1500s, most educated people received some artistic instruction.

* **composition** arrangement of objects in a work of art

Art texts originated in Italy, but they soon spread to northern Europe. The German painter and printmaker Albrecht DURER published two works on the subject in the 1520s. As books about art increased in number and popularity, they focused increasingly on theory. Many emphasized the Italian idea of *disegno,* which referred to the importance of design in painting. Others showed the relationship between fields such as mathematics or philosophy and art. Over time, knowledge of these other subjects became a necessary part of a serious artist's education.

Art Academies. Another important development in art education was the rise of art schools, or academies. The earliest academies were not formal schools but groups of apprentices who met at the end of the workday to practice drawing and other skills. Eventually such meetings grew into academies with an organized curriculum and regular classes. Over time the academies introduced new areas of study such as anatomy. They also began to set standards for training artists, a function previously performed by the guilds. For example, by 1571 artists in Florence no longer had to join a guild.

Italy led the way in founding art academies. Some of the early ones included the Compagnia e Accademia del Disegno in Florence, the Accademia del Disegno in Perugia, and the Accademia di San Luca in Rome. By the 1600s other European cities, such as Paris, Vienna, Madrid, and St. Petersburg, had academies devoted to educating artists. (*See also* **Academies; Art; Education.**)

Art in Britain

During the Renaissance a wave of new ideas about art swept across Europe. Many of these ideas were adopted in Britain in the 1500s, and by 1600 Britain had become an center for the development of Renaissance styles in art and architecture.

British Art to 1600. During the 1500s some British artists—particularly portrait painters—began to move away from the stylistic traditions of the Middle Ages. Artists such as Hans Holbein the Younger, who painted many individuals in the court of HENRY VIII of England, experimented with new approaches and techniques. However, in architecture and other fields the people of Britain were less enthusiastic about Renaissance ideas. They hesitated to adopt the *all'antica* (antique) style, which used classical forms based on ancient Greek and Roman models. The English associated this style with Italy, where it had emerged. Because Italy was a Catholic country and Britain was largely Protestant, some people in the British Isles were reluctant to accept this approach to design.

By the mid-1500s, however, British writers on architecture were promoting the use of the *all'antica* style. Designers began to incorporate more classical forms in official buildings and private residences. The English architect Inigo JONES used elements such as columns, triangular ornaments over windows, and carved foliage in the Banqueting House at Whitehall Palace in London (completed 1622).

Some writers also highlighted new artistic theories and techniques and emphasized the cultural value of art. In 1570 the English author John Dee introduced to Britain the Renaissance concept of applying mathematical principles such as proportion and perspective* to works of art. Dee challenged the traditional view of artists as members of a low social class. Moreover, he and other writers declared that well-educated people should have a basic knowledge and appreciation of art.

* **perspective** artistic technique for creating the illusion of three-dimensional space on a flat surface

British Art after 1600. In 1603 JAMES I became king of England, marking the beginning of the STUART DYNASTY and a period of great achievement in British art. James's son Henry helped make Renaissance art popular in Britain. After Henry's death in 1612, English nobles continued to follow his example. Thomas Howard, Earl of Arundel, traveled to Italy between 1613 and 1615 and brought back to England many antique and Renaissance works of art. These pieces provided models for artists to study.

The English court employed several famous artists, including the Flemish* masters Peter Paul RUBENS and Anthony Van Dyck. Artists at the court were expected to create works glorifying the English monarchs and reinforcing the idea that they ruled by divine right*. Rubens painted a series of ceiling panels that showed James I as a Christ-like figure bringing a new golden age to Britain. Other works depicting monarchs compared them with the great leaders of history. A bronze statue of CHARLES I (ruled 1625–1649) echoed images of the Roman emperor and philosopher Marcus Aurelius.

* **Flemish** relating to Flanders, a region along the coasts of present-day Belgium, France, and the Netherlands
* **divine right** idea that a monarch receives the right to rule directly from God

The English court masque, a type of play, brought together many Renaissance ideas. The masques were based on performances held at the courts of Italian nobles. For a number of productions, Inigo Jones created costumes decorated with popular Renaissance symbols. He also designed stage sets that used techniques such as perspective to create a scenic illusion. Yet the scenery often depicted a traditional English scene. Like other court artists, Jones used images drawn from British history and culture to create a uniquely English form of Renaissance art. (*See also* **Art; Art in Italy; England; Holbeins, The; Ireland; Scotland.**)

Art in Central Europe

During the Renaissance, many artists in central Europe looked to Italy for inspiration. They studied examples of Italian painting, sculpture, and architecture to learn about new theories and techniques. This interest and activity helped make the cities of Cracow in Poland, Prague in Bohemia (the present-day Czech Republic), and Buda in Hungary centers of Renaissance art and learning. Wealthy patrons*, including royalty, supported the production of art in these and other cities.

* **patron** supporter or financial sponsor of an artist or writer

Matthias Corvinus, the king of Hungary (ruled 1458–1490), was one of the earliest patrons of Renaissance culture in central Europe. Corvinus maintained close contacts in Florence, Milan, and other Italian cities throughout his reign. His successor, Vladislav II Jagiello, united Poland, Bohemia, and Hungary both politically and culturally. Vladislav and his brother, Sigismund I, helped spread Renaissance ideas throughout central Europe.

In 1526 Ferdinand I, a member of the Habsburg dynasty, took over as king of Bohemia and Hungary. Under the Habsburgs, royal patronage of the arts expanded dramatically, reaching a peak during the reign of Rudolf II (1572–1611).

Hungary. King Matthias Corvinus helped make the city of Buda (part of present-day Budapest) a center of Renaissance art in the 1400s. His first major artistic project was rebuilding the royal palace. Directed by an Italian architect, the reconstruction included grand courtyards that were enclosed by arcades*. Sculptures of Greek and Roman gods appeared alongside those of the king and his family.

* **arcade** series of arches resting on columns or pillars

Toward the end of his reign, Corvinus focused on assembling a great library, the Bibliotheca Corvina, which contained nearly 1,000 manuscripts. The collection reflected the king's interest in art and humanism* and included many richly decorated manuscripts produced by Hungarian and Italian artists.

* **humanism** Renaissance cultural movement promoting the study of the humanities (the languages, literature, and history of ancient Greece and Rome) as a guide to living

The first church building in Hungary designed entirely in Renaissance style was the Bakócz Chapel in the town of Esztergom. Begun in 1506, the chapel was built of red Hungarian marble and featured circular windows on the upper level and a dome held up by curved triangular supports. Commissioned by Vladislav II Jagiello, the chapel echoed the work of Italian architect Filippo Brunelleschi. In turn, it inspired a series

Sigismund Chapel in Cracow, Poland, contains the mixture of Italian Renaissance styles and earlier Gothic styles common to that city's art. The design of the chapel, which included such classical elements as a dome, statues, and images from mythology, influenced buildings throughout the kingdom.

of similar buildings in central Europe, including the Sigismund Chapel in Cracow.

The mid-1500s brought political turmoil to Hungary, including invasions by the OTTOMAN EMPIRE, based in present-day Turkey. Although part of Hungary fell under Ottoman control, the other areas continued to produce art in the Renaissance style well into the 1600s. In fact, the threat of Turkish attack led the Hungarians to build a number of new castles and to fortify some old ones, often with the help of Italian architects.

Poland. The Polish city of Cracow became one of the most important centers of Renaissance art. Although artists in Cracow, particularly

* **Gothic** style of architecture characterized by pointed arches and high, thin walls supported by flying buttresses; also, artistic style marked by bright colors, elongated proportions, and intricate detail

* **classical** in the tradition of ancient Greece and Rome

* **motif** theme or subject

architects and sculptors, employed certain Italian techniques, their work took on a distinctive form of its own. They mixed Renaissance styles with more traditional Gothic* ones. Moreover, most of the painting and decorative arts in Cracow followed styles popular in Germany, Poland, and the Netherlands.

The royal tomb of King Jan Olbracht (1505) was one of the first major works in Cracow to reflect Italian style. The tomb featured a classical* arch and decorations. However, the sculptor carved the figure of the king on the tomb in a style drawn from northern Europe, rather than from Italy. Another important example of Italian style is the Sigismund Chapel in Cracow Cathedral, which incorporated classical motifs* such as a dome, statues, and mythological images. Dedicated to Sigismund I (ruled 1506–1548), the chapel inspired many similar buildings throughout Poland.

In the late 1500s, a burst of artistic activity produced a "second" Renaissance in Poland. It was inspired partly by the work of artists from Venice and Lombardy in northern Italy. Polish architects and sculptors of this period combined ideas from Italy, Germany, and the Netherlands in an innovative way. In addition, Cracow developed a particularly distinctive tradition of miniature painting.

Bohemia. During the late 1400s and early 1500s, artists in Bohemia tended to merge the Gothic and Renaissance styles. Vladislav Jagiello commissioned several buildings for Hradcany Castle in Prague that displayed this tendency. The castle's Ludvik Wing, for example, featured a Gothic vaulted ceiling but Renaissance frames around the windows.

From the mid-1500s, the main artistic patrons in Prague were the Habsburg rulers, such as Ferdinand I, who brought a number of Italian artists to the city. In the 1530s Ferdinand ordered the construction of the Villa Belvedere on the castle hill in Prague. Based on the design of Italian Renaissance country houses, Belvedere had an arcade made up of columns capped by arches. The decorations included carvings of Greek and Roman subjects.

* **allegorical** referring to a literary or artistic device in which characters, events, and settings represent abstract qualities, and in which the author intends a different meaning to be read beneath the surface

* **still life** picture of inanimate objects, such as flowers or fruit

Bohemian artistic culture reached new heights under Habsburg ruler Rudolf II. In 1583 Rudolf set up his court in Prague and invited artists and humanists from throughout Europe to work there. Painters and sculptors at the court studied many of the pieces in Rudolf's outstanding art collection. Rudolf commissioned artists to produce portraits, allegorical* paintings, still lifes*, landscapes, sculpture, and decorative items in gold and ivory. In 1604 one observer described the Prague court as the most important place for an art lover to visit. (*See also* **Architecture; Art; Austria; Croatia and Dalmatia; Decorative Arts; Prague.**)

Art in France

Many historians consider the reign of Francis I (1515–1547) to be the beginning of the Renaissance in France. However, French artists of this period still carried on the traditions of the Middle Ages. Eventually, new styles from Italy began to have an influence in France. The nation's artists blended these foreign ideas with local traditions to

The royal château of Fontainebleau brought the Italian Renaissance to France with its architecture and decor, artworks and books. The lavish style of Fontainebleau had a great influence on the homes of French nobles and on the work of decorative artists in France. Artist Gilles Le Breton painted this view of Fontainebleau in the early 1500s.

create a distinctively French Renaissance style, particularly in architecture and the decorative arts.

Transition from Gothic to Renaissance. During the late Middle Ages, the focus of art in France was largely religious. The major artworks of this time were Gothic* cathedrals. Stonework on the outside of churches, sculptures in their interiors, stained glass windows, and illuminated* manuscripts all played a role in creating the religious background.

During the 1400s developments in neighboring states had an impact on the arts in France. The duchy* of BURGUNDY to the northeast became a artistic center with a tradition of courtly, or worldly, art. This tradition spread to France and began to flourish alongside religious art. Members of the nobility collected beautiful books, tapestries, and portraits. Meanwhile, artistic ties between France and Italy grew stronger. In the early 1500s styles of the Italian Renaissance gained a large following in France, though Gothic styles did not disappear. Sculptors, for example, blended Renaissance forms into traditional groupings of figures, making them livelier and more dramatic. The new Renaissance styles updated French artistic tradition, rather than revolutionizing it.

* **Gothic** style of architecture characterized by pointed arches and high, thin walls supported by flying buttresses; also, artistic style marked by bright colors, elongated proportions, and intricate detail

* **illuminated** having pages ornamented with hand-painted color decorations and illustrations

* **duchy** territory ruled by a duke or duchess

Italian designs also influenced French architecture. Buildings that were basically Gothic in style began to include classical* decorations. Several French churches built in the 1500s and 1600s, for example, feature classical columns and rounded rather than pointed arches. However, the greatest architectural changes in France appeared in the design of châteaus, or castles. The French king Francis I built several new châteaus during his reign and updated others. The most famous of his projects was the royal château of Fontainebleau, outside Paris.

* **classical** in the tradition of ancient Greece and Rome

Fontainebleau. Around 1528 Francis I began to expand and renovate the château of Fontainebleau, using Italian Renaissance ideas. His plan was to bring the best parts of Italian culture into France. He had already sent agents to Italy to collect books, paintings, and other works of art. A violent attack on Rome in 1527 by an army of the Holy Roman Empire* gave an unexpected boost to the king's project. Numerous artists fled Italy and sought work in France. They brought with them an elegant and ornate style that blended well with French Gothic forms.

* **Holy Roman Empire** political body in central Europe composed of several states; existed until 1806

Many of the artists who worked on Fontainebleau were part of a new movement called Mannerism*. The collection of art housed at Fontainebleau included pieces by leading Mannerist artists such as Benvenuto CELLINI. The room in the château called the Galerie François I (Gallery of Francis I) is widely viewed as the finest work of Mannerist art outside Italy. It features many large frescoes*, some based on stories from ancient mythology and others portraying the king in a variety of allegorical* settings. These large works appear alongside smaller paintings on wall panels and on the tops of columns. The gallery also includes decorative designs in woodwork and stucco*.

* **Mannerism** artistic style of the 1500s characterized by vivid colors and exaggeration, such as elongated figures in complex poses
* **fresco** mural painted on a plaster wall
* **allegorical** referring to a literary or artistic device in which characters, events, and settings represent abstract qualities and in which the author intends a different meaning to be read beneath the surface
* **stucco** building material made of cement, sand, and lime and used as a hard surface for exterior walls

The lavish decoration of Fontainebleau expressed the king's grand political and cultural ambitions. Images of this new style spread quickly throughout France thanks to the growth of printing in the late 1400s and early 1500s. Members of the nobility soon adopted it in their own homes and other buildings. In fact, by the late 1500s many observers were criticizing the excessive luxury and ornamentation of French buildings.

The ornamental designs of Fontainebleau also had a tremendous impact on French decorative arts, such as furniture, ceramics (objects made from clay), metalwork, and textiles. Many artists in these fields combined classical decorations with local styles. Bernard Palissy, one of the most famous decorative artists in France in the 1500s, was a naturalist as well as an artist. He dotted his brightly colored ceramics with figures of plants and animals.

See color plate 9, vol. 1

The French National Style. French artists who used classical styles wanted to do more than imitate the Italians. Their goal was to capture the spirit of the Renaissance and make it their own. They hoped to transform France into the "new Rome," the cultural heir to the glory of the ancient Roman Empire. Many French writers and artists traveled to Rome or copied Italian prints to capture the classical style.

French architects gradually began to incorporate Italian design into their work and to add classical decoration to the outer surfaces of buildings. However, they adapted the ancient designs to create a French clas-

sical style. Elements of this new style included ornamental brickwork and columns broken by roughened stone rings. These features became popular throughout France.

The French classical style of architecture reached its peak in the mid-1500s with the redesign of the Louvre palace in Paris. The architect, Pierre Lescot, blended classical forms with typically French design elements such as slate roofs. The building's sharply slanted roof, large windows, and abundant surface decoration soon became common elements of château design. Artist Jean Goujon decorated the upper levels of the building's exterior with relief* sculptures. These pieces feature heavy, yet graceful figures covered in elaborately molded drapery.

* **relief** type of sculpture in which figures are raised slightly from a flat surface

Meanwhile, French artists such as Jean and François Clouet were creating a national style in painting. They created many half-length nude portraits of women in curtained interiors, seated at dressing tables or in the bath. Later French historians considered these elegant paintings the best examples of a pure French national style, untouched by Italian influence. The Clouets also worked as court portraitists, producing formal paintings of kings and nobles. The other name most associated with the French national style, Jean Cousin, actually belongs to two artists—a father and son. Although few of their paintings survive, they are famous for their prints and their designs for decorative arts, such as stained glass and goldwork.

End of the Renaissance in France. The late 1500s and early 1600s were a period of crisis in France and elsewhere. The Protestant Reformation* brought great conflict and change to Europe, and it also had a crushing effect on the world of art. In the second half of the 1500s, France became a battlefield between Catholics and Protestants. The Wars of Religion (1562–1598) devastated the population and economy. The religious wars consumed much of the money and energy that might have been used to produce art.

* **Protestant Reformation** religious movement that began in the 1500s as a protest against certain practices of the Roman Catholic Church and eventually led to the establishment of a variety of Protestant churches

One art form that continued to flourish was the elaborate performances in the French court. Throughout the 1500s, French monarchs had employed artists such as Jean Cousin and poets such as Pierre de Ronsard to help them plan weddings, religious ceremonies, and other celebrations. These events generally involved elaborate processions and feasts. Artists created illustrated books, paintings, and tapestries in honor of the festivities. In the 1580s performances at court began to feature ballets, complete with music, dance, costume, and mythological themes.

Political conflicts shook France in the late 1500s. Paintings and prints from the 1580s often featured tiny figures engaged in acts of war or religious violence. Various groups used prints to promote their political positions. Some particularly vicious images attacked the king, Henry III, and his mother, Catherine de Médicis. In 1589 Henry was assassinated, and five years of bitter civil war followed. When Henry IV won the civil war in 1594, he showed little interest in promoting the arts. However, he did invest a great deal in modernizing the city of Paris. New buildings, bridges, and gardens encouraged nobles to make their homes in

Art of the Unusual

The style of art called Mannerism developed in Italy during the late Renaissance period. It focused on unusual images, such as figures of exaggerated length and twisted poses, and used bright and sometimes strange colors. Mannerist painters brought considerable emotion and expressiveness to their work. They often left the subjects of their works deliberately unclear, requiring viewers to guess at their meaning.

the city. These changes set the stage for the growth of new styles in French art. (*See also* **Architecture; Art; Châteaus and Villas; Decorative Arts; Protestant Reformation; Sculpture.**)

Art in Germany

During the Renaissance, the art of German-speaking lands was remarkably varied and inventive. Between 1400 and the late 1500s, printmaking and book publishing began in Germany, painting and sculpture rose to new artistic levels, and several German artists gained international fame. More than ever before, art became available and affordable to people at all levels of society. A simple woodcut* cost just pennies, and members of the growing merchant class adorned their homes with portraits and small collectible objects. They also filled their churches with statues, stained glass windows, and other works of art.

* **woodcut** print made from a block of wood with an image carved into it

The German Style. The Renaissance did not take hold in most German-speaking lands until about 100 years after it began in Italy. Even then, German art maintained a strong link to the traditional Gothic* styles of the Middle Ages. German painters adopted elements of the Renaissance style in creating more realistic forms and using perspective*. However, the bright colors and the stiffness of the figures in their work show the lingering influence of Gothic art.

* **Gothic** style of architecture characterized by pointed arches and high, thin walls supported by flying buttresses; also, artistic style marked by bright colors, elongated proportions, and intricate detail

* **perspective** artistic technique for creating the illusion of three-dimensional space on a flat surface

Most of the art in German-speaking countries was religious in nature. Religious images had two functions in society. First, they served as an aid to devotion, providing people with a focus for their faith. Second, religious art could reflect personal goals, both heavenly and earthly. For example, if a wealthy patron* donated an altarpiece to a church, the work might indicate the patron's desire for religious salvation. However, it would also remind other members of the community of the donor's prominent social or financial status.

* **patron** supporter or financial sponsor of an artist or writer

Most German painters and sculptors limited their work to a specific city or region. Only a few of the biggest towns, such as AUGSBURG, Cologne, and NÜRNBERG, could support a community of artists. Smaller communities looked to nearby market towns or to cities to find talented masters for important projects. At no point in the Renaissance was there a single German style. Instead, a rich variety of individual, local, and regional styles developed.

See color plate 12, vol. 1

Influence of the Netherlands. Throughout the Renaissance, German art reflected the new styles that were developing in other parts of northern Europe. In the 1400s the art of the Netherlands had a particularly strong influence on Germany. The city of Cologne, located near the Netherlands, was an important religious and commercial center. The city attracted a large community of artists and emerged as a major art center that followed the Netherlandish style.

During the 1400s, the focus of art in Cologne shifted from architecture to painting. Although work on the cathedral and a few monasteries continued, the city's great age of church building was over. Now wealthy patrons in Cologne sought to decorate religious buildings as well as their

Famed German artist Albrecht Dürer, shown here in a self-portrait, was best known for his engravings and woodcuts. He played a key role in blending the traditional art of northern Europe with the Italian styles popular during the Renaissance.

own residences with new works of art, contributing to a great era of painting.

Like the artists of the Netherlands, painters in Cologne developed an increasingly naturalistic* style during the Renaissance. They combined this naturalism with soft lines and rich, intense colors. This expressive style of painting remained popular with masters in Cologne for a long time. The artistic ties between Cologne and the Netherlands became even stronger after the mid-1400s. The work of Flemish* painters such as Hans MEMLING and Rogier van der WEYDEN had a great influence on later generations of Cologne artists.

The impact of artistic styles from other parts of Europe could also be seen in German-speaking lands. In Hamburg, for example, one of the most noted painters of the late 1300s was an artist known as Master Bertram. He produced simple, heavyset figures that strongly reflected the art of Bohemia (the present-day Czech Republic). During the 1400s this style gave way to the intensely emotional art of Master Francke, which reflected the new naturalistic style of northern Renaissance art. This style also spread to southern Germany, where it found favor with the influential painter and sculptor Hans Multscher.

In the mid-1400s, sculptor Nikolaus Gerhaert played a significant role in introducing northern Renaissance ideas into Germany. Originally from the city of Leiden in the Netherlands, Gerhaert worked in several German cities throughout his career. His carved figures are much more lifelike than those of earlier artists. Engravings based on Gerhaert's works helped spread his style far and wide.

Later Developments. By 1500 the cities of Nürnberg and Augsburg had become the liveliest centers of art in Germany. Painter and engraver Albrecht DÜRER, one of the most celebrated German artists of the Renaissance, helped bring fame to Nürnberg. More than any other artist, Dürer created a distinctly German Renaissance style that blended the qualities of Italian Renaissance art with the traditional Gothic art of northern Europe. Although a fine painter, Dürer became best known for his woodcuts and engravings, which reflect the many influences on German Renaissance art. The human body fascinated Dürer, and his figures are extremely realistic.

The other recognized master of the 1500s was painter Lucas CRANACH. A close friend of religious reformer Martin LUTHER, Cranach became the first great artist of the Protestant Reformation*. His pictures combined themes from the Old and New Testaments of the Bible. The Reformation had a dramatic effect on art in Germany. It reduced the demand for new religious images, which many Protestants saw as idols. In Basel, the arts went into such a decline that the noted painter Hans HOLBEIN the Younger left the city and moved to England. Other painters adapted to the times by switching to other art forms, such as portraits and landscapes.

In the years between about 1540 and 1580, Germany had very few artists of the stature of Dürer or Cranach, and patrons often brought foreign artists to Germany for major projects. However, by the late 1570s

* **naturalistic** realistic, showing the world as it is without idealization

* **Flemish** relating to Flanders, a region along the coasts of present-day Belgium, France, and the Netherlands

* **Protestant Reformation** religious movement that began in the 1500s as a protest against certain practices of the Roman Catholic Church and eventually led to the establishment of a variety of Protestant churches

and 1580s a gifted new generation of German artists emerged. These artists, such as the sculptor Hubert Gerhard and painter Hans von Aachen, often worked alongside skilled masters from the Netherlands and Italy. The arts continued to flourish in Germany until the early 1600s, when wars and religious conflicts had a devastating effect on the region's artistic life. (*See also* **Architecture; Art; Art in Central Europe; Art in Italy; Art in the Netherlands; Printing and Publishing; Wars of Religion.**)

Art in Italy

The Renaissance was a time of incredible artistic activity in Europe. Many of the new ideas and artistic developments of the time originated in Italy, and towering figures, such as the great Florentine artist MICHELANGELO, created masterpieces that others studied. The influence of Italian painters, sculptors, and architects could be seen all over Europe. However, Italian artists also received ideas and inspiration from other countries, and various regions of Italy developed distinctive artistic traditions.

THE ROLE OF ITALY IN THE RENAISSANCE

Several aspects of Italian culture help explain the important role played by Italy in the Renaissance. First, some of the ideas that led to the development of Renaissance art—such as humanism* and a renewed interest in the civilizations of ancient Greece and Rome—appeared first in Italy. Second, Italian artists and scholars took a very analytical approach to their artistic traditions. They were the first to write about Renaissance art, and their writings, naturally enough, focused on Italian artists and works.

* **humanism** Renaissance cultural movement promoting the study of the humanities (the languages, literature, and history of ancient Greece and Rome) as a guide to living

The early histories of Renaissance art came from Italian authors who were also practicing artists. Works such as Leon Battista ALBERTI's *On Painting* (1435) and *On Architecture* (1452), RAPHAEL's *Letter to Pope Leo X* (1519), Giorgio Vasari's *Lives of the Most Excellent Architects, Painters, and Sculptors* (1550), and Benvenuto CELLINI's *Autobiography* (1562) all discuss the history of art while examining Renaissance artistic practices and techniques.

The writings of Vasari, a painter and architect from FLORENCE, helped establish the idea that Renaissance art originated in Italy. According to Vasari, the Florentine painter GIOTTO DI BONDONE (d. 1337) had introduced a new style of painting inspired by nature. While earlier artists had used decorative lines and colors and elaborate detail, Giotto created powerful, realistic figures within settings that appeared to have spatial depth—characteristics that made his paintings surprisingly lifelike. Admiration for Giotto's naturalistic* style spread throughout the regions of Italy and helped launch the era of Renaissance art.

* **naturalistic** realistic, showing the world as it is without idealization

During the Renaissance, Italy was not a single, unified country. It consisted of a patchwork of small states, each with its own history, government, and traditions. Artistic styles varied significantly from region to

region. Although Florence, Rome, and Venice were the main centers of artistic activity, skilled artists produced significant work in other areas as well.

ART IN FLORENCE

* **patron** supporter or financial sponsor of an artist or writer

Florence, the major city of the Italian region of Tuscany, earned lasting fame for the richness and creativity of its culture during the Renaissance. Wealthy and powerful patrons* in the city, such as the Medici family, played an important role in shaping and supporting this culture. They built churches, monasteries, and palaces in and around the city and commissioned paintings and sculpture from the best artists of the day to decorate them.

See color plate 3, vol. 1

* **baptistery** building where baptisms are performed

Competitions for artistic and architectural projects attracted many participants and spurred creativity. In 1401, for example, a contest to design new doors for Florence's Baptistery* drew entries from such prominent artists as Filippo Brunelleschi, Donatello, and Lorenzo Ghiberti.

See color plate 4, vol. 1

A number of the city's well-known artworks feature David, the biblical hero who slew the giant Goliath. Florentines identified with David, seeing their city as a small republic battling tyranny all around it. Michelangelo's statue *David* (1504), modeled on ancient Greek sculpture, is the most famous representation of Florence's hero.

* **classical** in the tradition of ancient Greece and Rome

* **guild** association of craft and trade owners and workers that set standards for and represented the interests of its members

Architecture and Sculpture. During the 1400s Brunelleschi transformed the physical appearance of Florence through a series of architectural projects based on the models of ancient Greece and Rome. In his plans for a foundling hospital commissioned by the Silk Guild, Brunelleschi reintroduced classical* principles of proportion and balance and developed a harmonious new style. He also designed a dome for the city's cathedral that still dominates the skyline.

During the same period, the Florentine guilds* commissioned sculptures to adorn public buildings. The Orsanmichele, Florence's granary, featured statues of each guild's patron saint. For the city's oldest guild, the refiners of woolen cloth, Lorenzo Ghiberti created a bronze statue of St. John the Baptist (1405–1417) that was more than eight feet tall—the largest bronze statue to be cast in Italy for centuries.

The Florentines also used sculpture to honor prominent citizens. In the church of Santa Croce, for example, the tomb of the humanist scholar Leonardo Bruni is decorated with a carved image of Bruni with his hands folded on one of his books. In the mid-1400s, portrait busts—sculptures of the subject's head and perhaps shoulders—became fashionable. Florentine sculptors, influenced by the ancient Romans' view that signs of age and wear were honorable marks of a life of public service, created busts of important citizens in minute and even unflattering detail.

* **fresco** mural painted on a plaster wall

Painting and Other Arts. A strong tradition of painting in both fresco* and panels developed in Florence. In the 1420s Masaccio creat-

Michelangelo's *David* stands in Florence, Italy, as a tribute to the biblical hero who slew the giant Goliath. Created in 1504 in the style of ancient Greek sculpture, the statue is the most famous Renaissance image of this heroic figure.

ed a fresco of the *Expulsion from Paradise* that shows the anguish and remorse of Adam and Eve through their gestures and facial expressions. Fra ANGELICO, a leading Florentine painter of the 1430s, filled the convent of San Marco with luminous frescoes of religious themes. In the 1470s and 1480s Sandro BOTTICELLI produced numerous works, including *Primavera (Spring)* and *The Birth of Venus,* and Domenico Ghirlandaio completed a series of frescoes based on the life of St. Francis. Many private homes featured splendid painted decorations, such as the frescoes of *Famous Men and Women* (1488) created by Andrea del Castagno at a villa outside Florence.

During the early 1500s, two of the greatest artists of the Renaissance, LEONARDO DA VINCI and Michelangelo, worked in Florence. Together, they brought about what is now called the high Renaissance classical style. They also inspired and educated other artists, including Raphael, a distinguished painter from Urbino, and Florentine painters Fra BARTOLOMMEO and Andrea del Sarto. Del Sarto's scenes from the *Life of St. Filippo Benizi* (1509–1510) display soft brushwork and well-drawn figures within luminous landscapes.

Del Sarto's assistants, Jacopo Carucci da Pontormo and Rosso Fiorentino, moved toward the Mannerist style, which had taken root throughout Italy by the mid-1500s. Mannerist painters used distortions of form and unnatural colors to convey a sense of elegance and heightened emotion in their works. According to one explanation, the artificial aspects of the Mannerist style were intended to provide glimpses of true beauty, which could not be known through the senses. By the late 1500s, some painters abandoned Mannerism and returned to the more naturalistic approach of the high Renaissance.

Many Florentine artists of the Renaissance practiced more than one art form, often excelling at several, such as sculpture and painting. Other important forms in Florence included manuscript illustration and intarsia—creating images on panels with inlaid pieces of colored wood. In the early 1400s Luca della Robbia developed a technique of glazing terra-cotta sculptures and reliefs*. Many of his works were installed on buildings around the city.

* **relief** type of sculpture in which figures are raised slightly from a flat surface

ART IN SIENA

In SIENA, another Tuscan city, culture revolved around the university founded there around 1240. Siena's contributions to Renaissance art began with painters of the 1300s, who introduced vivid colors, figures enlivened with emotional power, and fresh images of landscapes and interiors. One of these artists, Simone Martini, painted the *Annunciation* (1333) for Siena's cathedral. The painting, which shows the angel Gabriel appearing to Mary, reveals the influence of French Gothic* art. Ambrogio Lorenzetti created a number of frescoes for the town hall, including *Effects of Good Government in the Country,* which provides a wide-angle view of the Tuscan countryside from above.

Sienese painters of the 1400s continued to work in the style of the previous century. Sassetta (Stefano di Giovanni) followed in the foot-

* **Gothic** style of architecture characterized by pointed arches and high, thin walls supported by flying buttresses; also artistic style marked by bright colors, elongated proportions, and intricate detail

steps of Lorenzetti, exploring techniques for painting landscapes and interiors. Giovanni di Paolo created paintings of the lives of saints, including a cycle of scenes featuring St. Catherine of Siena, one of the city's most important religious figures.

During the 1500s some Sienese artists took the city's painting tradition in new directions. The most important was Domenico Beccafumi, who experimented with extreme distortions of the human form in the Mannerist tradition. In his *Fall of the Rebel Angels* (1524 and 1528), long-limbed figures strain violently and convey strong emotion.

Siena was also home to Jacopo della Quercia, a great Renaissance sculptor of the early 1400s. He sculpted the relief figures for the fountain in front of the government building in Siena and for the cathedral in Bologna.

ART IN EMILIA-ROMAGNA

Located in north-central Italy between Florence and Venice, the region of Emilia-Romagna contributed to important developments in Renaissance art, especially painting. The influential ESTE family, rulers of the city of FERRARA, promoted humanist ideals and were active patrons of the arts. Leonello d'Este, who governed the city in the 1440s, had a humanist education and was well acquainted with the latest artistic theories and styles. He hired the Ferrarese painter Cosmè Tura to paint a series of images of the Muses* for his study. In the 1490s Duke Ercole I d'Este worked closely with architects on a vast city-planning project that included new streets and a major new square in Ferrara.

* **Muses** in ancient myth, nine sisters who inspired and represented the various arts and branches of learning

By the early 1500s, artistic taste in Emilia-Romagna had moved toward a more naturalistic style. This is reflected in the decision of Duke Alfonso I d'Este to engage Giovanni BELLINI and TITIAN to create mythological paintings for his study. In the city of BOLOGNA, many were inspired by the naturalism, grace, and beauty of *St. Cecilia,* a painting by Raphael installed in the church of San Giovanni in Monte in 1515. Naturalism reached a high point in the work of CORREGGIO (1494–1534), a painter from the city of Parma. His lyrical style was based on theories of human proportions, anatomy, and color technique.

The paintings of PARMIGIANINO (1503–1540), who came from Parma, display many of the characteristics of Mannerism. In Bologna, the painters Prospero Fontana, Tommaso Laureti, and Ercole Procaccini produced Mannerist pieces. In the late 1500s, some artists, including the three painters of Bologna's CARRACCI FAMILY, began to reject Mannerism in favor of a more natural style. Tracing their roots to the work of artists such as Correggio and Titian, the Carracci established an art academy in which they taught this new naturalism.

ART IN GENOA AND MILAN

During the Renaissance, GENOA and MILAN were the major urban centers of northwestern Italy. Genoa was ruled by various noble, military, and

The Italian artist Masaccio created a celebrated series of frescoes in Florence in the late 1420s. The *Tribute Money,* shown here, illustrates a biblical tale in which Christ instructs one of his followers to fetch money from a fish's mouth to give to a Roman tax collector.

merchant families, and they shaped the city's appearance with their patronage of artists and architects. Many members of the nobility built tall palaces, complete with finely carved entryways that highlighted the owners' power and privilege.

Genoa's churches and public buildings were decorated with an array of carved images, including coats of arms, symbols of peace and abundance, and portraits of Roman emperors. Painters produced frescoes of saints, historical scenes, and allegorical* figures for structures such as the Bank of St. George, a powerful financial institution. In 1528 the Genoese admiral Andrea Doria overthrew the rulers of Genoa and founded a new government. Thereafter, Doria's villa on the harbor became the focus of Genoese culture. Formal gardens and decorations based on classical models created a triumphant style that linked Doria's Genoa with the greatness of the ancient Roman republic.

* **allegorical** referring to a literary or artistic device in which characters, events, and settings represent abstract qualities and in which the author intends a different meaning to be read beneath the surface

Benefiting from close contacts with France and other parts of northern Europe, Milan became a leading cultural center in the 1300s and 1400s. Renaissance ideas, including a renewed interest in classical style, reached the region in the 1460s. Some of the greatest writers and artists of the Renaissance, including PETRARCH, BRAMANTE, and Leonardo da Vinci, worked in Milan.

The city undertook several major architectural projects during the Renaissance, including its cathedral. Some projects were so large in scope that they required many artists to work together. Architects often consulted each other about building plans, while sculptors followed designs made by painters. Construction on the cathedral began in 1386. In the early stages, architects, sculptors, and stonecutters from Germany and France came to work on it. By the early 1400s, however, local Lombard artisans* had taken over. Although the cathedral is basically Gothic in style, its decorations draw on all the artistic styles and trends of the Renaissance.

* **artisan** skilled worker or craftsperson

The Inside Story

The Italian artist Giorgio Vasari was not only an accomplished painter but also a historian of art who inspired a new literary form, the artistic biography. In 1550 he published *The Lives of the Most Excellent Architects, Painters, and Sculptors,* a massive work that included the life stories of many Italian artists of the time. Although Vasari often got the facts wrong, his biographies are of great interest because of his firsthand knowledge of the subjects, his lively writing style and sharp opinions, and the colorful anecdotes he included about some of the world's most famous artists.

Other important monuments in Milan and the surrounding region include the Certosa di Pavia (founded in 1396), an elaborately decorated monastery, as well as castles built by the ruling families. Prominent Milanese artists, such as Vincenzo Foppa and Bernardino Luini, completed paintings for some of these buildings. In the 1490s Leonardo da Vinci painted one of his most famous works, *The Last Supper,* in the church of Santa Maria delle Grazie in Milan.

ART IN UMBRIA

The mountainous province of Umbria lies in the heart of central Italy. During the Renaissance the region contained hundreds of churches, monasteries, and other religious institutions, which commissioned artworks for their buildings. For example, the painter PIERO DELLA FRANCESCA produced a group of religious panels for St. Anthony's convent in Perugia in the 1460s. Umbrian artists adopted some classical elements in their work, but they tended to focus on Christian subjects rather than mythological or historical figures.

By the end of the 1400s most of Umbria had fallen under the control of the pope in Rome. The popes sponsored artistic and architectural projects in the region, such as rebuilding the monastery of St. Francis in Assisi, but they also removed works of art and sent them to Rome. In 1540, after a revolt in Perugia, the pope ordered the destruction of the city's Baglioni palace, which possessed a hall decorated with portraits.

See color plate 1, vol. 1

Umbrian artists worked in numerous cities and towns throughout the region. In Foligno, the Trinci Palace, completed in 1408, contains several series of frescoes on subjects such as *Heroes of Roman History,* the *Liberal Arts,* and the *Planets.* In Orvieto the cathedral's chapel boasts a famous fresco series, *The Renaissance Antichrist* (1504), by Luca Signorelli. Often even the smallest Umbrian communities possessed one great piece of art. The town of Fontignano, for example, has a *Nativity* (1523) that was the last work of the Umbrian artist Pietro Vannucci, known as PERUGINO. Raphael spent time in Umbria in the 1490s and worked closely with Perugino.

ART IN ROME

During the Renaissance two different artistic styles flourished in Rome and the surrounding region. Some artists clung to the medieval* style that had been popular for generations, while others drew inspiration from the new movement of humanism. When a renewed interest in classical civilization took hold in the early 1500s, Rome—with its wealth of ancient monuments and its remarkable history—came to the forefront of the arts.

* **medieval** referring to the Middle Ages, a period that began around A.D. 400 and ended around 1400 in Italy and 1500 in the rest of Europe

Beginning in the mid-1400s, Roman artists developed their skills in fresco decoration, large-scale construction, and marble carving. Local artists became familiar with Renaissance ideas and studied the works of master artists from Tuscany and other northern regions. Painters, sculp-

tors, and architects from the cultural centers of northern Italy worked in Rome on grand projects sponsored by various popes. One of the most impressive examples of Roman painting from the 1400s was Melozzo da Forli's *Ascension* (ca. 1479), showing the triumphant figure of Christ surrounded by angels. Only fragments of this fresco cycle survive.

Rome entered the high Renaissance after 1500. At the Vatican, the seat of the Roman Catholic Church, Pope Julius II embarked on an ambitious construction program that included decorating the Sistine Chapel and building the new church of St. Peter. For these projects, the pope commissioned the greatest artists of the era, such as Raphael, Michelangelo, Leonardo da Vinci, and architect Donato Bramante. The classical forms, monumental dimensions, and expressive content of their work influenced all aspects of Roman culture.

* **Holy Roman Empire** political body in central Europe composed of several states; existed until 1806

* **sack** to loot a captured city

In 1527 troops of the Holy Roman Empire* attacked and sacked* Rome, bringing the city's immense artistic flowering to an abrupt halt. Artists and patrons fled the city, and the popes lost authority over political matters. When artistic life resumed, Roman art and culture took on new values of simplicity and clarity. Sebastiano del Piombo was one of the few artists whose career continued after the sacking of Rome. He gained a reputation as a portrait painter with bold, insightful works such as his studies of Pope Clement VII.

The city's largest architectural project, the building of St. Peter's, continued throughout the 1500s, with each new pope shifting its direction. Michelangelo became architect of the project in 1547. Although later architects changed his designs, his imprint remained in certain areas, such as the central dome.

ART IN NAPLES

Between 1400 and 1600, the city of Naples on Italy's southwestern coast was ruled successively by the Angevin dynasty of France, the Aragon family of Spain, and finally by a viceroy who governed on behalf of the Spanish crown. Each government favored a particular artistic style. The culture of Naples stretched back to ancient Greek and Roman times. Ancient ruins standing in the city ensured that Neapolitan artists remained connected with classical traditions. In addition, trade with merchants from the Middle East brought the people of Naples into contact with Arab art and design.

Capturing a City's History

Art and government were often intertwined in the Renaissance, as shown in a distinctive art form produced in Siena for centuries. *Tavolette* or *biccherne* were small paintings on panels, originally used as decorative wooden covers for the financial books of the city's treasury offices. These modest paintings, some of them fashioned by master artists, provide a pictorial history of events in Siena from the 1200s to the 1600s.

In the 1400s the Angevin rulers brought to the city a taste for Gothic architecture and finely detailed oil paintings from Burgundy. A notable work from this period, a royal tomb (1428) in the Church of San Giovanni a Carbonara, combines Gothic spires and classical columns.

After Naples came under the control of the Aragon family in 1442, the city's rulers restored some classical features, such as wide Roman streets, and added spacious new squares. The best example of Neapolitan art from this time is the marble arch at the Castel Nuovo, based on Roman arches and decorated with sculpture inspired by Roman coins, carving, and portraits. Meanwhile, important local families left their mark on the cityscape by building imposing palaces and churches.

The most famous artist to work in Naples was a Lombard painter known as Caravaggio. His style featured dramatic effects of light and dark and an element of naturalism, providing a refreshing contrast to the more formal works of most other painters. Although Caravaggio spent only a short time in Naples (1606–1610), his presence lent new energy to Neapolitan painters, and the city became an international center of Baroque* art in the 1600s.

* **Baroque** artistic style of the 1600s characterized by movement, drama, and grandness of scale

ART IN VENICE

The art of Venice, a city of islands and canals on Italy's northeastern coast, reflects the city's special circumstances. Venice's Renaissance culture was shaped by its maritime* setting, its position as a crossroads between Europe and the Middle East, its prosperity based on trade, and the stability of its government and society. Venetian artists blended influences from abroad with deeply rooted local traditions. They showed a devotion to the city's main religious figures, the Virgin Mary and St. Mark. In addition, their works glorified Venice, suggesting that it enjoyed divine protection and was destined for greatness.

* **maritime** relating to the sea or shipping

St. Mark's Basilica (1063–1094), the imposing church at the mouth of Venice's Grand Canal, displays a mixture of artistic traditions. Gothic sculptures on top of the church pierce the sky, while paintings inside the basilica mingle Gothic, Venetian, and Byzantine* styles. A wooden cover for the altarpiece, made in the mid-1300s by Paolo Veneziano, echoes the brilliant colors of the local mosaic* work.

* **Byzantine** referring to the Eastern Christian Empire based in Constantinople (A.D. 476–1453)

* **mosaic** picture made up of many small colored stones or tiles

By the 1450s classical elements of Renaissance art began to appear in Venice. Illustrating this new style is the entrance to the Arsenale (the center of the city's shipbuilding industry), which was modeled on a Roman triumphal arch. During most of the 1400s, painting in Venice was dominated by members of the Bellini and Vivarini families. The Bellinis (Jacopo, Gentile, and Giovanni) pioneered the Renaissance style, and the Vivarinis produced many works for export to other cities in the region. Giovanni Bellini experimented with the oil paints used in the Netherlands, an important step for Venetian art as these paints allowed artists to portray the city's glowing colors and shimmering gold mosaics.

See color plate 7, vol. 1

The palace of the Doge, the head of the Venetian government, contained a council chamber decorated with scenes of the history of Venice. Originally painted as frescoes, by the mid-1400s these decorations had decayed in the damp salt air and were replaced with paintings on canvas.

During the 1500s, many talented artists carried Venetian painting to new heights. Artists continued to experiment with color and light, to focus on creating visually splendid effects, and to explore the uses of oil paints. Key artists of this period include Giorgione da Castelfranco, Titian, Vittore Carpaccio, the architect Andrea Palladio, Tintoretto, and Paolo Veronese. Works such as the *Assumption of the Virgin* (1518) helped make Titian the city's most celebrated painter in the mid-1500s. After

the death of Titian, Tintoretto and Veronese emerged as the leading Venetian artists.

In 1577 a fire destroyed the paintings in the council chamber at the Doge's Palace in Venice. To return the hall to its former glory, the city launched a massive restoration program to which many artists from Venice and other cities contributed their efforts and talent. (*See also* **Architecture; Art; Decorative Arts; Humanism; Italy; Sculpture.**)

Art in the Netherlands

* **duchy** territory ruled by a duke or duchess

* **patron** supporter or financial sponsor of an artist or writer

* **artisan** skilled worker or craftsperson

During the Renaissance, much of present-day Belgium, Holland, and Luxembourg were part of the duchy* of BURGUNDY. This region, called the Burgundian Netherlands, experienced a great flowering of the arts in the 1400s and early 1500s. Wealthy patrons* such as the Burgundian ruler MARGARET OF AUSTRIA promoted the arts and shaped artistic tastes.

Artists and artisans* in the Netherlands produced a great variety of artworks and luxury goods, ranging from paintings and sculptures to fine jewelry and tapestries. These works were in great demand not only within the Netherlands, but also across the continent. The cities of Bruges and ANTWERP were major centers for the distribution of art, helping to spread Netherlandish art and styles throughout Europe.

Painting. The Netherlands became famous for painting during the Renaissance. The artists of the Netherlands worked in several kinds of paint, including watercolor and tempera (egg-based) paints. However, they were best known as masters of oil painting.

Since the Middle Ages, painters had used oil-based glazes to add a shiny finish to tempera paintings. However, the painters Jan and Hubert van EYCK revolutionized oil painting in the early 1400s by mixing the oil directly into the pigments (colored powders). This produced a glossy paint that caught the light. By applying multiple layers of this thin, tinted oil, artists could build up a painted image gradually, in great detail. The thin coats of oil paint enabled artists to blend brush strokes so finely that they were nearly invisible.

See color plate 11, vol. 1

Thanks in part to the use of oils, Netherlandish painters were able to capture the intricate details and light effects of the physical world. Their works reveal the textures of fabrics and metals, reflections in objects, the glimmer of jewels, and the brilliance of natural light. Landscapes and city scenes are elaborate. The Netherlandish masters were also praised for their ability to portray deep emotion in religious paintings.

The reputation of artists of the Netherlands spread throughout Europe. Perhaps the best known was Jan van Eyck, court painter to the Burgundian ruler Philip the Good. His fame reached as far as Italy, and ruling families such as the MEDICI in Florence and the ESTE in Ferrara sought to acquire his works. Rogier van der WEYDEN, another painter who worked for Philip the Good, also attracted many admirers in Italy, Germany, and Spain. He ran a busy workshop, and his paintings and style were widely imitated. Hieronymus BOSCH gained renown for the

As individuals collected gold jewelry and artwork as a way to display their wealth, the fine work of Netherlandish goldsmiths became popular throughout Europe. The goldsmiths, like the one shown in this painting by Petrus Christus from the mid-1400s, sometimes met with wealthy clients to design custom-made pieces.

elements of fantasy he brought to scenes based on biblical themes. Spanish, French, and Austrian monarchs collected his works, and weavers based tapestries on them.

Several Netherlandish painters of the 1500s traveled to Italy and imitated Italian classical* styles and subject matter. Painter Jan Gossaert, who visited Rome in 1508, worked many Italian elements into his pictures while following the style and technique of Flemish* art. Other well-known Netherlandish painters included Dirck BOUTS, Hugo van der GOES, and Hans MEMLING. One of the last great Netherlandish painters of the Renaissance was Pieter BRUEGHEL the Elder. Many of his masterful paintings present scenes from country life.

* **classical** in the tradition of ancient Greece and Rome

* **Flemish** relating to Flanders, a region along the coasts of present-day Belgium, France, and the Netherlands

Gold and Other Metalwork. During the Renaissance, fine works of gold and gems had a larger role than just adorning a person or decorating a building. They also reflected an individual's power and status. People wore gold jewelry to show membership in knightly orders, loyalty to a ruler, or friendship with another nation. The dukes of

Burgundy collected vast amounts of precious gold work. In addition to jewelry, they owned statues, busts, and reliquaries*, as well as fine enameled cups and spoons decorated with elaborate pictures.

* **reliquary** container for storing pieces of bone or items belonging to a saint or other holy person

During the 1400s the cities of Brussels and Bruges served as the main centers of the goldsmith's art. In the 1500s, the jewelry production shifted to Antwerp, which still enjoys a reputation for gem cutting. Netherlandish gold work also reached other parts of Europe. In Italy, Lorenzo de' Medici owned a Burgundian-made reliquary in the shape of a crystal goblet, with a gold lid decorated with gems and pearls.

The names of only a few master goldsmiths still survive. Jan de Leeuw, the head of the goldsmiths' guild* in Bruges in 1441, appears in a 1436 portrait by Jan van Eyck. Another famous goldsmith, Gérard Loyet, created an exquisite gold reliquary and life-size statues of his patron, Duke Charles the Bold of Burgundy.

* **guild** association of craft and trade owners and workers that set standards for and represented the interests of its members

Artists in the Netherlands also produced works in other metals, notably bronze. At St. Michael's Abbey in Antwerp, the tomb of Isabella of Bourbon, the second wife of Charles the Bold, has ten magnificent bronze statuettes by Brussels artist Jacque de Gérines. A bronze sculpture of Mary of Burgundy, Isabella's daughter, appears on her tomb at the Church of Nôtre-Dame in Bruges. In the southern Netherlands, artists working in brass created pieces for religious monuments, chandeliers, and tableware.

Tapestry and Embroidery. Tapestries—heavy cloths with elaborate pictures woven into the fabric—were among the most valued art forms in the Renaissance. They varied widely in quality and price. The finest pieces often contained silk, silver, gold, and even gems. They required considerable time and effort to produce.

Renaissance tapestries illustrated a wide variety of subjects, ranging from religious and historical images to scenes from everyday life. People hung tapestries to decorate their homes and to set the scene for special events. Rulers proclaimed their high status by lining their war tents and barges with splendid tapestries and displaying them during processions. In 1461 Philip the Good, duke of Burgundy, dazzled the citizens of Paris by hanging a wealth of tapestries in and on the building where he stayed while attending the coronation of the French king Louis XI.

Merchants managed the manufacture and sale of tapestries. They financed the work, kept stocks of designs, and hired weavers, often dividing large orders among many weavers in different cities. Buyers could purchase tapestries new or used or have them made to order. The greatest tapestry centers of Europe were the Burgundian cities of Arras, Tournai, and Brussels. By the mid-1500s, Antwerp had become the hub of the international tapestry trade. The Burgundian court sponsored and promoted the tapestry industry.

Nobles throughout Europe sought out Netherlandish tapestries and the weavers who produced them. The Medici family in Florence not only collected Netherlandish tapestries but also made a profit by selling them to other Italian rulers. Pope Leo X hired the highly admired weavers of Brussels to produce a series of tapestries for the Vatican's Sistine Chapel, using designs by the Italian artist Raphael.

The King of Prints

Lucas van Leyden, an artist of the early 1500s, was the most famous printmaker in the Netherlands. His fine use of shading gives his prints a remarkably soft quality, as if they were paintings rather than line drawings. He also had a rare ability to express a sense of light and darkness in the print medium. His best-known print, *David Playing the Harp Before Saul,* captures the complex emotions of a mad king soothed by music.

Embroidery was another specialty of the Netherlands. Many pieces contained the finest silk, gold thread, and seed pearls. Skilled embroiderers could "paint" with thread by using tiny stitches in extremely delicate color ranges of silk. Workers in Burgundy employed this technique to produce beautiful altar hangings and religious garments.

* **illumination** hand-painted color decorations and illustrations on the pages of a manuscript

Illuminated Manuscripts. The art of manuscript illumination* had flourished in the Netherlands since the 1300s, and Burgundian rulers promoted it in the 1400s. Philip the Good assembled the largest library in northern Europe, with roughly 1,000 volumes, and about half of these were illustrated. The manufacture of manuscripts became a highly organized industry. Studios divided work among various specialists who created text, borders, and artwork.

The decorations in Philip's books are in a formal, somewhat artificial style. In the late 1400s and early 1500s, the so-called Ghent-Bruges school in the southern Netherlands introduced a new style of illumination. It featured more realistic figures and spacious interior and exterior settings. Pastel shades increasingly replaced the primary colors favored in earlier manuscripts. Decorations in the margins of the books changed from plant designs to realistic optical illusions—flowers and other objects that seemed to cast shadows onto the pages of the manuscript.

* **altarpiece** work of art that decorates the altar of a church

Woodwork and Other Sculpture. Wooden altarpieces* carved in the Burgundian Netherlands were in great demand throughout Europe. Inexpensive compared to art forms such as gold work and tapestries, these works appealed to members of the middle class. Burgundy's position as a center of international trade helped promote sales of sculpted altarpieces. The great trade fairs at Antwerp were especially important. Items that passed through this city carried a mark guaranteeing their quality. Foreign merchants who sold their goods in Antwerp often brought back carved altarpieces, among other products, to sell in their native lands.

The production of carved altarpieces developed into an important industry. Workshops were run by master woodworkers, who took orders, purchased raw materials, divided the work, and sold the finished products. Altarpieces were fairly standard in their size and subject matter, making them easier to manufacture in bulk. A typical altarpiece generally consisted of a raised, rectangular center panel with separate sections on each side. The center panel featured a carving of a story or scene, and the side panels were often painted.

* **Moor** Muslim from North Africa; Moorish invaders conquered much of Spain during the Middle Ages

Netherlandish artists also produced freestanding sculptures in wood, stone, or plaster. Typical sculptures represented Christ, the Virgin Mary, and crucifixes. One statue of Mary made in Antwerp, called the *Granada Madonna,* is said to have been carried into battle against the Moors* by the Spanish monarchs Isabella of Castile and Ferdinand of Aragon. (*See also* **Art; Books and Manuscripts; Fairs and Festivals; Illumination; Netherlands.**)

Art in Spain and Portugal

During the Renaissance, Spanish and Portuguese art was influenced by cultural movements in other parts of Europe, particularly those in Italy. However, the art of the Iberian Peninsula* already possessed a distinctive character that was shaped by the region's history, social conditions, and landscape. In addition, different areas of the peninsula had developed their own unique styles based on local culture and traditions.

* **Iberian Peninsula** part of Western Europe occupied by present-day Spain and Portugal

Moorish Legacy. The Moors, Muslims who conquered large parts of Spain in the 700s and held it for most of the Middle Ages, had a major impact on Spanish and Portuguese culture. For nearly 700 years, the Moorish style, which combined plain, flat surfaces with elaborate decorations, dominated Iberian art and architecture. This style, known as *mudejar* for the Muslim artisans* who remained in Spain after its reconquest by Christians, appeared in many major buildings. The most famous example is the Alhambra palace, built around 1358 in Granada in southern Spain. A masterpiece of *mudejar* design, the Alhambra is lavishly decorated with delicate carving and colorful mosaics*.

* **artisan** skilled worker or craftsperson

* **mosaic** picture made up of many small colored stones or tiles

Characteristics of Iberian Art. After the expulsion of the Moors at the end of the 1400s, Spanish and Portuguese artists looked increasingly to the rest of Europe for inspiration. Architects created a new style that combined Gothic* and *mudejar* elements. Their designs made use of the bright Iberian sunlight, which highlighted the intricate carvings on outer walls and in courtyards.

* **Gothic** style of architecture characterized by pointed arches and high, thin walls supported by flying buttresses; also, artistic style marked by bright colors, elongated proportions, and intricate detail

Sculpture and architecture were closely connected in *mudejar* buildings. Finely sculpted decorations often covered columns, window frames, and other architectural elements. *Mudejar* work influenced Spanish artists, who developed a style known as *plateresco* (from *plata,* meaning silver) because it resembled the work of silversmiths. *Plateresco* walls and sculptures featured intricately carved designs.

Plateresco style gave rise to the most distinctive element of Iberian churches—the retable, an elaborately decorated high altar. Most retables were huge constructions made up of indentations filled with paintings and statues. In the 1480s and 1490s, the Spanish sculptor Gil de Siloé created enormous retables crowded with carved images of religious figures.

See color plate 14, vol. 1

During the 1400s artistic developments in northern Europe had an influence on Iberian painters. Artists in Spain and Portugal began to use oil paints, which were popular in the north. They also tended to dwell on the harsh and cruel aspects of daily life and of biblical scenes, as northern painters did. One reason for this emphasis in Iberian paintings may have been the violent atmosphere of the late 1400s and early 1500s that was created by the expulsion of Jews and Muslims.

Another source of inspiration for Iberian art was the rise of overseas exploration. Expeditions to Africa, India, East Asia, and the Americas brought the Spanish and Portuguese into contact with a wide variety of peoples. The artwork from these exotic lands influenced Iberian artists. At the same time, the colonial empires of Spain and Portugal developed distinctive cultures that blended European and local traditions.

In the 1560s Philip II of Spain began the construction of the sprawling Escorial palace and monastery complex. It symbolized the power of the king and his devotion to Catholicism. Built of golden limestone, the structure has a classical style that features repeated patterns and geometric forms.

Development of Renaissance Style. Spain's involvement with Italian Renaissance culture began around 1442, when King Alfonso of Aragon conquered the kingdom of Naples and moved his court from Spain to Italy. Alfonso commissioned work from a variety of painters, architects, sculptors, and illustrators in Naples. The work of these artists reflected the city's strong classical* tradition as well as its close links with Florence, one of the centers of Italian Renaissance art.

* **classical** in the tradition of ancient Greece and Rome

The first buildings in the Renaissance style appeared on the Iberian Peninsula in the late 1400s. One notable example is the facade* of the University of Salamanca. Constructed in 1494, it combines delicate Gothic spires and pointed arches with classical columns and rounded arches.

* **facade** front of a building; outward appearance

In Portugal a style known as Manuelino developed during the rule of King Manuel I in the late 1400s and early 1500s. It too combined Gothic features with structural elements and a sense of proportion typical of the Renaissance. Diogo Boytac, one of the king's principal architects, built convents, monasteries, and other major religious buildings in the Manuelino style. Portuguese Renaissance architecture is also noted for using *azulejos,* colored tiles, on facades, floors, and fountains. The church of São Roque in the city of Coimbra contains spectacular examples of *azulejo* decoration.

Spanish and Portuguese artists became familiar with Italian art in the early to mid-1500s, and their style reflected the influence of the Italian Renaissance. This was due in part to the emergence of internationally known Italian artists such as TITIAN and RAPHAEL. The publication of books on the arts, including the works of Leon Battista ALBERTI, also helped spread Renaissance art theory. In addition, many Portuguese and Spanish artists studied in Italy and then returned to Iberia to put their training into practice. Spanish painter Pedro Berruguete, who worked in Italy for the duke of URBINO from about 1475 to 1482, was one of these.

Berruguete adopted many Italian and northern European painting techniques, which he used throughout his career in Spain.

Various Iberian monarchs took an active role in encouraging the flowering of Renaissance art. CHARLES V of Spain (ruled 1516–1555) asked the Italian-trained architect Pedro Machuca to design a building attached to the Alhambra in Granada. Intended as a royal residence, the structure combined elements of ancient Roman and Renaissance Italian style.

* **patron** supporter or financial sponsor of an artist or writer

Charles's son, PHILIP II (ruled 1556–1598), was also an enthusiastic patron* and collector of Renaissance art. Philip bought Italian paintings for his palaces and Renaissance sketchbooks and art texts for his library. He ordered the construction of the vast Escorial palace and monastery complex north of MADRID. Designed by Spanish architect Juan de Herrera, the Escorial was an imposing structure that highlighted the power of both the king and the Roman Catholic Church in Spain. It was built in golden limestone in a classical style that emphasized repeated patterns and geometric forms. Philip invited Italian artists to create vivid, lively paintings like those popular in Florence and Rome to decorate the interior.

Philip II supported the work of many Spanish artists and architects. However, he did not like the paintings of the man known as EL GRECO (the Greek). After studying in Rome, El Greco moved to the Spanish city of TOLEDO. He received a commission to create a work for the church at the Escorial and painted *The Martyrdom of St. Maurice and the Theban Legion.* Philip rejected the picture for the church, so it was placed out of the way in the monastery. Nevertheless, El Greco found numerous other wealthy patrons in Spain and created many paintings in an intense emotional style. (*See also* **Architecture; Art; Moriscos; Portugal; Spain.**)

Artisans

During the Renaissance, most finished goods, such as shoes and jewelry, were produced by skilled crafts workers known as artisans. The artisan class first emerged in the late Middle Ages, when increased trade made many European cities centers of production. A growing population increased the demand for food and clothing. At the same time, the wealth of merchants encouraged the production of more luxury goods, such as jewelry and fine cloth.

* **guild** association of craft and trade owners and workers that set standards for and represented the interests of its members

Most artisans were members of craft guilds*. In general, these guilds were only open to men. Each guild set standards of quality for its products. It also set limits on how many hours a member could work, how many assistants he could have, and how much material he could use. These rules prevented any single artisan from dominating the market in his town. In most cities, local guilds controlled all production of goods. Only their members could work as artisans in that city.

* **apprentice** person bound by legal agreement to work for another for a specified period of time in return for instruction in a trade or craft

Guilds also set standards for the training of new members. A person began work as an apprentice* under the supervision of a master craftsman. An apprentice spent several years working for, and usually living with, one master. He or his parents paid the master for his training. At the end of this period he became a journeyman, who was allowed to

travel from master to master, gaining skill and experience. To become a master, a journeyman had to produce a masterpiece, a work that had to be approved by other masters.

Once a craftsman became a master, he could open his own shop. He was also allowed to marry. In fact, most guilds required masters to be married, because wives played a major role in running both shops and households. An artisan's wife and daughters could work in his shop alongside the apprentices and journeymen. If a master died, his widow could continue to run his shop, but she could not vote or hold office in the guild.

The fact that artisans usually owned their homes and kept large households set them apart from unskilled laborers. In many cities, craft guilds became a political force. They often struggled for power against city councils, usually dominated by merchants. Guilds also provided a social network for artisans. They offered financial support to aging masters, widows, and orphans, and also paid for members' funerals and for their children's baptism. Guild members often displayed their unity by marching together in city parades. The close-knit structure of the guilds created a unique artisan culture. Each guild was proud of its traditions and often hostile to outsiders. (*See also* **Guilds; Industry.**)

Asia, East

During the Renaissance, trade goods produced in East Asia, such as silk and spices, found a ready market in Europe. As a result, European merchants established bases in Asia and sought trading arrangements with local rulers. However, in some countries Europeans faced significant challenges in their attempts to form commercial relationships.

China and Malaysia. European merchants and missionaries visited East Asia throughout the 1200s and 1300s. Then in 1368 the rulers of the Ming dynasty in China cut off contacts with the West. China remained closed to Europeans until the early 1500s, when Portuguese merchants gained access to the port city of Malacca, in Malaysia.

The Portuguese planned to use Malacca as a base for journeys between India and China. When they arrived in the city, their commander asked the local sultan* for permission to engage in trade. However, Muslim merchants in the region viewed the Europeans as a threat and attacked the Portuguese expedition. After a ten-day battle in 1511, the Portuguese defeated the Muslims, driving them out of Malacca.

*** sultan** ruler of a Muslim state

Portuguese merchants resumed trade with China around 1512. Five years later Portugal sent Tomé Pires to serve as its first ambassador to China. Pires established good relations with the Chinese. But as more ships began to arrive from Portugal, the Chinese became anxious. They arrested Pires and executed several Portuguese. In 1521 China expelled all Portuguese ships and issued a decree calling the traders "barbarian devils" and banning business dealings with them.

Despite this decree, the Portuguese did not completely stop trading with China. They continued to do business in secret until 1554, when

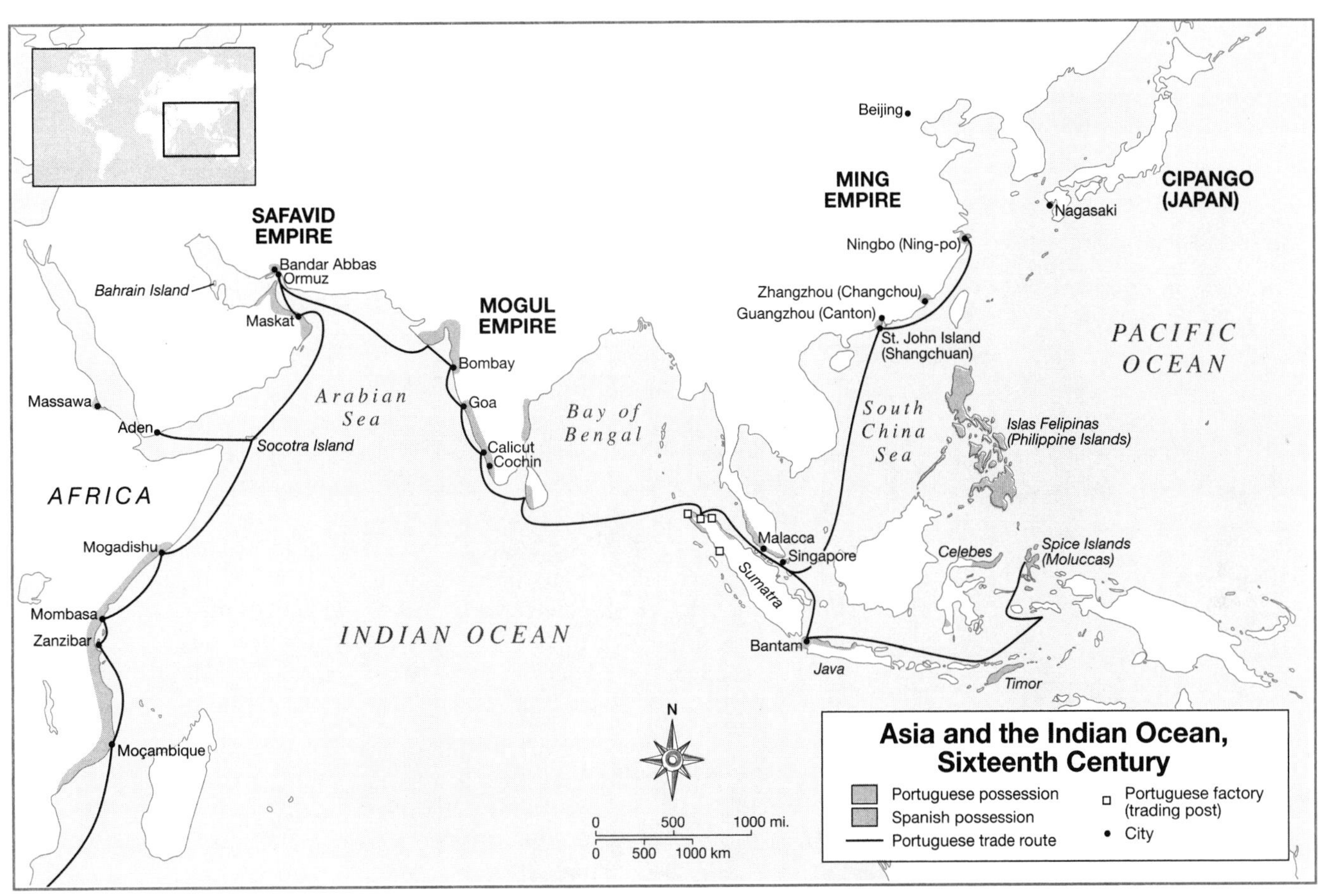

they received permission to establish a base of operations on the South China coast. Their first port on St. John's Island was later transferred to Macao, a peninsula in the South China Sea. Macao became a Portuguese colony and remained so until December 1999.

The Spice Islands and Japan. Another focus of European interest in East Asia was the Spice Islands (Moluccas) in Indonesia. A source of valuable spices, the islands eventually attracted merchants from Portugal, Spain, the Netherlands, and England. A Spanish expedition reached the islands in 1521, hoping to challenge the Portuguese monopoly* on trade in East Asia. The Spanish also built a capital in Manila in the Philippine Islands and forts in Formosa (present-day Taiwan). The Spanish gradually established trading routes between Manila and Acapulco in Mexico.

* **monopoly** exclusive right to engage in a particular type of business

In the 1540s the Portuguese gained a foothold in Japan. A fleet of Portuguese traders sailed off course in 1543 and landed on a Japanese island known as Tanegashima. For the next 50 years the Portuguese and Japanese engaged in a lively cultural and economic exchange. Japanese art and goods soon displayed Western decorative motifs*. In addition, Jesuit* missionaries arrived in Japan in 1549 and quickly converted more than 150,000 Japanese to Christianity.

* **motif** theme or subject

* **Jesuit** belonging to a Roman Catholic religious order founded by St. Ignatius Loyola and approved in 1540

This open relationship changed when the Spanish and Portuguese began to compete for Japan's trade, and the number of Europeans in the

region increased. The Japanese rulers came to see Western culture and Christianity as a threat to their traditional values and civilization and grew hostile toward Europeans. In 1637 they expelled all Japanese Christians from the country. Two years later Japan also forced the remaining Portuguese to leave. (*See also* **Exploration; Magellan, Ferdinand.**)

Astrology

See *Magic and Astrology.*

Astronomy

Astronomy, the scientific study of bodies in space, underwent a revolution during the Renaissance. Three great astronomers—Nicolaus COPERNICUS, Johannes KEPLER, and Galileo GALILEI—challenged the old notion that Earth was the center of the universe by showing that Earth and the other planets revolve around the Sun. Other Renaissance thinkers developed the concepts of infinity and of a universe containing many worlds.

Since ancient times, people had learned astronomy alongside astrology and cosmology. Astrology is the study of the influences of the heavens on earthly events. Renaissance astrologers believed that they could predict the future by observing the stars. Cosmology is the study of the nature and structure of the universe. It is linked to theology* and PHILOSOPHY. The ideas of philosophers, such as the ancient Greek thinker ARISTOTLE, affected Renaissance views of the universe as much as the observations of scientists did. Aristotle believed that the world was changing and imperfect, but that the heavens were unchanging and pure. PTOLEMY, the leading astronomer of the ancient world, thought that the study of heavenly motion should encourage people to think about its cause, which was God. Because they saw astronomy as being linked to faith, some Renaissance thinkers were very slow to change the ideas about the universe that they had inherited from Ptolemy.

* **theology** study of the nature of God and of religion

From Ptolemy to Copernicus. Ptolemy had described his view of the universe in a book called *Almagest.* Renaissance scholars translated and commented on this text in the 1400s. Ptolemy's model of the universe was geocentric, or earth-centered. In it, the Sun and planets revolved around Earth. Most Renaissance scholars accepted this theory.

Copernicus, the greatest astronomer of the first half of the 1500s, had a new vision of the universe. In *On the Revolutions of the Heavenly Spheres* (1543), Copernicus described a heliocentric, or sun-centered, universe. In this model, the planets, including Earth, circled the Sun. Copernicus believed that this entire system existed within a sphere of unmoving stars. He used ancient, medieval*, and Renaissance astronomical works to defend his ideas. He combined these sources with his own observations of the sky to create a complex mathematical theory of the movements of the heavens.

* **medieval** referring to the Middle Ages, a period than began around A.D. 400 and ended around 1400 in Italy and 1500 in the rest of Europe

Reactions to Copernicus. Most professional astronomers during the second half of the 1500s had high regard for Copernicus. However, they refused to believe in his heliocentric model.

See color plate 1, vol. 4

The greatest astronomer of this period was Tycho BRAHE. He possessed great skills as an observer and a maker of scientific instruments. Brahe presented a system called geoheliocentrism, in which the planets circled the Sun, which in turn circled an unmoving Earth. This theory enabled him to take advantage of some of Copernicus's discoveries. At the same time, Brahe rejected the disturbing notion that Earth was not the central and most important body of the universe.

Johannes Kepler (1571–1630) and Galileo Galilei (1564–1642) supported the heliocentric view. Kepler used mathematical principles to explain how planets move in a sun-centered system. He was also the first to describe gravity as a force that attracts all bodies in the universe to each other. Galileo used the telescope—a new invention—to study the heavens in greater detail than had ever been possible before. His observations led him to question established ideas about the universe. He saw that heavenly bodies were not perfect and unchanging when he found mountains and valleys on the Moon's surface. He realized that not everything in the heavens revolved around Earth when he discovered moons orbiting Jupiter. He carefully watched the phases of Venus (the cycle of changes in its appearance) and argued that they would not be visible in an earth-centered universe.

Galileo published his discoveries and theories in *Dialogue Concerning the Two Chief World Systems* in 1632. The book described Copernicus's view of a universe centered on the Sun as a physical reality, rather than simply a theory. By publishing this claim, Galileo disobeyed a papal* order. In response, the Roman Catholic Church banned his book and placed Galileo under house arrest for life.

* **papal** referring to the office and authority of the pope

Contributions from Theology. Modern views of the universe grew out of the findings of Copernicus, Kepler, and Galileo. However, they also reflect the ideas of Renaissance theologians.

Medieval models of the universe had claimed that the universe had boundaries. Cardinal Nicolas Cusanus (1401–1464) argued that the universe was boundless. He also believed that it had no single center and that it contained many inhabited worlds. In the late 1500s, Italian philosopher Giordano BRUNO took up Cusanus's ideas. Bruno was the first to claim that the Sun was a star and that the stars were suns. He was burned at the stake in 1600. Some Renaissance astronomers, including Copernicus, continued to see the universe as limited in size. However, by the end of the 1600s, the idea of an infinite universe with many solar systems had become common. (*See also* **Magic and Astrology.**)

Augsburg

Augsburg, one of the most important cities of Renaissance Germany, was located along a major trade route from Italy. It became a thriving center for both commerce and the arts. Augsburg was also one of the

largest cities in the region, with 30,000 people in 1520. By 1618 its population had reached 40,000.

Much of Augsburg's wealth came from its textile industry and from investments by merchants in banking and mining. After textiles, the main industries in Augsburg were crafts and gold working. By 1615 there were 185 master goldsmiths working in Augsburg. Other artisans* in the city included clock makers, jewel cutters, and cabinetmakers, who built fine furniture. The demand for their skills increased as production of luxury items grew in the 1600s.

* **artisan** skilled worker or craftsperson

Wealthy patrons* financed the growth of the arts in Augsburg, and the city supported many artists and sculptors. In 1529 the town had 34 masters in its painter's guild*, including Hans HOLBEIN the Elder. The city's most important patrons belonged to the FUGGER FAMILY. These prominent merchants made their biggest contribution to the city by financing the funeral chapel in the church of St. Anna. Completed in 1518, this was the first building in Germany designed and decorated in the Renaissance style. Augsburg's impressive town hall, built in 1624, was another noteworthy example of Renaissance architecture. Its design combined Renaissance forms with local styles, such as its pair of domed towers.

* **patron** supporter or financial sponsor of an artist or writer

* **guild** association of craft and trade owners and workers that set standards for and represented the interests of its members

Along with the arts, other forms of learning flourished in Augsburg during the Renaissance. The city's first humanist* group formed in the 1450s. Augsburg did not have a university, but in 1531 the city council established a Protestant school and a city library. In 1582 the Jesuits* founded the College of St. Salvator in Augsburg.

* **humanist** referring to a Renaissance cultural movement promoting the study of the humanities (the languages, literature, and history of ancient Greece and Rome) as a guide to living

* **Jesuit** belonging to a Roman Catholic religious order founded by St. Ignatius Loyola and approved in 1540

The Protestant Reformation* gained support quickly in Augsburg. In 1537 the city adopted a form of Protestantism called Zwinglianism as its official religion. However, the Holy Roman Emperor* CHARLES V changed the city's constitution in 1548 to restore the Catholic Church. He also did away with the city's guilds and gave political power to the nobility. A 1555 compromise called the Peace of Augsburg allowed citizens to worship as either Lutherans or Catholics. (*See also* **Architecture; Catholic Reformation and Counter-Reformation; Humanism; Patronage; Protestant Reformation.**)

* **Protestant Reformation** religious movement that began in the 1500s as a protest against certain practices of the Roman Catholic Church and eventually led to the establishment of a variety of Protestant churches

* **Holy Roman Emperor** ruler of the Holy Roman Empire, a political body in central Europe composed of several states that existed until 1806

Augustine of Hippo

354–430
Bishop and author

Augustine of Hippo, also known as St. Augustine, was an early bishop of the Catholic Church. His religious writings earned him the title of church father. His best-known work, the *City of God,* laid out many of his basic ideas on religion and morality. Augustine's ideas were popular thorough the Middle Ages. They also had a strong influence on religious scholars and philosophers of the Renaissance. However, most Renaissance scholars focused on specific ideas and did not accept all of Augustine's teachings.

Augustine had both supporters and critics in Italy. PETRARCH, an early humanist*, greatly admired Augustine's *Confessions,* an account of his youth and his conversion to Christianity. A later humanist, Lorenzo VALLA, criticized Augustine's views on the Bible, morals, and sin. Augustine's writing inspired philosophers such as Marsilio FICINO and

* **humanist** Renaissance expert in the humanities (the languages, literature, history, and speech and writing techniques of ancient Greece and Rome)

Tommaso CAMPANELLA. Ficino built on Augustine's idea that every human soul longs for God. Campanella argued that all people are born with a knowledge of God.

During the 1500s, many humanists outside Italy drew ideas from *City of God*. Thomas MORE lectured on it in London around 1501. Spanish humanist Juan Luis VIVES published a study of the work in 1522. He focused on its historical and literary references. In the late 1520s, the prominent Dutch humanist Desiderius ERASMUS published Augustine's complete works. Erasmus did not agree with Augustine's ideas about sin and the natural wickedness of humanity. However, he used his works as a historical source. He also cited Augustine to support his own religious views. Early Protestant leaders such as Martin LUTHER and John CALVIN took a similar approach to Augustine's work. They used specific arguments without embracing all of his ideas. For example, they referred to Augustine to support their views about predestination, or fate. (*See also* **Protestant Reformation; Religious Literature; Religious Thought.**)

Austria

* **patron** supporter or financial sponsor of an artist or writer

During the Renaissance, Austria was not a single nation, but an assortment of lands in central Europe. It included parts of modern Germany, Hungary, Czechoslovakia, the Netherlands, and Italy. Austria's rulers, the HABSBURGS, were major patrons* of the arts during the Renaissance. Artists, musicians, and scholars flocked to Austria from many parts of Europe, bringing with them Renaissance art and ideas.

POLITICS AND RELIGION

The Habsburg family, a powerful dynasty, ruled Austria for most of the Renaissance. Although the greater part of the lands that made up Austria came under the family's control in the 1200s and 1300s, few Habsburg rulers had power over all these lands at the same time. The Habsburgs typically divided their territory among their sons. They did not adopt the custom of primogeniture—which held that the eldest son should inherit all the family's property—until the mid-1600s. Even then, the Habsburgs did not always follow this practice strictly.

* **Holy Roman Emperor** ruler of the Holy Roman Empire, a political body in central Europe composed of several states that existed until 1806

Rudolf I, the first Habsburg to rule Austria, was also a German king and Holy Roman Emperor* during the late 1200s. Many of his descendants held those titles as well, and others tried hard to acquire them. The Habsburgs occupied the position of Holy Roman Emperor almost without interruption from the mid-1400s until 1806, when the empire ceased to exist. By the mid-1500s the family also came to rule Spain, the Netherlands, and southern Italy.

* **Protestant Reformation** religious movement that began in the 1500s as a protest against certain practices of the Roman Catholic Church and eventually led to the establishment of a variety of Protestant churches

Like other European rulers, the Austrian Habsburgs faced threats to their control over their lands. Princes, minor nobles, and local leaders all sought to increase their own power and influence at the expense of the ruling family. At the same time, the Protestant Reformation* created religious tensions within Austria. Most of the lands that made up Austria

The Habsburgs, a powerful dynasty that ruled Austria for most of the Renaissance, typically divided their territory among all their sons rather than leaving everything to the oldest son. This painting shows Rudolf I splitting his lands between his sons Albert and Rudolf in the late 1200s.

were divided along religious lines. For this reason, the Austrian Habsburgs adopted policies that aimed for a balance between the two religions.

Because the rulers of Austria controlled so much of Europe, Austria did not have a distinct national identity. In fact, modern scholars have trouble identifying an exact dividing line between Austria and Germany.

Ruling such a diverse empire proved difficult and costly, and the Austrian Habsburgs were constantly in need of more money. The search for cash was a driving force in their political activity.

CULTURE

Austria shared strong cultural ties with northern Germany. German artists, writers, and scholars played a significant role in the development of Renaissance culture in Austria. At the same time, Austrian arts and culture strongly influenced the German Renaissance. Cultural currents also flowed into Austria from places as diverse as Italy, Hungary, and the Netherlands.

Frederick's Secret Code?

During the reign of Frederick III (1440–1493), the initials AEIOU appeared in the archways of many castles, cathedrals, and other public buildings. Scholars have suggested over 300 different possible meanings for these letters, usually assuming that *A* stood for Austria. The most popular interpretation is *"Austria erit in orbe ultima,"* a Latin phrase meaning "Austria will outlive all others on Earth." It is not clear, however, whether this optimistic view referred to the land and the people of Austria, or to the dynasty that controlled it.

Learning and Literature. Arriving in VIENNA in 1490, Conrad CELTIS led the field of German writers and humanists* who worked in Austria. Vienna's university had already built up an excellent reputation in the fields of science and mathematics. Celtis broadened its curriculum by teaching poetry and rhetoric*, and Emperor MAXIMILIAN I created a professorship in these fields just for him. Celtis later established a college of poetry and mathematics apart from the university to promote humanist learning.

The works of Celtis and his successors added to the knowledge of German history and enriched German culture. They included editions of early German poetry and literature and histories of both Germany and Austria. Humanists from other countries also contributed. The Italian Enea Silvio Piccolomini (1405–1464), who later became Pope PIUS II, served the Habsburg family as a poet and secretary during the 1440s and 1450s. He wrote a history of Austria that includes a vivid description of Vienna.

Music and Theater. The Habsburgs were early and eager patrons of music, bringing to Austria composers from the music centers of Europe. Composers from the Netherlands introduced many of the latest developments, including new forms such as OPERA, a shift toward instrumental music, and new techniques such as dissonance*. Italian musicians and composers also played leading roles at the Habsburg court and helped establish Austria's reputation as a musical center.

The theater became an important element in Austrian culture as well. In Vienna, students of Conrad Celtis staged comedies by ancient Roman playwrights and by Celtis himself. Later, Catholic and Protestant writers used the theater to promote their religious and theological* ideas. Their shows often featured costumes, stage effects, and music. Even plays presented in Latin attracted audiences that numbered in the thousands.

Art and Architecture. Both the Catholic Habsburgs and the Protestant nobles of Austria supported the arts. Many German artists, such as Albrecht DÜRER and Albrecht Altdorfer, worked for the Habsburgs. In addition, the Habsburgs promoted the arts in other parts of their realm, such as BOHEMIA.

Emperor Maximilian I was the first Habsburg ruler to support the major artists of northern Europe. He commissioned several works that focused on his family's role in history, including two huge woodcuts* produced by German artists between 1516 and 1518. Maximilian also used the new technology of printing to illustrate his own works of literature with woodcuts from famous artists.

Maximilian's most ambitious artistic project was the monument he requested to decorate his own tomb. Many of the leading artists of the day contributed to the design, which featured plans for over 200 larger-than-life bronze statues of famous historical and mythical figures. Some of these statues portrayed Habsburgs of previous generations. Others were legendary rulers, such as King Arthur and the French king Clovis, representing the virtues of kingship. Work on the monument began in 1502 and continued until 1585. However, the project was often sus-

* **humanist** Renaissance expert in the humanities (the languages, literature, history, and speech and writing techniques of ancient Greece and Rome)

* **rhetoric** art of speaking or writing effectively

* **dissonance** musical technique of combining different tones to produce harsh sounds that create a feeling of tension

* **theological** relating to theology, the study of the nature of God and of religion

* **woodcut** print made from a block of wood with an image carved into it

pended for lack of funds, and only a fraction of the planned statues were ever completed.

During the 1400s and 1500s, a shortage of money, and the threat of the OTTOMAN EMPIRE on Austria's eastern border, limited construction of elaborate palaces or public buildings. However, a few remarkable architectural projects date back to this period. Maximilian's grandson FERDINAND I commissioned the striking palace called Belvedere in the city of PRAGUE. Constructed between 1534 and 1563, it is a beautiful example of architecture in the Italian style.

Two other notable Austrian castles are Schloss Porcia (Porcia Castle) and Schloss Schallaburg, both built for Austrian nobles. Completed in the 1590s, Schloss Porcia in the city of Spittal an der Drau is a square structure with two round towers. Its most notable feature is its three-story courtyard decorated with elaborate columns, sculptures, and scenes from classical* mythology. Schloss Schallaburg, in Lower Austria, dates back to the Middle Ages. However, builders remodeled it between 1572 and 1600. It has a similar courtyard featuring terra-cotta ornaments in the classical style. (*See also* **Architecture; Art in Central Europe; Art in Germany; Drama; German Language and Literature; Holy Roman Empire; Margaret of Austria; Music; Printing and Publishing.**)

* **classical** in the tradition of ancient Greece and Rome

Bacon, Francis

1561–1626
English politician and philosopher

Francis Bacon was an important figure in both the public world of politics and the private world of scholarship in Renaissance England. His public life was a drama in which he fell from high office to prison, while his achievements as a thinker helped transform the sciences.

Political Rise and Fall. Bacon was born in London to a family with political connections—his father held a position at the court of Queen ELIZABETH I. At the age of 12, Bacon entered Trinity College, Cambridge. Two years later he left Cambridge without a degree. Soon afterward, in his only trip abroad, he accompanied a diplomatic* mission to France. Bacon returned to England after his father died in 1579. He studied law and entered politics as an elected member of Parliament.

* **diplomatic** having to do with formal relations between nations

During Elizabeth's reign, Bacon hoped to gain a desirable position in government. His rivals kept him from advancing, so he formed an alliance with the powerful Earl of Essex. However, Essex was unsuccessful in obtaining a position for Bacon. When Essex went to trial for treason in 1601, Bacon had the disagreeable task of presenting the case against him in court. The episode haunted him for years.

After JAMES I came to the throne in 1603, Bacon's fortunes improved. He received a knighthood and in 1613 became attorney general of the kingdom. Five years later the king made him lord chancellor, the highest appointed post in the land. Bacon also received two noble titles, becoming Baron Verulam and Viscount St. Albans.

Although Bacon was among the most talented men of his time, he did not remain in power long. A former rival, whom Bacon had helped to remove from an earlier position, led a movement against the privileges of nobles. To save a more favored member of the court, King James reluctantly allowed investigators to accuse Bacon of bribery and corruption. In reality, Bacon had accepted only the usual fees of office, and no one could show that they had affected his judgment. Nonetheless, he was forced to resign from his post, briefly imprisoned, and banished from the court and from politics. He devoted the rest of his life to intellectual pursuits.

One of the leading political figures in Renaissance England, Francis Bacon fell from power after being falsely charged with bribery. Unable to clear his good name, he devoted the rest of his life to scholarship.

The Science of Knowing. "I have taken all knowledge for my province [realm]," Bacon wrote in 1592, and he was true to his word. During his career, he wrote masterful histories, religious translations, and literary essays. Bacon's major works, however, dealt with science and logic.

Rather than contributing new information to particular fields, Bacon examined ways to achieve and organize knowledge. He divided human reasoning into two distinct processes, invention and judgment. People showed invention when they discovered the basic principles of an art or science and how they related to knowledge in general. They used judgment, by contrast, when they applied these principles to specific questions or problems. Each realm of understanding, Bacon thought, had its own fundamental ideas and its own particular pitfalls and errors. He believed that his theory applied to all areas of knowledge except society, politics, and divine revelation*.

Bacon's overall intellectual goal was to develop a science of reasoning and an empirical* method for achieving knowledge. In works such as *The Advancement of Learning* (1605), *Description of the World of Thought* (1612), *New Instrument* (1620), and *Natural and Experimental History* (1622), he helped establish concepts of critical thinking and organized knowledge that became part of modern science. (*See also* **Government, Forms of; Science; Shakespeare, William.**)

* **revelation** communication of divine truth or divine will

* **empirical** based on observation or experimentation

Baltic States

The Baltic region is the part of northeastern Europe on the eastern shore of the Baltic Sea. During the Renaissance, this area contained many small states. The new ideas and artistic styles of the Renaissance had considerable influence in the states of Prussia and Livonia and helped create enduring links between these areas and western Europe.

A religious military order known as the Teutonic Knights had considerable influence and land in the Baltic region. The Knights played a major role in bringing the ideas of the Renaissance to eastern Europe. Members of the order visited Rome and the court of the Holy Roman Emperor* on a regular basis. Young Knights traveled to Germany and brought back the latest styles in art and literature. The Knights also sent many young men to be educated in Italy.

* **Holy Roman Emperor** ruler of the Holy Roman Empire, a political body in central Europe composed of several states that existed until 1806

Two other factors helped link the Baltic region with the rest of Renaissance Europe. The first was its closeness to the Polish city of Cracow. Home to a major university, Cracow was a famous center of Renaissance thought, art, and architecture. The second factor was the influence of merchants and burghers* in Baltic cities such as Riga,

* **burgher** well-to-do middle-class inhabitant of a town or city in central Europe

Königsberg, and Danzig (also known as Gdansk). These wealthy eastern Europeans followed the examples of their German peers in sending their sons away for a university education. They also copied the architectural styles of Germany and Poland. The Prussian city of Danzig contained many notable examples of northern Renaissance architecture, some of which still exist.

The influence of the Renaissance was strongest in Prussia. Education helped promote Renaissance thought, especially among the upper and middle classes. The Prussian city of Königsberg was home to the most famous university in northeastern Europe, founded by a leader of the Teutonic Knights. In addition, many towns had their own schools for local youths. Between 1450 and 1540 Prussia produced several important Renaissance scholars, including the great astronomer Nicolaus COPERNICUS. Although Polish by birth, Copernicus lived most of his life in Prussia.

To the northeast, the state of Livonia was more remote and difficult to reach than Prussia. It also had a smaller population and lacked the resources to develop Renaissance ideas and styles fully. Local clergy, nobles, and merchants could only afford to support modest building projects and a handful of artists and humanists*. Unlike Prussia, which followed the examples of Poland and Germany, Livonia had little contact with the rest of Europe and its new ideas. As a result, Livonia lagged far behind Prussia in adopting Renaissance ideas and styles. However, several striking buildings from the period survive in the cities of Riga (now in Latvia) and Reval (in present-day Estonia). (*See also* **Art in Central Europe; Humanism; Poland.**)

* **humanist** Renaissance expert in the humanities (the languages, literature, history, and speech and writing techniques of ancient Greece and Rome)

Banking

See *Money and Banking.*

Barocci, Federico

ca. 1535–1612
Italian painter

The work of painter Federico Barocci helped introduce the Baroque* movement in art. He broke with the artistic style of his day by using colors in a natural way and by portraying heartfelt emotions. Barocci's many religious paintings illustrated the spiritual ideas of the Catholic Reformation, a reform movement within the Roman Catholic Church.

Barocci learned painting in his hometown of URBINO, Italy. Early influences on his style included the rich colors of the paintings of TITIAN and RAPHAEL. However, his mature work most strongly reflects the style of CORREGGIO, with its vibrant colors and passionate feelings. Barocci's first notable piece in this style was *Deposition* (1567–1569), which shows the body of Christ being taken down from the cross. Barocci combined the intense grief of the women in the painting with the motion of a powerful wind through the hair and clothes of the figures. *Madonna del Popolo* ("mother of the people"), completed about a decade later, shows the Virgin Mary gazing down from heaven at her worshipers. The picture illustrates the idea of a direct connection with God, a concept that played a role in the Catholic reform movement then taking shape in Rome.

* **Baroque** artistic style of the 1600s characterized by movement, drama, and grandness of scale

Barocci was also a skilled portrait painter. He excelled at capturing fine shadings of expression in his subjects' faces. His 1572 portrait of *Duke Francesco Maria II Della Rovere,* his chief patron*, shows the soldier delicately caressing his helmet, a soft blush on his cheek. Barocci's *Self-Portrait,* painted when he was around 60 years old, captures the artist's thoughtful and moody character. (*See also* **Art in Italy; Baroque.**)

* **patron** supporter or financial sponsor of an artist or writer

Baroque

Scholars often use the term *baroque* to refer to the art, music, and literature of the 1600s, a period of great social and political upheaval. During this time many writers and artists moved away from the orderly, classical* principles of the Renaissance and adopted a more dramatic and expressive style in their work.

* **classical** in the tradition of ancient Greece and Rome

The word *baroque* was first used in the 1700s to describe the style that emerged toward the end of the Renaissance. A negative term—possibly derived from the Spanish *barrueco* (a misshapen pearl), it was applied to works considered distorted or excessive. In the late 1800s scholars began to refer to Baroque art in a more positive way, identifying it as a distinct movement and noting its grandeur, exuberance, and vitality.

Baroque architecture conveys a sense of movement and emotion through the use of massive forms, soaring heights, and rich interior decorations. Prominent baroque architects include Francesco Borromini and Giovanni Lorenzo Bernini, who was also a noted sculptor.

Artists who worked in the baroque style include the Italian painter Pietro da Cortona and the Flemish* painter Peter Paul RUBENS. Pietro da Cortona created magnificent ceiling frescoes* that seem to open up to the sky. Rubens portrayed groups of figures displaying deep emotion or energy but finished with the intricate details typical of northern European painting.

* **Flemish** relating to Flanders, a region along the coasts of present-day Belgium, France, and the Netherlands

* **fresco** mural painted on a plaster wall

A similar move toward a dramatic style appeared in baroque music. OPERA, which developed around 1600, provides a prime example of this trend toward the dramatic. Italian composer Claudio MONTEVERDI took the form to a new level. Over time opera productions became increasingly elaborate, captivating audiences in many parts of Europe. At the same time, writers such as the Spaniard Lope Félix de VEGA CARPIO produced plays in the baroque style, ranging from light comedies to dramas about history, religion, love, and honor. (*See also* **Art; Drama; Music; Renaissance: Influence and Interpretations.**)

Bartolommeo della Porta, Fra

1472–1517
Italian painter

Fra Bartolommeo della Porta, a leading painter in Florence in the early 1500s, influenced artists at home and in other cities of Italy. Born Baccio della Porta, he had joined an artist's workshop by the age of 15. In time he set up his own workshop with another painter. His early fresco *Last Judgment* shows a unity of tone and balanced composition typical of high Renaissance art.

* **Dominican** religious order of brothers and priests founded by St. Dominic

In 1500 the artist abandoned painting to join a convent. After taking the vows of the Dominican* order, he changed his name to Fra Bartolommeo. However, four years later Bartolommeo returned to painting. His career flourished, and he received commissions for paintings in churches and public buildings. He was a fine draftsman who always made many drawings before painting.

On a visit to Rome in 1513, Bartolommeo saw RAPHAEL's frescoes in the pope's apartments and MICHELANGELO's ceiling in the Sistine Chapel. The influence of these artists is evident in some of Bartolommeo's later work. (*See also* **Art in Italy; Florence.**)

Basel

* **humanist** referring to a Renaissance cultural movement promoting the study of the humanities (the languages, literature, and history of ancient Greece and Rome) as a guide to living

* **Holy Roman Empire** political body in central Europe composed of several states; existed until 1806

* **guild** association of craft and trade owners and workers that set standards for and represented the interests of its members

* **Protestant Reformation** religious movement that began in the 1500s as a protest against certain practices of the Roman Catholic Church and eventually led to the establishment of a variety of Protestant churches

Located on the Rhine River in Switzerland, the city of Basel was a center of publishing and humanist* scholarship during the Renaissance. Basel had been part of the Holy Roman Empire* during the Middle Ages. However, in 1501 it declared itself a "free city" and joined the Swiss Confederation, a group of cantons, or states, that had banded together for defense. With a population of about 10,000, Basel was one of the largest cities in the confederation.

The famous scholar Desiderius ERASMUS made his home in Basel in the 1520s. Thanks largely to his influence, the city became a major center of humanist scholarship. Erasmus had come to the city to work with his friend the publisher Johann Froben, who printed many of Erasmus's works. He and other humanists played an important role in Basel's publishing industry. They served as editors and proofreaders on books of history and literature in Latin, Greek, and German. Basel also dominated the field of religious publishing in northern Europe. It produced high-quality Bibles and works of biblical scholarship.

Most of the city's printers belonged to the powerful Safran guild*, an organization that included such workers as papermakers, booksellers, mapmakers, and even goldsmiths and jewelers. The publishing industry helped support a great variety of artists, who provided illustrations for books. Many of Basel's artists specialized in religious images for religious services or personal prayers. Hans HOLBEIN the Younger, who lived in the city, was known for his paintings, engravings, and illustrations.

Turmoil broke out in Basel during the Protestant Reformation*. On February 9, 1529, a Protestant mob attacked the Roman Catholic cathedral and many other churches in the city. Their four-hour rampage destroyed most of the city's religious art from the Middle Ages. After the attack, members of the town council who supported Catholicism fled the city. Those that remained behind voted to support the Reformation. Most Catholics left Basel, and the city became a center of Protestantism in northern Europe. As a result, its production of religious images ceased. The city lost its prominence in the arts and did not recover it until the 1800s. (*See also* **Humanism; Printing and Publishing; Protestant Reformation.**)

Basel, Council of

See *Councils.*

Battles

See *name of individual battle.*

Bavaria

* **duchy** territory ruled by a duke or duchess

* **Holy Roman Empire** political body in central Europe composed of several states; existed until 1806

* **absolutist** refers to complete control by a single ruler

* **humanist** Renaissance expert in the humanities (the languages, literature, history, and speech and writing techniques of ancient Greece and Rome)

* **patron** supporter or financial sponsor of an artist or writer

The duchy* of Bavaria, a territory in the southeastern part of the Holy Roman Empire*, was ruled by the Wittelsbach family from 1180 until the early 1900s. However, by the early 1400s Bavaria had been divided into four separate duchies, ruled by different members of the family. The Wittelsbach dukes battled for control of the duchies, and in 1504 their struggle led to war. Duke Albrecht IV of Bavaria-Munich emerged the victor and united all the duchies under his rule. From then on, leadership of the duchy passed to the oldest living male heir.

During the 1400s, the dukes shared their power with nobles and high church officials. In the 1500s they expanded their power, taking greater control over legal matters and the church. They also set up councils to oversee finances, military matters, and church affairs. Duke Maximilian I, who became ruler in 1597, increased his power further. He raised taxes and made military decisions without consulting minor nobles and lesser officials. Under his rule, Bavaria became one of the earliest absolutist* states in Europe.

Bavaria's economy at this time was almost entirely based on agriculture. Four of every five Bavarians were peasants who lived in small villages and produced crops for their own use and for local markets. Bavaria also had a small textile industry based in the city of Munich, its largest city. In 1500 Munich had a population of about 12,000.

In the 1550s Protestant nobles asked Duke Albrecht V for the right to practice their religion in Catholic Bavaria. At first, the duke agreed. However, when he learned that Protestants were plotting against him, he took back many of their privileges. By the 1580s Bavaria was once again a solidly Catholic state, and during the Thirty Years' War (1618–1648) it supported the Catholic powers. However, invading Swedish and French troops devastated Bavaria during the war, and the Wittelsbach dukes lost most of their territory.

Bavaria was a cultural center during the 1400s and 1500s. Its University of Ingolstadt, founded in 1472, was home to several noted scholars. By the 1490s many humanists* had gathered in Bavaria. The duchy's churches and other religious institutions supported many painters and sculptors. After the unification of Bavaria, its dukes became major patrons* of the arts. Many Italian artists and sculptors arrived to work on new museums and churches, such as the Michaelkirche in Munich. However, the Thirty Years' War brought an end to this golden age of Bavarian art. (*See also* **Art in Germany; Holy Roman Empire; Humanism; Protestant Reformation.**)

Behn, Aphra

1640–1689
English writer

Aphra Behn, playwright, novelist, and poet, was the first Englishwoman to make an independent living as a writer. She was the most productive female author of the late 1600s, a period that wit-

nessed a surge of female writers in England. Many of her works highlight the position of women in English society.

Behn lived an adventurous life. As a young woman, she traveled with her family to the South American colony of Suriname. In the 1660s, she served as a spy for the English crown. Behn gained fame as a writer by composing 16 plays for the English stage during the 1670s and 1680s. Behn's plays are typical of the period, featuring bawdy* language and sexual situations. However, her female characters are better developed than those of her male contemporaries. She also addressed serious issues, such as women's lack of power in romantic relationships and the role of the monarchy in England.

* **bawdy** indecent; lewd

Along with her plays, Behn penned several poems and some of England's earliest novels. Her novel *Oroonoko; or, the Royal Slave* (1688) describes a slave revolt she witnessed during her visit to Suriname. It focuses on some of her favorite themes, such as the importance of honor and the evil influence of wealth. In 1688 Behn translated the book *A Discovery of New Worlds,* by French author Bernard Le Bovier de Fontenelle. This work featured a young woman who pursued scientific studies. However, Behn noted that the author seemed to mock his main character's intellect by making her "say a great many very silly things." (*See also* **English Language and Literature.**)

Bellarmine, Robert

1542–1621
Catholic Church leader and author

Robert Bellarmine, an Italian theologian*, was an influential writer on the Catholic faith. As a man of strong religious convictions and a defender of the Catholic faith, Bellarmine emerged as a respected leader and adviser within the church. He was not afraid, however, to challenge papal* authority in civil matters.

* **theologian** person who studies religion and the nature of God
* **papal** referring to the office and authority of the pope
* **Jesuit** belonging to a Roman Catholic religious order founded by St. Ignatius Loyola and approved in 1540
* **heresy** belief that is contrary to the doctrine of an established church

Bellarmine was born in Montepulciano, Italy. He studied for the priesthood and entered the Jesuit* community in 1560. Ten years later, he became a priest. He spent the next several years teaching theology, first at Louvain in the Netherlands, and later in Rome. His lectures focused on defending Catholicism against Protestant criticism. These lectures were later published as the *Controversies,* a highly regarded work.

Pope Clement VIII (1592–1605) made Bellarmine a cardinal in 1599. He became archbishop of Capua three years later. Bellarmine spent his last 16 years working for various church organizations, including the INQUISITION, which investigated charges of heresy*. In 1616 Bellarmine was the official who forbade the astronomer Galileo GALILEI to hold or defend the theory that Earth circles the Sun.

As a writer, Bellarmine played a key role in preparing the Sixto-Clementine Vulgate (1592), which served as the official Catholic Bible for centuries. His most popular work was a short book of religious instruction for children, *Dottrina cristiana breve* (Short Christian Doctrine). During his last years, Bellarmine wrote several short religious books that sold widely. Pope Pius XI declared Bellarmine a saint in 1930. (*See also* **Catholic Reformation and Counter-Reformation; Clergy; Popes and Papacy; Protestant Reformation.**)

Bellini Family

Venetian painters

Jacopo Bellini and his sons Gentile and Giovanni were among the most famous and successful artists of the Italian Renaissance. Working separately and together, they made important contributions to Renaissance painting in Venice. The Bellinis developed new techniques and strongly influenced later generations of Italian painters.

Jacopo Bellini. Jacopo Bellini (ca. 1400–1470) began his career as the pupil of Gentile da Fabriano, a renowned painter from central Italy. From Fabriano, Jacopo learned how to represent light in paint. By studying the theory of perspective* of architect Leon Battista ALBERTI, Jacopo learned how to add depth to his paintings. His altarpiece the *Annunciation* (early 1400s) reveals his interest in both light and perspective. Jacopo was also a skilled portraitist. Few of his paintings have survived, but those that still exist show him to be the most advanced Venetian painter of his generation.

* **perspective** artistic technique for creating the illusion of three-dimensional space on a flat surface

Among Jacopo Bellini's most important works are two bound volumes of drawings produced between the mid-1430s and the mid-1460s. Highly prized in their day, the volumes show the inventive process of a Renaissance artist at work. The drawings include real and imagined views of nature, objects from ancient Greece and Rome, and religious subjects. In many cases, the artist combines grand architecture, figures in action, and scenes of the Venetian landscape. After Jacopo's death, one volume went to each of his sons.

Jacopo's influence on other artists is as noteworthy as his own work. He shared his interests in perspective and classical* art with his son-in-law Andrea MANTEGNA, an artist from Padua, and with the Florentine sculptor DONATELLO. Jacopo also had an impact on the next generation of Venetian painters. He trained his sons Gentile and Giovanni and later worked with them. Gentile's paintings resembled Jacopo's bound drawings, and Giovanni continued his father's experiments with light and landscapes.

* **classical** in the tradition of ancient Greece and Rome

Gentile Bellini. The lesser known of Jacopo Bellini's sons, Gentile (ca. 1429–1507) worked with his father and brother on altarpieces and a number of projects. His contemporaries held him in high esteem. After Holy Roman Emperor* Frederick III granted him a knighthood in 1463, Gentile received his most important assignment—redecorating the Chamber of the Great Council in Venice. Unfortunately, a fire destroyed his work in 1577.

* **Holy Roman Emperor** ruler of the Holy Roman Empire, a political body in central Europe composed of several states that existed until 1806

In 1479 the Venetian government sent Gentile on a diplomatic mission to CONSTANTINOPLE. While there, he painted a portrait of MEHMED II, the ruler of the OTTOMAN EMPIRE. Upon his return to Venice, Gentile completed a number of large paintings that have become his best-known works. These include numerous portraits and detailed pictures of buildings, clothing, and customs. His precise style features strong, straight lines.

Giovanni Bellini. Giovanni (ca. 1431–1516) began his career in his father's workshop. His religious paintings and landscapes have made

Giovanni Bellini's *Madonna of the Meadow,* painted around 1500, showcases the artist's use of perspective and sensitive portrayal of religious figures. These qualities, as well as his skill with new oil painting techniques, made Bellini one of the leading painters in Renaissance Venice.

him one of the greatest Venetian painters and the most famous member of the Bellini family.

Giovanni revolutionized painting in Venice by adopting oil painting techniques developed in the Netherlands. Unlike the fresco* techniques that were popular in Italy, the Netherlandish process mixed colors with oil. By applying the mixture in very thin layers, an artist could create a smooth, glassy image with a feeling of depth. In *Coronation of the Virgin,* Giovanni used a similar technique. He may have been introduced to this new process by PIERO DELLA FRANCESCA, a painter from Tuscany. In any case, the technique enabled him to experiment further with his father's specialties, light and perspective.

*** fresco** mural painted on a plaster wall

See color plate 6, vol. 1

Giovanni excelled in every category of painting. He also tried out new styles throughout his career. In his altarpiece for San Giobbe church in Venice (late 1400s), he used perspective to paint his figures as if they were in a chapel of the church. To the observer, it appeared that the Madonna and several saints had gathered in a nearby room. In 1479 he went to Venice to work on historical narrative* paintings with his brother Gentile in the Chamber of the Great Council. There he produced his lifelike portrait *Doge Leonardo Loredan* (ca. 1501). Later works, such as *The Drunkenness of Noah* (ca. 1514) and *Nude Woman Holding a Mirror* (1515), show Giovanni's flexibility as an artist.

*** narrative** storytelling

By about 1490, the demand for Giovanni's religious paintings had become enormous, and his workshop was one of the largest and best organized of the Renaissance. Giovanni trained or directed numerous painters of the next generation. Many of them, known as the "belliniani," practiced his style. Others, such as Venetian painters GIORGIONE and TITIAN, developed distinct personal styles and became the great

artistic pioneers of the 1500s. (*See also* **Art; Art in Italy; Art in the Netherlands.**)

Bible

Several major changes during the Renaissance affected the way Europeans read and interpreted the Bible. The first development was a renewed interest in Greek and Hebrew, the original languages of the New and Old Testaments. The second was the production of Bibles in the vernacular—the languages common people used in their daily lives—rather than in Latin. And finally, the invention of printing made widespread distribution of the Bible possible for the first time.

TRANSLATION AND INTERPRETATION

At the beginning of the Renaissance, the accepted version of the Bible was a Latin translation known as the Vulgate. Many scholars believed it to be the work of St. Jerome, a church father who lived in the late 300s and early 400s. During the Renaissance, humanist* biblical scholars analyzed the Vulgate and wrote new translations from the original Greek and Hebrew texts.

* **humanist** referring to a Renaissance cultural movement promoting the study of the humanities (the languages, literature, and history of ancient Greece and Rome) as a guide to living

Recovering the Greek Text. During the Middle Ages, scholars had little knowledge of ancient Greek, the language of the New Testament. Around 1400 a revival of Greek scholarship began. Many teachers entered Italy from Greece, and many western Europeans traveled to Greece to learn. When the Ottoman Empire conquered CONSTANTINOPLE in 1453, even more Christian scholars with a knowledge of ancient Greek came to the West.

* **Ottoman Empire** Islamic empire founded by Ottoman Turks in the 1300s that reached the height of its power in the 1500s; it eventually included large areas of eastern Europe, the Middle East, and northern Africa

Armed with new knowledge of ancient Greek, several scholars set out to improve their understanding of the New Testament. Lorenzo VALLA undertook one of the earliest and most influential efforts in 1444 with his *Collatio Novi Testamenti.* In this work he made a comparison *(collatio)* between the Vulgate's New Testament and a Greek text. Valla noted differences between the two versions, but he did not favor one text over the other. However, his work opened the door for later biblical criticism.

Interpretation and Criticism. Scholars who followed Valla not only translated the Bible, but also offered their own commentaries on the text. In 1509 Jacques Lefèvre d'Étaples published an edition of the Book of Psalms that presented five different versions of each psalm. Each page showed four traditional versions and Lefèvre's personal interpretation. His was the first work to use this technique, which many other translators and commentators later adopted. Lefèvre carefully explained each word and verse of the text in every psalm. Despite its importance, Lefèvre's work suffered from his limited knowledge of Greek and Hebrew.

The great humanist scholar Desiderius ERASMUS published his own Greek version of the New Testament in 1516 and revised it in 1519. The second edition upset many religious scholars because it contained cor-

rections and changes that affected the meaning of the text. In 1517 he published the first of his *Paraphrases on the New Testament,* a series that rewrote Biblical passages in simpler terms. Between 1516 and 1536, Erasmus also published several volumes of *Annotations* on the New Testament. In these works he commented on questions of language and theology* that interested him or that were subjects of debate.

* **theology** study of the nature of God and of religion

Polyglot Bibles. Some scholars prepared polyglot editions of the Bible, which presented the text in several different languages. The first and most familiar is the Complutensian Polyglot. Cardinal Francisco Jiménes de Cisneros, the founder of a Spanish university, began work on the text in 1502. Each page of the Old Testament showed a single passage in Latin, Greek, and Hebrew. It provided both the text of the Vulgate edition and a new Latin translation. The book also included the Targum of Onkelos, a paraphrase of the first five books of the Old Testament in the ancient language of Aramaic. The Targum appeared with its own Latin translation. The New Testament included both the original Greek and the Vulgate.

The Complutensian Polyglot was completed in 1517, but a wait for permission from the pope delayed its distribution until 1522. Over the next 135 years, scholars in Antwerp, Paris, and London produced three more polyglot Bibles. Scholars consider the London Polyglot (1655–1657) the most accurate of the four.

THE PROTESTANT REFORMATION AND THE VERNACULAR BIBLE

The year 1517 marked the beginning of the PROTESTANT REFORMATION, a religious movement that divided Christians into Catholics and Protestants. Protestant leader Martin LUTHER argued that the true source of salvation was the Bible, rather than the traditions and practices of the church. Catholic religious scholars of the 1500s and 1600s spoke out against Luther's view. They held that the Bible was not clear and that the Catholic Church had the final say in determining its meaning.

The Reformation strongly influenced later versions of the Bible in two ways. First, it encouraged the production of vernacular Bibles, which people could read without knowing Latin. Protestants strongly supported vernacular Bibles, but the Catholic Church continued to rely on the Vulgate. It approved some vernacular Bibles prepared by Catholics but banned others. The Reformation also affected the focus of new versions of the Bible. The way translators interpreted specific passages often reflected their religious views.

German Versions. The first printed vernacular Bible, a German translation of the Vulgate, appeared in 1466. Seventeen more German Bibles based on the Vulgate followed. In September of 1522 Luther published a translation of the New Testament from Erasmus's Greek Bible. Over the next 12 years, he gradually translated the Old Testament from Hebrew into German. Luther worked with Greek and Hebrew scholars

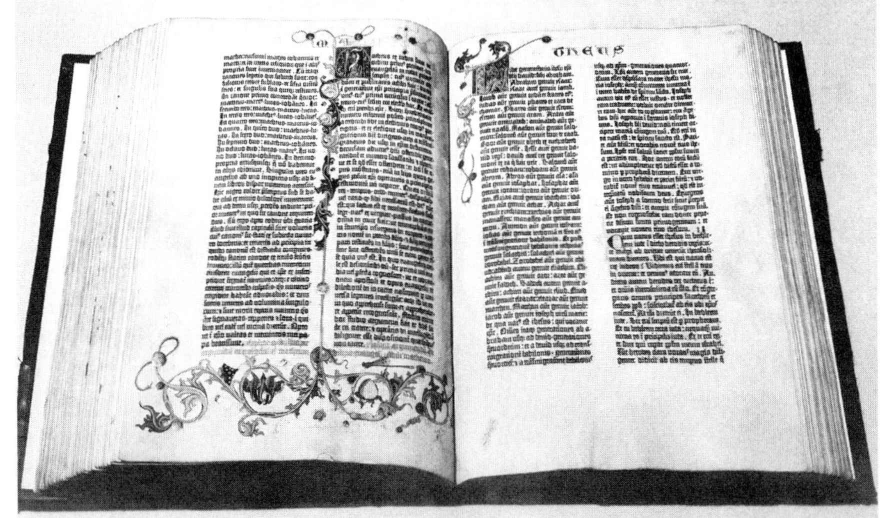

The first major book to appear in print, the Gutenberg Bible is an outstanding example of Renaissance print work. Each page consists of 42 lines of crisp, sharp type set along perfectly straight right-hand margins. Artists decorated the pages by hand to enhance the appearance of the books.

to create a Bible that would be clear and easy to read. He was careful to use language that was familiar to the common people.

By the time Luther died in 1546, his Wittenberg Bible had sold over 500,000 partial or complete copies throughout Europe. It was the most widely printed book in the German language. The Wittenberg Bible drew criticism from Catholics, who offered their own German translations as alternatives. However, they based most of these Catholic versions on Luther's translation. Soon, Germany was flooded with Bibles.

English Versions. The first complete English Bible was translated in the 1300s by John Wycliffe, an outspoken critic of the Catholic Church. After church officials accused Wycliffe of heresy* and banned his books, creating an English Bible became a crime. However, in the 1520s humanist William Tyndale believed that the English people were hungry for a vernacular Bible. To get around the law, Tyndale traveled to Germany to prepare an English version of the New Testament.

* **heresy** belief that is contrary to the doctrine of an established church

Authorities in the city of Cologne stopped Tyndale's first attempt in 1525. The following year, he published some 3,000 copies of a full New Testament in the city of Worms and sent them to England. Tyndale then moved to Antwerp, where authorities arrested him in 1535. A year later he was executed for heresy. Only two complete copies of his Bible survive, yet it formed the basis for all later English versions.

Meanwhile another translator, Miles Coverdale, had obtained permission from HENRY VIII to create an English Bible. He produced his first translation in 1535. Four years later he used Tyndale's work to create a new version, the Great Bible. The Church of England authorized this version and planned to set up a copy in every church. However, the most influential English Bible was the King James Version, published in 1611. Unlike many other Bibles of the day, it included no commentaries or notes on the text. Disliked at first, it became very popular in the late 1700s. The King James is still the most widely published edition of the Bible in English.

"Perfection in This World"

Jewish scholars during the Middle Ages and Renaissance developed a rich tradition of biblical study and interpretation. Jewish thinkers saw the Torah—the most holy text in the Jewish religion, containing the first five books of the Bible—as vastly complex, requiring intense study and questioning. Preachers and teachers connected passages from Scripture to subjects as diverse as physics, politics, and psychology. One scholar claimed that the Torah "provides us with perfection in this world, as well as in the world to come ... contained within it are all the sciences."

French Versions. In 1530, Jacques Lefèvre published the first complete French Bible, using the Vulgate as its basis. The first French translation from original languages appeared in Geneva five years later. The famous Protestant leader John CALVIN contributed an introduction to this book, called the French Geneva Bible. It became one of the most popular versions of Scripture in any language. New versions added notes and commentaries, many of which took strong Protestant stands on questions of theology.

The first Catholic edition of the Bible in French appeared in 1566. However, it relied on the Protestant French Geneva Bible, so Catholic scholars condemned it. In 1578 Christophe Plantin published a revision of the earlier Catholic edition. This version is called the Louvain Bible because it received the approval of theologians at the Catholic university in Louvain.

PRINTING AND THE BIBLE

The development of printing spread the text of the Bible throughout Europe on a scale never known before. It also helped promote new biblical scholarship.

Early Printed Bibles. Johann GUTENBERG's revolutionary invention, movable type, made widespread distribution of books possible. The first book he printed with movable type, around 1455, was a Bible. Gutenberg's Bible had less visual detail than manuscript Bibles of his day, but it used the same layout—two columns of text on each page. Gutenberg used a style of type that was similar to handwriting, and he left space so that scribes* could insert decorative initial letters by hand. Most Bibles used this approach until printers developed new methods of printing initial letters.

German and Italian Bibles of the 1400s often featured woodcut* illustrations, with some editions having hundreds. The Italian Malermi Bible of 1490 included 387 woodcuts. Printed Vulgate Bibles, by contrast, did not have illustrations before about 1500. In 1498 the great German artist Albrecht DÜRER published an illustrated copy of the Book of Revelation in both Latin and German. His work greatly influenced the illustrations of later Bibles.

* **scribe** person who copies manuscripts

* **woodcut** print made from a block of wood with an image carved into it

Technical Improvements. Two important technical advances in Bible printing during the 1400s were the creation of smaller type and the ability to print Hebrew text accurately. Early Bibles were printed on large pages called folios. They were so large that the Bibles often consisted of more than one volume. As smaller type became available, Bibles shrank. The first quarto edition Bible (half the size of a folio) appeared in 1475, followed by an even smaller octavo Bible (half the size of a quarto) in 1491.

In 1477 printers in Bologna made the first attempt to produce a book of the Bible in Hebrew. The Hebrew letters in their Book of Psalms did not align with their vowel points, the small markings that indicate

vowel sounds. Five years later Abraham ben Hayyim overcame this problem. His edition of the Pentateuch (the first five books of the Old Testament) also included the Targums. Ben Hayyim later joined the Soncino press in Italy, which printed the first complete Hebrew Bible in 1488. (*See also* **Books and Manuscripts; Catholic Reformation and Counter-Reformation; Censorship; Christianity; Humanism; Illumination; Jewish Languages and Literature; Ottoman Empire; Printing and Publishing; Translation.**)

Biography and Autobiography

* **genre** literary form

* **classical** in the tradition of ancient Greece and Rome

* **medieval** referring to the Middle Ages, a period that began around A.D. 400 and ended around 1400 in Italy and 1500 in the rest of Europe

* **humanist** referring to a Renaissance cultural movement promoting the study of the humanities (the languages, literature, and history of ancient Greece and Rome) as a guide to living

* **exemplary** serving as a model or example; worthy of imitation

Renaissance authors did not recognize biography as a specific genre* of writing. However, they produced many written works about people's lives. A "life" of a famous person was more like a portrait than a detailed story. In fact, the arts of "life-writing" and portrait painting shared many similarities.

Biography. Renaissance life-writing had its roots in the ancient world. Many Greek authors had written lives of famous people. The most famous was Xenophon, who included biographies in his historical writing. Collections of biographies by the Roman authors Suetonius and Plutarch were popular in the Renaissance. Suetonius stressed his subjects' deeds. Plutarch, by contrast, focused on his subjects' personalities. These classical* works became important models for later writers. Ancient and medieval* Christian authors followed their style in creating hagiographies, or lives of holy people.

In the 1300s, ordinary people began to record their lives in diaries. The best known of these are the *ricordanze* (remembrances) written in Florence, Italy. At the same time, humanist* writers created a new form of life-writing called the exemplary* life. In these works, writers used their subjects as models for others. The first example of this style was *Life of Dante* (1348) by Italian writer Giovanni Boccaccio. Boccaccio was more concerned with using Dante as a model than with portraying his life accurately. In 1436, Italian historian Leonardo Bruni wrote another life of Dante to eliminate the fiction in Boccaccio's work.

In the mid-1300s, Italian writer Petrarch created a form of biography called collected lives. His *On Famous Men* is a series of biographies gathered into one volume. Collected lives became a common Renaissance form. Boccaccio published two collections in the mid-1300s, *The Fates of Illustrious Men* and *On Famous Women*. They became very popular outside Italy, particularly in England. One of the most famous collections was *Lives of the Artists*, published in 1550 by Italian artist and historian Giorgio Vasari. It combined biography with the new field of art history.

Later English biographers followed the style of exemplary biography. Instead of trying to portray their subjects accurately, they tried to show them in a particular light. An example is the harsh life of King Richard III written around 1513 by English statesman and author Thomas More. This work may have had a political motive. More supported the Tudor family, which had taken control of England after defeating Richard. William Roper, a friend of More, wrote *Life of Sir Thomas More* around

1556. This book resembles a hagiography more than a balanced perspective. *The Life and Death of Dr. Donne, Late Deane of St. Pauls London* (1640), by English biographer Izaak Walton, focuses on the religious life of English poet John Donne. However, it ignores Donne's love poetry.

Autobiography. Renaissance autobiographies also drew on ancient models. *Confessions,* by Augustine of Hippo, influenced many later writers. Dante imitated its style in *The New Life* (1293–1294). Petrarch also copied it in a letter called "The Ascent of Mount Ventoux," written around 1352. *Confessions* also formed the basis for the spiritual autobiographies created by Protestant authors of the 1600s. *Commentaries,* by Julius Caesar, also influenced some writers of the 1400s.

Renaissance autobiographies were diverse. Some took the form of collections of letters. Petrarch introduced this style, and it became popular with female authors of the 1400s and 1500s. Other women recorded their lives in poetry. French writer Michel de Montaigne closely examined his own existence in his *Essays,* written between 1572 and 1588. These pieces offer strong opinions on a broad range of topics. Donne's *Devotions upon Emergent Occasions* (1624) focused on his spiritual and intellectual thought. The most famous autobiographer of the Renaissance was Benvenuto Cellini, an Italian artist, soldier, and writer. He wrote his autobiography between 1558 and 1566. It portrayed him as a mysterious and fantastic figure who could do absolutely everything.

Portraits. During the Renaissance, formal portraits served the same goal as biographies. A portrait provided a permanent memorial to a remarkable individual. Group portraits presented the lives of various individuals in one grand image. In Italy, for example, two artist brothers, Taddeo and Francesco Zuccaro, created detailed frescoes* showing the lives and famous deeds of the prominent Farnese family.

* **fresco** mural painted on a plaster wall

Advances in printing enabled artists to share their work with the public. For example, the image of German religious leader Martin Luther appeared in pamphlets distributed widely during the 1500s. German artist Albrecht Dürer reproduced portraits of himself using a method called copperplate engraving. This and other new methods helped bring images and text closer together. In some cases, portraits appeared in printed biographies. (*See also* **Books and Manuscripts; History, Writing of; Literature; Printing and Publishing.**)

Boccaccio, Giovanni

1313–1375
Italian author

* **classical** in the tradition of ancient Greece and Rome

Scholars disagree about whether Boccaccio's writings belong to the Middle Ages or to the Renaissance. However, there is no question that he helped to define the Renaissance literary tradition. Boccaccio was a devout Christian, but the ancient world fascinated him. In his works, he revived classical* mythology and literature and used them to comment on his own era. He had a strong influence on later Renaissance authors. His most famous work is the *Decameron,* a collection of prose tales that continues to influence writers and filmmakers today.

Author Giovanni Boccaccio was one of the most influential writers of the early Renaissance. His most famous work, the *Decameron,* inspired authors and artists from Italy to England.

The Early Years. Giovanni Boccaccio was born near Florence, Italy. His father, a successful banker, wanted him to have a practical education. Boccaccio studied banking and religious law, but he showed a stronger interest in literature and classical learning. When he and his father moved to Naples, Boccaccio found many teachers at the university and court. He learned Italian poetry, ancient mythology, astronomy, and Greek. He also began to write.

Boccaccio's writing reflected his interest in classical literature, but he did not try to copy the classics. Instead, he combined ancient works with elements of his own times to create something completely new. For example, Boccaccio's *Il Filostrato* (1335), a long narrative* poem, uses classical settings and names. However, its style is similar to the love poetry of Boccaccio's time. *Il Filostrato* is an example of Boccaccio's strong influence on later writers. The English poet Geoffrey Chaucer used it as the basis for his poem *Troilus and Criseyde* (1385). SHAKESPEARE, in turn, used Chaucer's poem to write *Troilus and Cressida* in the early 1600s.

Boccaccio also wrote *Thesiad of the Marriage of Emilia* (1340–1341) while he was in Naples. This work was the first epic* written in Italian verse. Boccaccio included comments to explain the ancient names, myths, and customs that he referred to in the text. He also made the epic form more modern by writing in his native language, or vernacular, instead of Latin. British poet Edmund SPENSER followed this example in his own epic, *The Faerie Queene* (1590).

Boccaccio in Florence. In 1341, Boccaccio and his father left Naples because his father had to return to his position in Florence. Boccaccio did not want to leave Naples because he felt that Florence was dull by comparison. However, he spent the rest of his life in or near Florence. There he composed his most famous work and built a lasting friendship with fellow Italian poet PETRARCH.

In Florence, Boccaccio continued to write works inspired by earlier literature. He based two pieces on *The Divine Comedy,* an epic by the medieval* poet Dante. In *Nymphs of Fiesole* (1344–1346), Boccaccio created his own mythology in the spirit of ancient mythology. Spenser later imitated this approach in *The Faerie Queene.* Even the *Elegy of Madam Fiammetta* (1343–1344), a novel set in the Naples of Boccaccio's time, described daily life in classical terms. Some scholars have called this work the first psychological novel because it traces its main character's thoughts and feelings. Boccaccio's use of a female main character was also a new idea. Women writers of the Renaissance later copied this approach.

Boccaccio's masterpiece is the *Decameron* (1348–1351). It features ten young men and women in Florence during the time of the Black Death*. The characters share 100 tales about topics such as love, trickery, and fortune. These tales fit together to form a larger story, although each can also stand alone. The *Decameron* was hugely popular. Readers enjoyed its lively speeches, witty wordplay, tight plots, and psychological insights. Several later writers discussed or imitated the *Decameron* in their own works. These include the Italian writer Baldassare CASTIGLIONE, the

* **narrative** storytelling

* **epic** long poem about the adventures of a hero

* **medieval** referring to the Middle Ages, a period that began around A.D. 400 and ended around 1400 in Italy and 1500 in the rest of Europe

* **Black Death** epidemic of the plague, a highly contagious and often fatal disease which spread throughout Europe from 1348 to 1350

Spanish dramatist Lope de Vega, and Shakespeare. In addition, the Italian painter Botticelli and other artists based paintings on scenes from the book.

Latin Writings. While Boccaccio was writing Italian fictions, he was also producing Latin texts. In *Buccolicum Carmen* (ca. 1341–1372), Boccaccio revived a classical form called the eclogue. This form is a poem in which shepherds converse. *Buccolicum Carmen* is a series of such conversations on religious and political issues. Later Renaissance poets continued to use the form in Latin and in the vernacular.

In *The Fates of Illustrious Men* (1355–1373) and *On Famous Women* (1361), Boccaccio used the lives of famous people to illustrate moral principles. He drew most of these figures from ancient history. He used their stories to show how even powerful people can suffer because of their own immoral behavior. *On Famous Women* praises women who became learned, wrote, or even waged battle and ruled kingdoms. Boccaccio's moral approach to history suited both medieval and Renaissance readers. Later Renaissance writers used the books as sources for their own works.

Boccaccio and Classical Studies. Boccaccio was determined to share his knowledge and love of the ancient world with others. In *Genealogy of the Pagan Gods* (1350–1373), he created a complete catalog of pagan* mythology. This book became a major reference work for much of the Renaissance. Boccaccio also promoted the study of ancient Greek literature. He established a position for a professor of Greek at the University of Florence. He encouraged the new professor to translate the great Greek writers Homer and Euripides into Latin. Through his writings and his contributions to the study of the ancient world, Boccaccio had a lasting impact on the Renaissance and on the rest of western history. (*See also* **Italian Language and Literature.**)

* **pagan** referring to ancient religions that worshiped many gods, or more generally, to any non-Christian religion

Bodin, Jean

1529–1596
French political philosopher and writer

Jean Bodin of Angers, France, was an important writer on the subjects of religion and politics in the late 1500s. His most famous work, *Six Books of the Commonwealth* (1576), discusses his belief in absolute monarchy and religious tolerance. He also published an original work on how to study history in 1566.

As a young, educated man trained in law, Bodin found a place at the court of Henry III in the 1570s. France at the time was torn by conflicts between Catholics and Protestants. Bodin argued in *Six Books of the Commonwealth* that the power of the monarch was absolute and that his subjects should never resist it, even if they considered his actions unfair. Bodin also claimed that one way to eliminate conflicts between the king and his subjects was to remove arguments about religion from the sphere of politics.

These very views caused Bodin to fall out of favor with the crown. The same year Bodin wrote his famous work, Henry III was attempting to raise funds for further religious wars. Bodin refused to support the

king's plan. Instead, he turned his support to the king's brother, the Duke of Anjou, who wanted to end the wars through a policy of religious toleration. After the duke's death in 1584, Bodin became a lawyer representing the affairs of the French crown in Laon, in northern France. However, his belief in tolerance for Protestants left him under a cloud of suspicion for the rest of his life.

Bodin's support for religious tolerance did not extend to those who had no religion. In 1580 he published a manual for witch-hunting, urging legal authorities to deal more harshly with people he saw as worshipers of Satan. In his last work, *Theater of All Nature* (1596), Bodin criticized those thinkers who discussed the laws of nature without reference to God. Bodin hoped that promoting respect for God and tolerating different religions could bring an end to the nation's religious wars. (*See also* **Constitutionalism; Government, Forms of.**)

Bohemia

* **Holy Roman Empire** political body in central Europe composed of several states; existed until 1806

Bohemia was a kingdom in central Europe that became a seat of power within the Holy Roman Empire*. During the Renaissance several Bohemian kings ruled this empire. Under their leadership, the Bohemian city of PRAGUE developed into a lively center of scholarship and artistic creativity.

Bohemia's Rise to Power. In the mid-1300s Charles IV became king of Bohemia. In 1348 he founded the University of Prague, the first university in central Europe. He also started an ambitious building program, designed to transform Prague into a major capital.

In 1355 Charles was crowned emperor of the Holy Roman Empire. The following year he issued the Golden Bull, a document establishing a system for electing the emperor. The king of Bohemia was one of the seven rulers who voted to choose the emperor. As the imperial residence of Charles, Prague attracted scholars and artists. The newcomers brought Renaissance learning and ideas to the city.

In the late 1400s, Bohemia emerged as a center of HUMANISM, a cultural movement promoting the study of the languages, literature, and history of ancient Greece and Rome as a guide to living. The Bohemian king Vladislav II Jagiello (ruled 1471–1516) increased cultural ties with Italy, where humanism had begun. About 20 years into his reign, Vladislav also became king of the neighboring kingdom of Hungary. Buda, Hungary's leading city, was an early center of humanism, and humanist views spread to Bohemia during Vladislav's rule. In addition, the king encouraged Italian artistic ideas. When he rebuilt Prague Castle, he added a wing based entirely on Italian Renaissance design.

Habsburg Rule. Vladislav's son, Louis II, ruled Bohemia from 1516 to 1526. Then FERDINAND I, who was Louis's brother-in-law and a member of the powerful HABSBURG family, claimed the throne. This led the Bohemian nobles to revolt against the monarchy. The Habsburgs were Roman Catholics. However, many members of the nobility were Hussites, a group of political and religious rebels. The Bohemian nobles

also opposed the Habsburg rulers' attempts to establish a powerful central government. In 1547 the Habsburgs put down the uprising and severely punished the rebellious nobles.

Throughout the 1500s the Bohemians made advances in farming (including the breeding of fish in ponds), brewing, mining, metalworking, and architecture. Italian-style mansions and villas* became popular. Some towns erected new city halls, schools, and other public buildings to highlight their prosperity and importance.

* **villa** luxurious country home and the land surrounding it

Ferdinand I commissioned a number of notable structures in Prague. His first project, the royal garden, was heavily influenced by Italian Renaissance design. It included a wooden orangery, an enclosure for raising plants that need protection from the cold. The development of Prague continued in the 1580s under RUDOLF II (ruled 1576–1611). In 1592 he appointed Boniface Wohlmut as court architect. Wohlmut built the Great Ball Court at Prague Castle, one of the first buildings dedicated to sport.

The Arts and Sciences. Under Rudolf II, Prague gained a reputation as a center of late Renaissance science. Many doctors, chemists, botanists, lawyers, and historians lived there. Specialized workshops produced precision instruments for astronomers such as Tycho BRAHE and Johannes KEPLER. The city's thriving printing industry made it possible to spread new ideas and information rapidly.

Rudolf also supported the work of Renaissance artists, such as the portrait painter Giuseppe Arcimboldo and still life and landscape painter Roelant Savery. Many wealthy citizens of Prague became generous patrons* of the arts. Their assistance encouraged a flood of foreign painters and sculptors to settle in the city. In addition, a flourishing Jewish community, which included many scholars, contributed to the city's intellectual environment. By the early 1600s Prague had grown into a sophisticated cultural center.

* **patron** supporter or financial sponsor of an artist or writer

Conflict and War. Religious tensions in Bohemia between the Catholic Habsburgs and the Hussite nobles continued into the 1600s. Both Rudolf II and Ferdinand II (ruled 1619–1637) tried to restore the power of the Roman Catholic Church. However, in 1619 the Bohemian nobles revolted and overthrew Ferdinand. The uprising led to the outbreak of the THIRTY YEARS' WAR, a conflict involving many states of Europe. The war ended with the Peace of Westphalia (1648), a treaty that confirmed the political and religious control of the Habsburgs over Bohemia. (*See also* **Catholic Reformation and Counter-Reformation; Holy Roman Empire; Protestant Reformation.**)

Bologna

The Italian city of Bologna was a major center of Europe's textile industry during the Renaissance and the home of a famous university. During the 1300s and 1400s, the city's population averaged about 50,000 and rose to about 70,000 at the end of the 1500s.

Politics and Economy. In 1278 Bologna became part of the Papal States, a group of territories ruled by the pope. Several local groups attempted to gain control of the city. By 1394 some nobles succeeded, governing through an executive body called the Reggimento. However, other Bolognese families and the popes still sought to rule the city. In 1447 the Reggimento and Pope NICHOLAS V signed an agreement known as Capitulations. It gave Bologna its own code of laws, government institutions, currency, and certain privileges, but the city remained part of the Papal States.

During the late 1400s the Bentivoglio family led efforts to gain more autonomy* for Bologna. Annibale, Santo, and Giovanni II Bentivoglio ruled the city and built up its power. But after a series of conspiracies and invasions, Pope JULIUS II expelled the family in 1506. He replaced the Reggimento with another ruling body, the Senate, and tried unsuccessfully to suspend the Capitulations. The pope appointed members of the Senate but did not otherwise interfere with its authority. By the 1500s, the Senate controlled all social, financial, and political affairs in Bologna.

* **autonomy** independent self-government

The silk industry was an important source of Bologna's wealth and fame. Local artisans* designed a mill that allowed them to spin a very strong, soft thread and to use fewer workers. During the 1500s about half of the city's residents relied on the silk industry. Bologna also boasted significant local agriculture and a major university famous for law and medicine. Its nearly 2,000 students, many from abroad, contributed a great deal to the economy. A number of famous scholars taught at the University of Bologna.

* **artisan** skilled worker or craftsperson

Art and Culture. Bologna produced few notable artists or architects until the late 1400s, when the Bentivoglio family became active patrons*. The family supported both foreign and local artists, such as the sculptor Niccolò dell'Arca. As a result of this support and Bologna's close ties with Rome, the city became a center of Baroque* art. Other nobles followed the Bentivoglios' example of supporting Bolognese artists. Impressive new public buildings, sculptures, and private villas* enriched the city. Bologna proved to be a particularly good environment for female artists. Several women became known for their portraits of Bolognese scholars, religious leaders, and society figures. Among these women was the noted sculptor Properzia de' Rossi. (*See also* **Baroque; Italy; Patronage; Pomponazzi, Pietro; Popes and Papacy; Universities.**)

* **patron** supporter or financial sponsor of an artist or writer
* **Baroque** artistic style of the 1600s characterized by movement, drama, and grandness of scale
* **villa** luxurious country home and the land surrounding it

Books and Manuscripts

During the Renaissance more books became available to more people than ever before. The invention of the printing press made books affordable to the lower classes, but handwritten manuscripts also remained popular. The flood of texts reflected not only scholarly humanist* ideals but also the growing emphasis on material goods during the Renaissance.

* **humanist** referring to a Renaissance cultural movement promoting the study of the humanities (the languages, literature, and history of ancient Greece and Rome) as a guide to living

Manuscripts. Before the invention of printing presses, the only texts were copied by hand. The earliest manuscripts were rare collector's items with unique designs and layouts. They had pages of rugged parchment—dried and prepared skins of sheep, goats, or calves. Parchment was extremely expensive. In Paris in the 1400s, for example, a single skin cost up to five times as much as a loaf of bread, and a single book used hundreds of pages of parchment. A less expensive alternative, paper, did not reach Europe until the 1100s.

* **medieval** referring to the Middle Ages, a period that began around A.D. 400 and ended around 1400 in Italy and 1500 in the rest of Europe

* **illumination** hand-painted color decorations and illustrations on the pages of a manuscript

The first people to copy works on a large scale were medieval* monks whose religious rules required them to perform some manual labor. Throughout the Middle Ages monks copied and produced thousands of texts. Some manuscripts included illumination*, such as designs, miniature artwork, or decorative lettering. Kings, queens, and other wealthy individuals collected illuminated manuscripts much like other forms of art.

* **guild** association of craft and trade owners and workers that set standards for and represented the interests of its members

* **scribe** person who copies manuscripts

As medieval UNIVERSITIES expanded in the 1200s, they demanded more and more manuscripts. The universities became thriving centers of manuscript production and distribution when the *stationarii,* a licensed guild* of scribes*, set up their stalls near university lecture halls and began to copy texts. The guild separated an original manuscript into sections, or *pecia,* and divided the *pecia* among its scribes. The scribes worked like an assembly line to create copies section by section. This method enabled them to generate many copies cheaply.

Even after the development of the printed book, manuscripts remained common in Europe. Many readers valued manuscripts for their fine craftsmanship. Also, many intellectuals preferred to spread their ideas in manuscript form before printing them, especially when their views were controversial. Another common form of manuscript was the personal copybook, a handwritten collection of passages from a person's favorite works.

Printing and Publishing. Most scholars credit Johann GUTENBERG, a German printer, with the invention of the printing press. Although other cultures had already developed printing, Gutenberg was the first to use the screw press—a viselike machine that had been used for making paper and wine—to print books. Gutenberg also refined movable type, which used one die (metal block) for each letter of the alphabet. He produced the Gutenberg Bible—the first book printed with movable type—around 1455.

It took a team of three men to print a book. The compositor—the most skilled of the three—set the type, placing letters one by one in two frames to create pages. It was a time-consuming process. To keep the press running without delay, the compositor set the next day's pages while two other men—the inker and the operator—ran the press. The inker set the two frames in the press, one above the other. After smearing the type in the frames with ink, he inserted a sheet of paper between them. The operator then swung the press's lever to bring the two frames together, making imprints on both sides of the paper sandwiched inside. Once he released the lever, the frames separated, and the inker

removed the printed page. The inker and the operator might repeat this process 1,000 times in a single day.

By the 1460s printers had set up presses in France and Italy. Spanish and English printers were at work by the 1470s. The spread of printing made more books available and drove the price of books down. In the late 1460s a printer might make 300 copies of a book. Ten years later that number reached 1,000. Printers also competed to make cheaper versions of popular titles, sometimes copying the books of rival printers. The development of the printing press and the business of publishing made books affordable to common people for the first time.

Books and Material Culture. During the Renaissance, people began to place more value on material possessions. Many collected expensive and exotic objects, such as paintings, tapestries, scientific specimens, and leather-bound books.

Books and manuscripts helped to fill the intellectual and material needs of many people. Some collectors read their texts carefully and cross-referenced ideas in their margins, while others prized books largely for their beauty. Illuminated manuscripts were treasures, but printed books also became central to Renaissance material culture. Collectors might pay for elaborate decorative bindings on their printed books to blend them in with the handsome manuscripts in their libraries. However, even members of the lower classes, who could not afford such fancy volumes, became eager consumers of books. The most popular works included religious texts and books on manners.

* **apothecary** pharmacist

Private collections grew greatly between 1350 and 1600. In Venice a wealthy person's library might house hundreds or even thousands of books. Professionals such as doctors, lawyers, and apothecaries* kept private collections of books about their professions. In Florence, many people had libraries of religious texts, although these rarely numbered more than 100 volumes. Some book collectors made their private libraries available to others. For example, Gian Vincenzo Pinelli (1535–1601) made his home in Padua a meeting place for local scholars. The great scientist Galileo GALILEI wrote several lectures while he was Pinelli's guest. Some private collections eventually formed the core of Europe's first public LIBRARIES. (*See also* **Bible; Humanism; Illumination; Patronage.**)

Borgia, House of

* **papacy** office and authority of the pope

During the 1400s, the Spanish Borja family established roots in Italy and became known there as the House of Borgia. This powerful family produced 2 popes, 11 cardinals, 1 saint, and several dukes and princes. Of all the Borgias, the two who made the greatest impact on Renaissance history were Rodrigo, later Pope ALEXANDER VI, and his son Cesare. They used the political and financial resources of the papacy* to advance family interests.

Rise to Power. Alfonso de Borja (1378–1458) founded the family fortunes. A Spanish religious scholar trained in church law, he served as

secretary to Alfonso V of Aragon. In 1429 he became bishop of Valencia. Within a few years he moved to Italy, where he helped King Alfonso gain control of the kingdom of Naples. He also played a key role in negotiating a treaty with the pope that recognized Aragon's claim to Naples. Soon after, Borja was made a cardinal, a high official of the Roman Catholic Church. In 1455 his fellow cardinals chose him as pope in the hope that his Spanish connections would be useful in a new crusade against the Ottoman Turks*.

* **Ottoman Turks** Turkish followers of Islam who founded the Ottoman Empire in the 1300s; the empire eventually included large areas of eastern Europe, the Middle East, and northern Africa

As pope, Alfonso took the name Calixtus III. He tried to rally European naval forces against the Ottoman Turks, but he failed to gain support for this plan. Even Alfonso of Aragon and Naples, his former employer, refused to cooperate. Pope Calixtus's most enduring legacy was the rise of his young nephew, Rodrigo Borgia (1431–1503).

Marked from an early age for a career in the church, Rodrigo was greatly helped along that path by Calixtus. In 1456 the pope appointed him cardinal. Rodrigo was only 25 years old at the time, and the appointment aroused sharp criticism. Calixtus also named Rodrigo vice-chancellor of the church, a position that gave him responsibility for much of the church's day-to-day administration. Although Calixtus died two years later, Rodrigo held the powerful post for 35 years and accumulated riches and influence.

Pope Alexander VI and His Descendants. Rodrigo became Pope Alexander VI in 1492. He was the most controversial of all Renaissance popes. Some feared him, and with reason. He threatened those who crossed him, and there were suspicious deaths among his opponents.

Alexander had several mistresses and fathered eight or nine illegitimate children. However, it was his unconcealed ambitions for his family that shocked people the most. He gave his children lands seized from noble Roman families and arranged advantageous marriages for them. His daughter Lucrezia (1480–1519) married three times, each time to advance the fortunes of the House of Borgia. Her third marriage sealed an alliance between the Borgias and Italy's powerful Este family. During this marriage, as Duchess of Ferrara, she presided over a court of highly influential and educated figures.

Alexander made Juan, his favorite child, a military leader. After Juan was murdered in 1497, Alexander shifted his attention to his oldest son, Cesare (1475–1507). Then Cesare, a cardinal, resigned his position in the church and took on military duties for his father. As part of Alexander's plan to create a permanent Borgia state, Cesare conquered several regions in central Italy. Alexander's death in 1503, however, deprived Cesare of necessary resources. Furthermore, the new pope, Julius II, did not support the Borgias. In an effort to win the pope's approval, King Ferdinand of Spain had Cesare jailed. Cesare escaped, only to die in a battle in 1507. Italian writer Niccolò Machiavelli discussed this Borgia in *The Prince,* his famous analysis of statecraft. He argued that Cesare failed because of his reliance on the power and money of his father.

* **Holy Roman Emperor** ruler of the Holy Roman Empire, a political body in central Europe composed of several states that existed until 1806

* **Jesuit** belonging to a Roman Catholic religious order founded by St. Ignatius Loyola and approved in 1540

After Alexander's death, the Borgias returned to Spain where they held a dukedom. Francisco Borgia (1510–1572), great-grandson of Alexander, was an important figure at the court of CHARLES V, Holy Roman Emperor*. After the death of his wife, Francisco joined the Jesuits*, becoming head of the order in 1565. A century after his death in 1572, the Roman Catholic Church declared Francisco a saint. (*See also* **Ferdinand of Aragon; Ottoman Empire; Popes and Papacy.**)

Bosch, Hieronymus

1450–1516
Dutch painter

* **patron** supporter or financial sponsor of an artist or writer

* **aristocracy** privileged upper classes of society; nobles or the nobility

* **allegorical** referring to a literary or artistic device in which characters, events, and settings represent abstract qualities and in which the author intends a different meaning to be read beneath the surface

In his paintings Hieronymus Bosch, of Hertogenbosch in the Netherlands, created a highly original world with a moral message. Bosch used his works, often based on Christian writings, to present his views on human sin and its consequences. He also produced some very fine landscapes.

A member of a family of painters called the van Akens, Bosch spent most of his life in Hertogenbosch. Sometime before 1481 he married Aleyt Goyaerts van den Meervenne. Over the years Bosch gained many influential patrons*, including leading members of the church and aristocracy*. Despite his success, his works were not well documented and are difficult to identify. Scholars using scientific methods of examination have estimated that Bosch produced 25 paintings and 14 drawings.

Bosch had a rather dark view of humanity—though his works were not without humor. Many of his paintings were allegorical* with images of Christ and saints, and they often told stories of the folly of humans. He painted a number of triptychs (three connected panels), which allowed him to tell a part of a story in each panel. His triptych the *Haywain,* for example, traces the development of sin. The left-hand panel shows the origin of sin (Adam and Eve), the large center panel illustrates sin's progress in the world, and the final panel shows the punishment of sinners in hell.

Scholars divide Bosch's works into three main periods. In the early years, from about 1470 to 1490, he began to focus on humanity's weakness toward sin. In his middle period, from 1490 through 1500, Bosch expanded on this topic and began to paint triptychs. Many of his works from this time are on a large scale and include numerous small people and creatures. This changed, however, during the final period of his career, from 1500 to his death in 1516. In these last years, Bosch painted on a smaller scale with close-up views of larger figures.

After Bosch's death, followers produced copies of his paintings. This made it more difficult for scholars to identify his original works. The influence of Bosch can also be seen in the paintings of artists such as Pieter Brueghel the Elder. (*See also* **Art in the Netherlands; Brueghel Family.**)

Botany

See *Science.*

Botticelli, Sandro

ca. 1444–1510
Italian painter

Alessandro Filipepi, known as Botticelli, was a great painter from FLORENCE, Italy. His work is typical of the Renaissance approach to the arts, which combined a new interest in the works of ancient Greece and Rome with a respect for religion. Although Botticelli often used themes from ancient mythology, he mixed and combined them to create a new vision rather than simply reproducing familiar images. At the same time, many of his works illustrated religious themes.

* **apprentice** person bound by legal agreement to work for another for a specified period of time in return for instruction in a trade or craft

Botticelli's Life. Botticelli began his career as an apprentice* to the painter Fra Filippo Lippi. The influence of Lippi is visible in many of Botticelli's early paintings. By 1470 Botticelli had become a master painter in the city of Florence, and two years later he joined the Compagnia di San Luca, a society of Florentine artists. He opened a studio, where he produced his own work and took on students. His former master's son, Filippino Lippi, was his most successful pupil.

During the 1470s and 1480s Florence was a thriving center of the arts, thanks to the influence of Lorenzo de' MEDICI, the ruler of Florence. Many of Botticelli's patrons* belonged to Lorenzo's inner circle. These prominent Florentines commissioned a variety of works, including paintings to decorate some of the chapels in Florence.

* **patron** supporter or financial sponsor of an artist or writer

* **fresco** mural painted on a plaster wall

Botticelli also traveled outside Florence to paint frescoes* in cathedrals and other buildings. In 1480 the pope asked Botticelli to join several artists who were decorating the walls of the newly built Sistine Chapel in Rome. In the decade that followed Botticelli produced some of his finest paintings, developing a style marked by smooth lines and rich colors.

Lorenzo de' Medici died in 1492, and the Medici family was exiled from Florence two years later. Soon after that, artistic activity in Florence began to decline. Projects for painters became scarce. Botticelli continued to paint during this period, but his style changed noticeably. His work became simpler and more severe, with a greater emphasis on moral and religious feeling.

By 1500 Botticelli had sunk into poverty and depression. He spent the last years of his life working on a series of illustrations for the *Divine Comedy* by the Italian poet Dante. However, he died before finishing the project. After Botticelli's death, his works were largely forgotten until the late 1800s, when critics recognized him as one of the great artists of the Renaissance.

Botticelli's Work. Botticelli's major paintings fall into two categories: works with religious themes and works based on ancient mythology. His best-known religious work, *The Adoration of the Magi* (1475–1476), portrays three foreign kings and their followers coming to pay tribute to the infant Christ. Botticelli gave several of the figures in the picture the faces of actual people, including himself and five members of the Medici family. The work won praise for the way the artist varied the positions of the figures' heads and for the detailed depictions of the king's followers.

Sandro Botticelli's *Primavera (Spring)* is a celebration of love, a popular Renaissance theme. In the painting, Venus, the Roman goddess of love, stands in a garden with Cupid hovering overhead. The piece borrows images from the work of classical authors, such as the Roman poet Ovid.

Botticelli's mythological works are more typical of the Renaissance as a whole. Like other artists of the period, Botticelli combined ancient themes with a fresh vision. This approach reflects two important ideas of the Renaissance. The first is a view of the ancient world as a symbol of the glory of human achievement. The second is the importance of the artist as a thinking, creative individual.

Many of Botticelli's works deal with the subject of love, which was a popular theme in the Renaissance. In *Primavera (Spring)* (ca. 1478), he shows Venus, the Roman goddess of love, standing in a garden. Surrounding her are other figures from Roman mythology, including the three Graces and Flora, the goddess of flowers. This painting (also called *The Realm of Venus*) borrows images from several classical authors, including the Roman poets Ovid and Horace, instead of illustrating a familiar story.

Another important work, *The Birth of Venus* (ca. 1484), uses a scene described in mythology. It portrays the goddess rising out of the sea, standing on a shell. Botticelli painted Venus in the nude, possibly for the first time since the ancient period. He based this piece on a description from a work by Angelo POLIZIANO, a Florentine poet. Its theme, the birth of love, suggests that Botticelli may have created the painting for a wedding. (*See also* **Art; Art in Italy; Classical Antiquity.**)

Bourbon Family and Dynasty

The Bourbon family, the leading noble house in Renaissance France, controlled vast amounts of wealth and territory. However, ambition occasionally led the Bourbons into conflicts with the French crown. The family's fortunes reached a peak in 1589, when a Bourbon became king of France.

Shifting Fortunes. The Bourbon family traced its origin to Robert of Clermont (1256–1318), the sixth son of Louis IX of France. The family grew steadily in wealth, power, and prestige. Through a series of strategic marriages, the Bourbons gained control of vast amounts of territory. Many members of the family obtained high positions in the church and in the government.

By the 1400s, the power of the Bourbons led them to challenge the French crown. In 1461 Jean II, duke of Bourbon (1426–1488), was tried for treason after supporting a revolt against the king of France, Charles VII. However, the new king, Louis XI, released Jean and made him commander of the royal army. The Bourbon family remained loyal to the crown throughout Louis's reign.

The Bourbon family faced a more serious threat in 1521. Louise of Savoy, mother of the French king Francis I (reigned 1515–1547), attempted to seize some of the Bourbons' family lands. The head of the Bourbon family, Charles III (1489–1524), responded by forming an alliance with the Holy Roman Emperor* Charles V against Francis. The emperor's forces captured the French king in 1525. However, Francis was released a year later and took control of the lands of Charles de Bourbon. After Charles died, the king tried him for treason and seized all the Bourbon lands.

* **Holy Roman Emperor** ruler of the Holy Roman Empire, a political body in central Europe composed of several states that existed until 1806

Return to Power. The younger brother of Charles III, Charles, duke of Vendôme (1489–1537), had remained loyal to Francis I during his brother's rebellion. The king recognized Charles as the new head of the Bourbon family and married him to his own sister-in-law, Françoise d'Alençon. Their son Antoine (1518–1562) wed Jeanne d'Albret, who became queen of Navarre, a tiny kingdom in the Pyrenees Mountains. These alliances gave the Bourbons control of much of central and southwestern France.

During the 1560s, the Bourbons became involved in the French Wars of Religion. Catholic and Protestant parties struggled for control of the French crown after the death of Henry II in 1559. Antoine de Bourbon and his son, Henry of Navarre (1553–1610), sided with the Protestants. Known as Huguenots, the Protestants were followers of John Calvin.

In 1572 Henry of Navarre married Margaret of Valois, daughter of Henry II. This marriage, which placed him in the line of succession to the French crown, was intended to bring peace between Catholics and Huguenots. Instead, it fueled an outbreak of violence known as the St. Bartholomew's Day Massacre in August 1572. Henry survived only by agreeing to convert to Catholicism. He was held captive at the court for four years. When he escaped in 1576, Henry reclaimed his role as protector of the Protestant faith.

In 1589 Henry mounted the throne as HENRY IV, becoming the founder of the Bourbon royal dynasty. However, he faced a challenge to his throne from his uncle Charles, cardinal of Bourbon. The Catholic Holy League, a group of nobles and other opponents, supported Charles against Henry. To secure his throne, Henry converted to Catholicism in 1593. Five years later, he signed treaties with French Huguenots and with the Spanish. These treaties brought a much-needed period of peace to France.

* **annulment** formal declaration that a marriage is legally invalid

Henry IV received an annulment* to his marriage in 1599 and took MARIE DE MÉDICIS as his second wife. Their son, Louis XIII, set France on a path toward absolute monarchy. The Bourbon dynasty controlled the French throne until a revolution toppled the monarchy in 1792. (*See also* **France; Francis I.**)

Bourgeoisie

All Renaissance societies were hierarchical, with some groups or classes having higher status than others. The bourgeoisie was the class of burghers, the respectable master craftsworkers, shopkeepers, and merchants who formed the backbone of urban society. Laws determined who had burgher status. However, unofficial social standards set aside certain members of the bourgeoisie as an urban elite*—a small group that controlled a great deal of wealth and political influence.

* **elite** privileged group; upper class

The law gave burghers certain political and social privileges. For example, only they could become full members of guilds*. Some towns gave legal protection to their burghers when they traveled to other areas. If one of them became involved in a dispute, the town would stand for him or her in court. Burghers also took part in cultural events in their cities, such as processions and plays. In the 1520s, Amsterdam opened an orphanage specifically for the children of burghers. Burghers supplied the manpower for urban militias*, and some took positions in government.

* **guild** association of craft and trade owners and workers that set standards for and represented the interests of its members

* **militia** army of citizens who may be called into action in times of emergency

Despite these privileges, only a few burghers enjoyed high social status. These were often members of old and respected families. Other factors linked to high status were wealth, public office, and professional positions (especially in the field of law). The urban elites guarded their position by choosing their members carefully. In some places, such as Venice, laws gave members of certain families the right to participate in government, keeping outsiders from joining the elite. Central and northern Italy and part of southern Germany adopted similar standards in the 1500s. "Golden books" listed the names of all male members of elite families, not including illegitimate* children. However, in some German towns, outsiders successfully challenged the dominance of old families.

* **illegitimate** refers to a child born outside of marriage

Economic change sometimes affected social status. In England, some trading families rose to the elite as they built wealth. However, a loss of wealth did not necessarily mean a loss of status. When the economies of Spain and Italy slowed in the early 1600s, elite families' fortunes shrank, but their social position stayed the same.

Members of the elite struggled to distance themselves from those of lower social ranking. They lived in certain areas within each city and married only within their own social group. Sumptuary laws, which specified what clothing people of different classes could wear, attempted to stop the lower classes from imitating the dress of the elites. Other laws limited the size of celebrations among the lower classes. However, members of the elite were often willing to use their social status to help their "inferiors." They took lower-status children as godchildren, acted as guardians of widows and orphans, and sponsored people who applied for burgher status. Such actions helped them earn the support of the lower classes, a useful political asset.

* **aristocracy** privileged upper classes of society; nobles or the nobility

* **coat of arms** set of symbols used to represent a noble family

The elites often imitated the lifestyles of the aristocracy*. They might spend money on luxuries, adopt coats of arms*, or use formal titles when addressing each other. In Italy and Spain nobles settled in towns and joined the local elite. In England and other places, members of the nobility and the elite intermarried. However, the elite remained separate from the aristocracy. Nobles suspected elites of social climbing, and elites did not always trust the nobles completely. Elites had strong loyalties to their towns, many of which had histories of clashes with nobles. (*See also* **Aristocracy; Cities and Urban Life; Clothing; Guilds; Luxury; Social Status.**)

Bouts, Dirck

ca. 1415–1475
Dutch painter

Painter Dirck Bouts of the Netherlands helped spread the influence of his homeland's art abroad. His style combined rich color with simple lines and an overall lack of movement. His works often suggest a feeling of quiet reflection. Critics particularly praised his landscapes for their sensitivity to the effect of natural light at different times of the day.

Born in Haarlem, Bouts probably received his training in art in that city. By 1457 he had settled in the town of Louvain and established a large workshop. Bouts trained his two sons in his workshop. One of them, Dirck Bouts the Younger, probably inherited the shop after his father's death. The other, Albert Bouts, established his own workshop in Louvain.

One of Bouts's major works is *Holy Sacrament* (1460s), a painting created to decorate the altar of the chapel at St. Peter's church in Louvain. The piece is a triptych, a set of three painted panels. The central panel shows a moment during the Last Supper of Christ, but it is set in a hall of the 1400s. The panels on either side of it illustrate scenes from the Old Testament of the Bible.

The high quality of this painting won Bouts a major assignment. The town council of Louvain hired Bouts to create two paintings for the new town hall: a triptych of the biblical *Last Judgment* and *Examples of Justice* from history. For his work on these projects, the council awarded Bouts the title of "city painter," a position that provided both good pay and high status. Bouts finished the *Last Judgment* in 1470 but died before completing *Examples of Justice*. (*See also* **Art in the Netherlands.**)

Brahe, Tycho

1546–1601
Danish astronomer

B efore the invention of the telescope, Danish noble Tycho Brahe mapped the stars far more accurately than any previous astronomer. Tycho's theories of the heavens were inaccurate. However, the data that he gathered helped to explain the structure of the solar system.

After completing his university education, Tycho studied alchemy*. However, a strange event on November 11, 1572, drew him to ASTRONOMY. That evening he noticed a bright new star in the constellation of Cassiopeia. Since this was supposed to be a "perfect," or unchanging, area of the heavens, Tycho knew he was witnessing something special. He carefully observed the new star and published his findings a year later in a book titled *De Stella Nova* (the new star). The work made him famous.

* **alchemy** early science that sought to explain the nature of matter and to transform base metals, such as lead, into gold

In 1576 the king of Denmark, Frederick II, granted Tycho an island on which to conduct his observation of the heavens. In return, Tycho was to give the king advice on astrology*. Tycho built a richly furnished, well-equipped villa* on the island. He called it Uraniborg, or the castle of astronomy. It served as both an astronomical observatory and a laboratory for his work in alchemy.

* **astrology** study of the supposed influences of the stars and planets on earthly events

* **villa** luxurious country home and the land surrounding it

Tycho had found errors in existing measurements of the movements of the Sun, Moon, planets, and stars. He reasoned that these errors were why many astrological predictions of his day were flawed. Therefore, he designed and built his own astronomical instruments, making them very large to increase their accuracy. Tycho carefully tested these tools to be certain that they were precise. He also established new methods of computing.

See color plate 1, vol. 4

The astronomical data Tycho collected were twice as accurate as any before this time. His findings led him to propose a new model of the universe. Like earlier scholars, Tycho believed that Earth stood at the center of the universe and the Sun revolved around it. However, like the Polish astronomer Nicolaus COPERNICUS, Tycho claimed that the other planets revolved around the Sun, not around the Earth. Copernicus argued that Earth, too, revolved around the Sun, but Tycho's observations did not appear to support this theory. Tycho's system was popular among Catholic astronomers and philosophers during the 1600s. The Catholic Church at that time rejected the idea that Earth was not the center of the universe.

When Frederik II died, his heir took away the grants that the king had awarded to Tycho. Tycho set up a new observatory near PRAGUE, but he died soon afterward. His pupil Johannes KEPLER would later use Tycho's findings to explain how planets orbit the Sun on oval-shaped paths.

Bramante, Donato

ca. 1444–1514
Italian architect

D onato Bramante, one of the leading architects of the Renaissance, developed a new style of architecture based on classical principles. Among his works are some of Rome's most notable monuments, including the Vatican Palace, St. Peter's Basilica, and the Tempietto in San Pietro in Montorio. Scholars have called the Tempietto a perfect Renaissance building.

Training and Theory. Bramante first studied to be a painter, not an architect, and he specialized in frescoes*. He began his career in the city of Urbino and later moved north to Lombardy, the region around Milan. According to the Renaissance author Giorgio Vasari, Bramante became interested in mathematics before turning to architecture. During this time, Bramante came in contact with the *cantiere,* a stonemason's organization in Milan. The *cantiere* combined Gothic* traditions of building with an interest in the architectural style called *all'antica,* based on classical principles.

* **fresco** mural painted on a plaster wall

* **Gothic** style of architecture characterized by pointed arches and high, thin walls supported by flying buttresses; also, artistic style marked by bright colors, elongated proportions, and intricate detail

During the 1400s, Italian scholars rediscovered classical writings on architecture that changed their ideas on building design. The ancients stressed the importance of precise mathematical proportions to achieve harmony and balance. They also had firm ideas about the proper use of orders, or types, of columns. Bramante created his own system of orders based on the classical types, and he was the first to use orders consistently in his designs.

Bramante in Milan. One of Bramante's first projects as an architect was the chapel of San Satiro in Milan, which he began in the early 1480s. The Duke of Milan, Gian Galeazzo Sforza, asked Bramante to rebuild the existing chapel and make it one of the city's jewels. Bramante's design drew from a variety of styles and the latest architectural ideas of the day. With the help of stucco and paint, he created the illusion of a large choir stall on a wall of the chapel.

During the 1490s, Bramante continued to work on projects in Milan for the next duke, Ludovico Sforza. These included the expansion of the abbey of Sant'Ambrogio and the construction of a magnificent tomb for Ludovico and his wife. Bramante may also have played a role in the planned reconstruction of Pavia Cathedral (1487–1505) under Ludovico's brother, Cardinal Ascanio Sforza. Parts of its design reveal ideas that Bramante later incorporated in his design for St. Peter's.

At Ludovico's court in Milan, Bramante mingled with many great figures in Renaissance art and learning. There he met the mathematician Luca Pacioli, formed a close friendship with LEONARDO DA VINCI, and learned more about classical theories from the sculptor Gian Cristoforo Romano. His contact with poets, artists, and humanist* scholars helped shape his ideas on architecture and design. This rich cultural court life ended in 1499, when the king of France invaded Milan. The court broke up, and Bramante fled to Rome.

* **humanist** referring to a Renaissance cultural movement promoting the study of the humanities (the languages, literature, and history of ancient Greece and Rome) as a guide to living

Bramante in Rome. With the court of the pope expanding rapidly at this time, Bramante had little trouble finding patrons* in Rome. He soon found work designing the Tempietto in San Pietro for Spanish monarchs FERDINAND OF ARAGON and ISABELLA OF CASTILE. The project had tremendous significance for Spain. Located at the traditional site of St. Peter's crucifixion, the monument served notice that Spain, its patron, had arrived as a world power.

* **patron** supporter or financial sponsor of an artist or writer

Construction of the Tempietto began in 1502. Bramante used a strict yet simple system of proportions, basing the design on the circle (an

Art & Architecture

Plate 1
The influence of the sculptures of the ancient world can be seen in the work of Italian painter Piero della Francesca (ca. 1412–1492). His solid figures set in a precisely defined space provide a sense of stillness and dignity. This scene is from *Legend of the True Cross,* a series of wall paintings that the artist worked on for 11 years.

Plate 2: Left
One of the great masters of Italian Renaissance painting, Raphael (1483–1520) reflected the ideals of his time. His works reveal the influence of two other giants of the period, Leonardo da Vinci and Michelangelo. From Leonardo, Raphael learned to use color and shading to define form; from Michelangelo, he gained an appreciation of human anatomy. This portrait of *Agnolo Doni* shows Raphael's sensitivity to his subject and his skill in presenting him as an individual.

Plate 3: Below
In 1401 Lorenzo Ghiberti, goldsmith and sculptor, won a commission to design the doors of the Baptistry of Florence. Over the next 50 years, he created two series of bronze panels illustrating the lives of saints and themes from the Bible. The panel shown here tells the story of Joseph and his brothers in Egypt.

Plate 4: Left
The city of Florence has three famous and very different statues of David: the graceful *David* (1430s) by Donatello; the confident bronze *David* (1460s) by Andrea del Verrocchio shown here; and the monumental marble *David* (1502–1504) by Michelangelo. Recent studies suggest that Verrocchio originally placed the giant's head slightly behind David's left foot but that it was moved between the feet so the statue would fit on a small pedestal.

Plate 5: Below
The green-and-white marble façade of the church of Santa Maria Novella, designed by Leon Battista Alberti in the mid-1400s, introduced a distinctive new look in Florence. Alberti successfully blended the Gothic style of the lower façade with geometric patterns above. He also used scroll buttresses (supports) to soften the outline and tie the two stories of the structure together.

Plate 6: Above
Renaissance artists loved allegory—the use of objects and figures to represent ideas or qualities. In *Sacred Allegory* (1490s), the great Venetian painter Giovanni Bellini shows the Virgin Mary and various saints on a platform with a Muslim figure passing by. Some have suggested that the picture represents the Catholic Church in relation to the rest of the world. Others see it as a vision of Paradise.

Plate 7: Left
Titian (ca. 1488–1576), another great master of Renaissance Venice, brought rich color and sensuality to his paintings. Here *Penitent Magdalene*, the Mary Magdalene saved by Christ in the Bible, is clearly inspired by religious feeling but remains a very earthly figure.

Plate 8

In 1534 Michelangelo, the great Renaissance artist, began work on a painting that would cover the entire altar wall of the Sistine Chapel in Rome. Called the *Last Judgment*, the monumental work presents the artist's vision of the end of the world when souls receive their eternal rewards. The powerful figure of Christ is the focal point of the painting. Surrounded by the Virgin Mary, saints, and ordinary mortals, he raises one arm to strike down the sinners and extends the other to raise up the virtuous.

Plate 9: Left
Jean Fouquet, the most important French artist of the 1400s, worked primarily for the members of the French court. Fouquet's painting of Étienne Chevalier with St. Stephen was originally part of a two-panel work known as the Diptych of Melun (ca. 1450). Chevalier, the treasurer of France, and St. Stephen were on the left panel; the Virgin and Child were on the right.

Plate 10: Below
Renaissance architecture took a unique form in France. The Château of Chambord, started in 1519, shows the influence of Italian style but remains essentially French. Its massive towers and the extraordinary roof overflowing with chimneys and turrets continue the inventive spirit of late Gothic design. The layout of the château also follows the tradition of medieval castles.

Plate 11: Left
Many scholars consider the Flemish painter Jan Van Eyck (1395–1441) to be the founder of the Renaissance artistic tradition of northern Europe. He and his brother Hubert created the Ghent Altarpiece, which consists of 24 panels with images of God (the panel shown here), Christ, the Virgin Mary, angels, saints, and many biblical figures. The work has been praised for its beauty, realism, and technical mastery.

Plate 12: Below
German artist Lucas Cranach the Elder (1472–1553) worked for three successive rulers of Saxony and created many portraits of them. This painting, *The Deer Hunt of Frederick III, the Wise, Elector of Saxony*, shows a royal hunt in progress. Cranach presents the scene in considerable detail, but the landscape seems more fanciful than realistic.

Plate 13: Above
The great Flemish painter Pieter Brueghel the Elder often illustrated the lives of ordinary people at work and play. In *The Return of the Hunters* (1565), the artist presents a sweeping panorama of village life and scenery in the gray-green tones of winter. Brueghel's down-to-earth peasant scenes and his landscapes had enormous influence on later Dutch and Flemish painters, such as Peter Paul Rubens.

Plate 14: Right
El Greco, a Greek from the island of Crete, became the leading painter of the Spanish Renaissance. He used color in an intense and original way and often created swirling backgrounds to express spirituality. In his dramatic *View of Toledo* (ca. 1600), the vibrant colors produce a sense of motion and suggest a coming storm.

Donato Bramante designed the Tempietto of San Pietro in the early 1500s. Built in a classical style, the structure is based on the ideal pattern of the circle. Scholars have called it the perfect Renaissance building.

ideal pattern). The building sits on a round platform and resembles a classical temple. A single row of columns rings the outside of the platform. It was the first building to use an authentic order of columns as described by the Roman architect Vitruvius.

In 1503 JULIUS II became pope. He named Bramante to head several impressive building projects. The first of these was an expansion of the Vatican palace that included the use of both classical and modern architectural features. Julius also planned to redesign the existing Basilica of St. Peter, originally built in the 300s. The structure was too old and small to reflect the glory of the Renaissance church.

Bramante sent the pope his model for a complete rebuilding of the basilica, featuring a huge dome set between four smaller domes and towers. The floor plan resembled that of Milan's San Lorenzo Cathedral—an enormous Greek cross with four arms of equal length—but included a dome at the crossing (center of the cross). Bramante's design also drew inspiration from great buildings of different eras: the Pantheon, Rome's ancient Greek temple; the Hagia Sophia in Constantinople, built in the mid-500s; and the Cathedral of Florence, dating from the 1300s with Filippo BRUNELLESCHI's magnificent dome added in the 1430s.

Workers laid the foundation stone for the new basilica in 1506, and the four supports for the crossing were soon in place. However,

Bramante died long before the basilica was complete, and records show numerous changes to the plans. Besides the dome crossing, little of Bramante's original plan for St. Peter's appeared in the final building. (*See also* **Art in Italy; Classical Antiquity; Milan; Patronage; Popes and Papacy; Rome.**)

Brandenburg

* **Holy Roman Empire** political body in central Europe composed of several states; existed until 1806

* **Protestant Reformation** religious movement that began in the 1500s as a protest against certain practices of the Roman Catholic Church and eventually led to the establishment of a variety of Protestant churches

During the Renaissance, Brandenburg was an independent state within the Holy Roman Empire*. It played a central role in the religious conflicts that divided Europe during the Protestant Reformation*. Although at first Brandenburg's rulers defended Roman Catholicism against reformers, they ended by adopting and modifying Protestant beliefs and practices.

Brandenburg and the Catholic Church. Brandenburg gained its independence in 1417. Holy Roman Emperor Sigismund gave control of the region to his lieutenant, Frederick of Hohenzollern. Frederick received the title of elector, which passed to his descendants after his death.

The state first became involved in the religious conflict sweeping across Europe under the rule of Joachim I, Frederick's great-grandson. Joachim and his brother, Albert II, were both fiercely opposed to Martin Luther and his movement to reform the Roman Catholic Church. In 1525 the brothers joined the Anti-Lutheran League, an alliance of political leaders against Luther. When Joachim I died later that year, his territory was divided between two sons. He had hoped that one of them would remain loyal to the Catholic Church.

Joachim's younger son, John of Küstrin, embraced Luther's views in 1537. His brother, Joachim II, was more cautious. He hoped a church council could work out a compromise between the Catholic and Protestant faiths. Pressured by his subjects, he finally declared his support for Luther in 1539. However, he insisted that Brandenburg's church maintain many of the ceremonies and practices of Catholicism. Because of this arrangement, Brandenburg gained the approval of both Luther and the Holy Roman Emperor Charles V. It was the only German Protestant church to do so.

Further Reforms. John George, the son of Joachim II, inherited both parts of Brandenburg from his father and his uncle. In 1577 he signed the Formula of Concord, which officially established the Lutheran church in Brandenburg. This offended members of other Protestant groups, such as the Reformed church of John Calvin.

John George's successors moved Brandenburg toward Calvinism. In 1613 the elector John Sigismund publicly converted to the Reformed church. This shift, known as the "Second Reformation," made Brandenburg the leading Calvinist state in Germany. However, most of the country remained faithful to Lutheranism. Conflicts with members of the aristocracy* forced John Sigismund to weaken his reforms.

* **aristocracy** privileged upper classes of society; nobles or the nobility

Brandenburg suffered heavy losses during the THIRTY YEARS' WAR, a series of conflicts in central Europe between 1618 and 1648. However, Brandenburg recovered its influence during the late 1600s, and by the end of the century it had become the leading Protestant state in the empire. (*See also* **Holy Roman Empire; Humanism.**)

Brittany

Brittany, a region in what is now northwestern France, lay at the center of European politics and economic development during the Renaissance. A struggle for control over Brittany, the Breton War of Succession, began in 1341. It became a focus of the early stages of the Hundred Years' War between England and France. John of Montfort won control of Brittany in 1364 with the help of the king of England. Montfort's son, Duke John IV, founded a dynasty that ruled Brittany as an independent duchy* until 1491.

* **duchy** territory ruled by a duke or duchess

In the late 1400s the French king Charles VIII made alliances with several important Breton nobles. He invaded the duchy in 1487 and defeated a combined force of Bretons and English the following year. Brittany's Duke Francis II, who signed a humiliating treaty with France, died soon afterward. His daughter ANNE OF BRITTANY succeeded him as ruler.

Seeking to maintain Brittany's independence from France, Anne became engaged to Austria's powerful Duke MAXIMILIAN I in 1491. Meanwhile, the French king was planning to wed Maximilian's daughter. However, he called off that marriage, canceled Anne's engagement, and married Anne himself. One of Anne's grandsons from a later marriage became France's King Henry II. Many Bretons still consider Anne to be a symbol of a golden age in Brittany. Besides ruling the duchy, she supported the arts as a patron* and assembled a court of artists and writers. During the Renaissance new artistic trends from Italy spread to the region.

* **patron** supporter or financial sponsor of an artist or writer

Brittany remained largely independent under Anne, but a treaty in 1532 made the duchy part of France. The French allowed Brittany to keep its customary laws, which gave male and female heirs equal rights (commoners only) and protected widows' property rights. Bretons controlled the region's taxes until 1789.

Socially, Brittany resembled other parts of France. It was dominated by two powerful noble families. The aristocrats modeled their form of government after that of France and maintained close ties to the French nobility. The Breton noble families married into the French royal family and, like most eastern Bretons, were culturally French. Western Brittany was strongly Celtic* in culture and language.

* **Celtic** referring to the ancient inhabitants of Europe, known as Gauls in France and Britons in Britain

Although Brittany's aristocracy* controlled politics into the 1600s, economic power shifted to the towns that ran Brittany's industries. Brittany's economy was diverse, exporting salt, wine, wheat, and rye throughout Europe. Breton ships dominated Europe's coastal trade from the early 1400s to the mid-1500s. Their fishing fleet probably discovered the Grand Banks of Newfoundland long before Columbus's first voyage. The region was also the center of a prosperous linen industry. (*See also* **Art in Italy; England; France.**)

* **aristocracy** privileged upper classes of society; nobles or the nobility

Brueghel Family

Flemish painters

*** Flemish** referring to Flanders, a region along the coasts of present-day Belgium, France, and the Netherlands

*** still life** picture of inanimate objects, such as flowers or fruit

*** guild** association of craft and trade owners and workers that set standards for and represented the interests of its members

*** satire** literary or artistic work ridiculing human wickedness and foolishness

*** allegory** literary or artistic device in which characters, events, and settings represent abstract qualities, and in which the author or artist intends a different meaning to be read beneath the surface

*** patron** supporter or financial sponsor of an artist or writer

*** realism** artistic treatment of a subject that strives to reflect its true nature or appearance

See color plate 13, vol. 1

The Brueghels were a family of Flemish* painters who worked primarily in the city of Antwerp in present-day Belgium. They are best known for their landscapes, still lifes*, and paintings of scenes from everyday life. The most famous member of the family was Pieter Brueghel the Elder. His sons, Pieter the Younger and Jan, also achieved considerable success.

Pieter Brueghel the Elder (ca. 1525–1569). Born in the Flemish village of Bruegel, Pieter studied with the prominent artist Pieter Coecke van Aelst and joined the artists' guild* in Antwerp. In the early 1550s Brueghel spent several years in southern France, Italy, and the Alps. Then he returned to Antwerp, where he worked until he moved to Brussels in 1563. He married Mayken Coecke, the daughter of his former teacher, and they had two children, Pieter the Younger and Jan.

Brueghel's career falls into two major phases, divided by his move from Antwerp to Brussels. While in Antwerp, he produced many prints, including landscapes, satires*, and scenes of peasant life. Brueghel also began to paint in Antwerp. These early works were allegories* inspired by Flemish culture and traditions.

After moving to Brussels, Brueghel concentrated on painting rather than on printmaking. He had many important patrons* in the city, including wealthy government officials and the Roman Catholic cardinal. He produced both individual paintings and groups of related works, such as the *Labors of the Months* (1565), which portray activities typical of different seasons.

Brueghel's art shows the influence of the Flemish tradition of realism*. He drew inspiration from the work of artists such as Jan van Eyck and Rogier van der Weyden. He was also fascinated by the art of Hieronymus Bosch, a leading Flemish painter of the late 1400s and early 1500s. Brueghel's interest in Bosch emerged in his early print designs and continued to inspire some of his later paintings.

Brueghel's works cover a wide variety of subjects, including landscapes, religious figures, allegories, peasant scenes, and illustrations of Flemish proverbs. His landscapes range from pictures of the local countryside to great vistas inspired by his travels in the Alps. The sweeping views reveal a sense of grandeur that sets him apart from earlier Flemish artists.

Brueghel's allegorical paintings present witty satires of human folly, often based on themes from Flemish literature. His peasant scenes also display a vigorous sense of humor. Two of his most famous paintings, *Peasant Dance* and *Peasant Wedding,* reveal keen observation of human behavior.

Highly prized for their realism, Brueghel's paintings became part of some of the major art collections of the Renaissance, including those of Rudolf II (Holy Roman Emperor, 1576–1612) and two of the governors of the Spanish Netherlands. Widely copied and imitated, the artist's peasant scenes and landscapes deeply influenced the work of later Dutch and Flemish painters, such as Peter Paul Rubens.

Pieter Brueghel the Elder gained fame for his realistic paintings featuring peasant scenes, landscapes, and religious figures. One of his best-known works, *Peasant Wedding* (painted around 1566), is a colorful view of country life.

Pieter Brueghel the Younger (1564–1638). The elder son of Pieter the Elder, Pieter the Younger spent his entire life in Antwerp. He joined the city's artists' guild in 1585. Pieter the Younger painted religious subjects as well as numerous scenes of fires and hell that earned him the nickname "Hell Brueghel." He also specialized in producing copies or reworked versions of his father's paintings, particularly the scenes of peasant festivities. In his finest works, Pieter the Younger came close to matching the quality achieved by his father. However, he also produced many less successful pictures.

Jan Brueghel the Elder (1568–1625). Born shortly before his father's death, Jan was raised by his grandmother, an artist who painted miniatures. She was one of Jan's early art teachers.

As a young man, Jan traveled to Germany. In about 1589 he went to Italy, where he painted a number of works for Cardinal Federigo Borromeo. Jan returned to Antwerp in 1596 and six years later became head of the artists' guild. He also served as court painter to the governors of the Spanish Netherlands. Jan was a close friend of the artist Peter Paul Rubens, who painted a portrait of Jan and his family.

Jan the Elder specialized in landscapes, still lifes, pictures of animals, and rural scenes showing people at work and play. His earliest landscapes reflect the influence of his father. However, he later developed his own style, creating extremely detailed scenes in glowing, jewellike colors. Often painted on copper, these rich images earned him the nickname "Velvet Brueghel." He often worked with other artists, including Rubens.

Jan's numerous works became extremely popular and were copied and imitated well into the 1700s. Two of his sons, Jan the Younger and Ambrosius, also became painters. Both of these sons had sons who carried on the Brueghel family tradition as artists. (*See also* **Art; Art in the Netherlands.**)

Brunelleschi, Filippo

1377–1446
Italian architect

Filippo Brunelleschi was an architect, sculptor, and engineer from FLORENCE, Italy. His ideas helped shape Renaissance art, architecture, and engineering. Brunelleschi's major work, the dome of Florence's cathedral, has been called the greatest architectural and engineering feat of the 1400s.

Early Works. From an early age, Brunelleschi enjoyed drawing and painting, and in his late 20s he became a master goldsmith. He also worked as a sculptor, creating four silver figures for the cathedral of Pistoia, near Florence, and a wooden statue of Mary Magdalene. In 1401 his reputation as a craftsman and artist earned him an invitation to enter a competition for creating the bronze doors of the baptistery* in Florence. The judges, unable to decide between Brunelleschi and Lorenzo GHIBERTI, offered the job to both as a joint project. Brunelleschi refused to work with Ghiberti, however, and turned his attention to architecture.

* **baptistery** building where baptisms are performed

Between 1402 and 1409, Brunelleschi traveled to Rome to study its architecture, make drawings and measurements, and examine the foundations of ancient Roman buildings. He used his findings to work out a system of structural proportion based on mathematics and the principles of perspective*. Brunelleschi's work on perspective drawing, though not new, led artists of his time to regard him as its inventor.

* **perspective** artistic technique for creating the illusion of three-dimensional space on a flat surface

Building a Dome. In 1417 the caretakers of the Cathedral of Santa Maria del Fiore in Florence called on Brunelleschi for advice on constructing a dome for the unfinished building. The cathedral's central octagonal space, 130 feet in diameter, made creating a suitable dome difficult. The large, heavy dome would need more support than a wooden structure could provide.

Borrowing ideas from the Roman buildings he had studied earlier, Brunelleschi suggested doing away with the wooden framework normally used in the construction of a dome. Instead, he proposed a cone-shaped dome with an inner and outer shell connected by eight ribs that were linked horizontally by rings of stone blocks. Used around the dome, the ribs provided the necessary support and became a design element.

Brunelleschi's plan faced ridicule and opposition, but it was accepted. Work began in 1420, and within a few years of construction Brunelleschi had full control of the project as chief architect. He invented special tools, cranes, hoists, and scaffolding to make the work go more smoothly. In 1436 Brunelleschi completed the dome, a major achievement of Renaissance architecture.

Other Works. During the early years of construction on the dome, Brunelleschi designed a shelter for orphans. It was for this structure that he created a much admired portico* in front of the church of Santissima Annunziata in Florence. The portico's harmonious design with wide semicircular arches supported by slender columns had a strong influence on later Renaissance architects.

* **portico** porch or walkway supported by regularly spaced columns

The dome of Florence's cathedral was a feat of engineering that borrowed design elements from ancient Roman buildings. Architect Filippo Brunelleschi used a series of eight ribs to support the large, heavy dome. Some consider the structure the greatest marvel of Renaissance architecture.

Brunelleschi also designed a chapel and family tomb for the Pazzi family of Florence. Due to a lack of funds, construction did not start until 1442 and was not completed until after Brunelleschi's death. Many consider the small, perfectly proportioned chapel as Brunelleschi's masterpiece. (*See also* **Alberti, Leon Battista; Architecture; Art in Italy.**)

Bruni, Leonardo

ca. 1370–1444
Italian historian and humanist

Leonardo Bruni, the most important Italian humanist of the early 1400s, gained famed for his histories and biographies and his translations of ancient Greek works. His most ambitious project was a history of the city of FLORENCE. Celebrated as the leading literary figure and best-selling author of his day, Bruni enjoyed great success in his lifetime.

Bruni's Life. Bruni was born to wealthy parents in the Tuscan city of Arezzo. In the early 1390s he entered the University of Florence. He intended to study law but instead fell into the literary circle of Coluccio Salutati, the chancellor of Florence. Salutati recommended his young friend for a position as secretary to Pope Innocent VII in Rome. Bruni held this post from 1405 to 1414, serving a series of popes. In 1414 he returned to Florence to begin a scholarly career, which brought him great fame. In 1427 he became chancellor of Florence. Other political and professional honors followed. When Bruni died in 1444, he was honored in Florence and famous throughout Europe.

Greek Translations. Bruni produced Latin versions of the works of numerous Greek writers and orators. He translated speeches by Demosthenes, biographies by Plutarch, and four of Plato's dialogues. He also created new translations of several of Aristotle's works. Bruni's methods of translation were controversial. Most translators of his time favored literal, word-for-word translations. Bruni, by contrast, preferred to translate a piece according to its "sense." He defended this method in *On Correct Translation* (ca. 1420).

Bruni's most popular translation from the Greek was St. Basil of Caesarea's *Letter to Young Men* (1400–1401). This piece, which argues that Christians can benefit from reading the works of pagan* authors, provided support for Salutati in an argument with clergy members over the value of the classics. The work came to embody the views of the humanist movement.

* **pagan** referring to ancient religions that worshiped many gods, or more generally, to any non-Christian religion

Historical Writings. Many scholars consider Bruni the first modern historian. He wrote on topics from ancient Greek and Rome to the Italy of his day. His works on ancient history used Greek sources to supplement the existing Latin histories of authors such as Livy. Many of Bruni's histories promoted particular political views. For example, in *Commentary on Greek Affairs* (1439), he implied that political decisions should be made by educated citizens rather than by the masses.

Bruni composed his masterwork, the *History of the Florentine People,* over the period between 1415 and 1444. It covers the history of Florence from the founding of the city in the first century B.C. to the beginning of the 1400s. The history focuses on how Florence maintained its freedom and expanded its empire but generally ignores the political struggles within the city. The work is both a celebration of the city's achievements and a model for good foreign policy.

Bruni's Humanism. In his own time Bruni was best known as a translator, orator, and historian. Modern scholars, however, focus on his role as a humanist thinker. In 1955 historian Hans Baron described Bruni as the first "civic* humanist," meaning someone who blended classical studies with a commitment to political involvement. The ideals of civic humanism were classical learning, liberty, and devotion to the common good. According to Baron, Florence in the early 1400s was the breeding ground for this new philosophy. Baron and some other schol-

* **civic** related to a city, a community, or citizens

ars claim that it influenced later writers from Machiavelli through Thomas Jefferson.

Baron's ideas about Bruni remain influential. However, many other historians have pointed out flaws in his argument. Some note that the republican* ideas Baron describes had been discussed at least 100 years before Bruni's time. Others argue that Bruni's writings did not really promote democracy. Instead, they claimed that the ideal state is one ruled by "the best and the wealthy." Like most humanists of his time, Bruni supported existing governments, controlled mostly by aristocrats. However, he tried to improve the character of these regimes by providing examples of wise and virtuous conduct. (*See also* **History, Writing of; Humanism; Italian Language and Literature; Translation.**)

* **republican** refers to a form of Renaissance government dominated by leading merchants with limited participation by others

Bruno, Giordano

1548–1600
Italian philosopher

Giordano Bruno spent his life challenging traditional views in the fields of philosophy, theology*, and science. He ended his controversial career by being burned at the stake for heresy*.

Born in the Italian city of Nola, Bruno entered the Dominican* order in 1565. By 1572 he had become a priest, but three years later he came under suspicion of heresy for reading the forbidden books of the humanist* Erasmus. He fled the order's residence in Naples and began a long series of travels that occupied much of his adult life.

Bruno passed through Rome and other northern Italian cities before reaching Geneva, Switzerland, where he taught theology. However, Bruno quarreled with Calvinists* in the city and eventually was sued for slander. Bruno left town and traveled through southern France, teaching philosophy and mathematics in the city of Toulouse. He then moved on to Paris, where he lectured and published three works concerned with the art and science of memory. Bruno's works attacked noted philosophers such as Aristotle and promoted his own system of learning and method of memorization.

Bruno next spent several years in England, where he lectured on the theories of astronomer Nicolaus Copernicus. He expanded on the views of Copernicus in his 1584 work *The Ash Wednesday Supper.* Bruno argued that space is infinite, with neither center nor boundary, and that multiple worlds exist. Bruno also published several other works that year that criticized traditional religion, which he saw as based on superstition, and discussed his view of the universe as the physical embodiment of God.

After a brief return to France in 1585, Bruno traveled to Germany, where he converted to Lutheranism. He also composed works on the writings of Aristotle and on his own system of thought. His ideas eventually led the Lutherans to excommunicate* Bruno, who had already been cast out of the Catholic and Calvinist religions. In 1591 Bruno returned to Italy at the invitation of a Venetian nobleman who wanted to learn Bruno's art of memory. However the noble soon accused Bruno of such heresies as practicing magical arts, believing in infinite worlds, and rejecting elements of Catholic doctrine. The Roman Inquisition, the arm of the church responsible for identifying and punishing heresy, subjected Bruno to a lengthy trial and executed him.

* **theology** study of the nature of God and of religion

* **heresy** belief that is contrary to the doctrine of an established church

* **Dominican** religious order of brothers and priests founded by St. Dominic

* **humanist** Renaissance expert in the humanities (the languages, literature, history, and speech and writing techniques of ancient Greece and Rome)

* **Calvinist** member of a Protestant church founded by John Calvin

* **excommunicate** to exclude from the church and its rituals

It is undoubtedly true that Bruno was attracted to magic and other systems of thought at odds with the church. Indeed, he wrote a series of works on magic in the 1580s, which remained unpublished until 1891. His lifelong quest was to question traditional philosophies and religions and to create his own view of God and the world. Many modern readers see him as a martyr for the cause of freedom of thought. (*See also* **Astronomy; Inquisition; Magic and Astrology; Philosophy; Religious Thought.**)

Brunswick-Wolfenbüttel

* **duchy** territory ruled by a duke or duchess

* **Protestant Reformation** religious movement that began in the 1500s as a protest against certain practices of the Roman Catholic Church and eventually led to the establishment of a variety of Protestant churches

* **humanist** referring to a Renaissance cultural movement promoting the study of the humanities (the languages, literature, and history of ancient Greece and Rome) as a guide to living

* **medieval** referring to the Middle Ages, a period that began around A.D. 400 and ended around 1400 in Italy and 1500 in the rest of Europe

The duchy* of Brunswick-Wolfenbüttel, in northern Germany, consisted of nine distinct areas that were not all connected to each other. During the Renaissance, it became a center of scholarship and home to one of the largest libraries in Europe.

Members of the merchant class in Brunswick-Wolfenbüttel joined the Protestant Reformation* early on. For many years, they pressured their Catholic dukes to become Protestant. When Duke Julius mounted the throne in 1568, he converted the duchy to Lutheranism. His reign brought a dramatic rise in humanist* learning to the court.

In 1572 Duke Julius founded a court library in Wolfenbüttel. He contributed many treasures from his own collection, including a variety of valuable medieval* manuscripts taken from former monasteries after he abolished Catholicism in his realm. Four years later, Julius founded the University of Helmstedt, mainly to educate Lutheran clergy members. However, the school's policies stressed the need for a broad humanist program. Later decades brought a series of independent-minded teachers to the university, including the philosopher Giordano Bruno.

During the rule of Duke August the Younger (1635–1666), the library expanded to over 135,000 works, becoming one of the largest in Europe. In contrast to other book-loving aristocrats, August was not just a collector but also a librarian. At a time when cataloging was rare, even in university libraries, he sorted and cataloged his library into 20 subject areas. August also acquired countless treasures of medieval and Renaissance book art.

Later dukes and duchesses of Wolfenbüttel donated valuable collections to the library, though none as systematically as August. At the beginning of the 1700s, the ruling duke commissioned a building to house the collection. Called the Bibliotheca Rotunda, this became the first library building in Europe that was not associated with a church. The philosopher Gottfried Wilhelm Leibniz, who served as librarian in Wolfenbüttel from 1691 to 1716, oversaw the planning for the Rotunda. The building later became a model for libraries at Oxford University and the British Museum. (*See also* **Books and Manuscripts; Libraries.**)

Brussels

The city of Brussels, in present-day Belgium, was an important political and cultural center during the Renaissance. At the time Brussels

lay within the Netherlands, also known as the Low Countries, which were under the control of Spain. In 1531 Mary of Hungary, the ruler of the Low Countries and the sister of Holy Roman Emperor* CHARLES V, moved her court to Brussels. Her arrival marks the beginning of the Renaissance in the city.

* **Holy Roman Emperor** ruler of the Holy Roman Empire, a political body in central Europe composed of several states that existed until 1806

Brussels had prospered in the Middle Ages thanks to its highly successful cloth industry. During the 1400s, carpet and tapestry weaving became major industries. The influence of Italian Renaissance styles can be seen in many of the beautiful tapestries produced in Brussels during the 1500s. The Italian Renaissance also influenced the city's painters, especially Pieter BRUEGHEL the Elder, the father of a notable family of artists.

Echoes of the Renaissance appeared in the city's architecture as well. The presence of the court prompted many nobles to build splendid homes for their families in Brussels. One outstanding Renaissance palace (now in ruins) belonged to Antoine Perrenot de Granvelle, who later became a Catholic cardinal. However, Renaissance styles had little effect on church architecture, which continued for many years in the Gothic* tradition of the Middle Ages.

* **Gothic** style of architecture characterized by pointed arches and high, thin walls supported by flying buttresses

A revolt during the reign of PHILIP II of Spain pulled the Netherlands into a civil war that lasted from 1568 to 1648. However, Brussels returned to Spanish rule in 1585 and came under the control of the archdukes of Austria in 1598. Brussels once again emerged as a thriving center for the arts, home to such noted painters as Peter Paul RUBENS. The city experienced a burst of new construction in the early 1600s, adding many buildings in the Baroque* style of architecture. (*See also* **Art in the Netherlands; Netherlands.**)

* **Baroque** artistic style of the 1600s characterized by movement, drama, and grandness of scale

Burckhardt, Jakob

1818–1897
Renaissance historian

Jakob Burckhardt, who lived in Switzerland, was one of the most influential commentators on the Renaissance. His masterwork, *Civilization of the Renaissance in Italy* (1860), shaped the direction of Renaissance studies for generations. It also inspired a popular fascination with the Renaissance period in the early 1900s.

Burckhardt's Life and Work. Born into an upper-class family in Basel, Switzerland, Burckhardt attended a high school that specialized in classical* languages and literature. He studied history at the University of Basel, receiving a doctorate in 1843 and a teaching position. He moved to the Federal Institute of Technology in Zurich in 1855. Three years later he returned to Basel to become professor of history. He continued to teach and lecture in Basel until his retirement in 1893. He also traveled throughout western and central Europe, particularly Italy, to visit famous museums and monuments.

* **classical** in the tradition of ancient Greece and Rome

Burckhardt came up with the idea for his most famous work while in Rome in 1848. It took him another ten years to begin writing the book. Burckhardt approached history in a new and unconventional manner. Most historians of his time focused on strict, provable facts. Burckhardt considered it more useful to examine the way people saw and experi-

enced the events of their time. Also, while most historians aimed to trace the causes and effects of specific events, Burckhardt chose to examine the overall trends that gave a period its unique character. His goal was to present a picture of an era, helping his reader understand the society and culture as a whole.

The Civilization of the Renaissance. Burckhardt divided his work into six sections. The first section focuses on forms of government during the Renaissance—princedoms (states ruled by one man, the prince*) and republics* (states ruled by many). Both forms encouraged individualism. In a princedom, the ruler had to rely on his own efforts. In a republic, the people were "subjects" of the government and saw themselves as individuals rather than as part of a group. The second section of the book explores this new concept of individualism. Burckhardt saw it as the key to the creative drive behind the greatest achievements of the Renaissance. He also believed that the new interest in individual works and deeds led to a renewed fascination with classical art and learning, which was central to the humanist* movement. He examined this topic in section three.

* **prince** Renaissance term for the ruler of an independent state

* **republic** form of Renaissance government dominated by leading merchants with limited participation by others

* **humanist** referring to a Renaissance cultural movement promoting the study of the humanities (the languages, literature, and history of ancient Greece and Rome) as a guide to living

Section four discusses the Renaissance fascination with the world of nature. In Burckhardt's view, Renaissance thinkers drew connections between the laws of science, the beauty of the natural world, and the inner nature of humanity. His fifth section discusses Renaissance society and festivals. This section is not as well developed as the others. However, Burckhardt's discoveries later proved useful in developing the new disciplines of social history and sociology.

The book's final section, on morality and religion, is the most controversial. Burckhardt saw the Renaissance as the beginning of the modern world's departure from religious faith. However, this departure was not a deliberate, logical choice. Instead, it resulted from "wavering" between a Roman Catholic Church that had become corrupt and immoral and a new, human-centered worldview. In Burckhardt's view, neither of these forces produced true spiritual reform in Italy.

Burckhardt's work is far from comprehensive. It does not deal with economic conditions, and it devotes little attention to the art of the Renaissance. However, the book had an enormous influence on later historians. Even those who criticized Burckhardt's views praised his ability to examine so many aspects of the Renaissance in such detail. (*See also* **Humanism; Renaissance: Influence and Interpretations.**)

Burgundy

The Renaissance state of Burgundy was a patchwork of territories that extended from the Netherlands to present-day Switzerland. Formed as a result of several historical accidents, the state survived for little more than 100 years. Nonetheless, it played an important role in the distribution of power in western Europe and left a legacy of great political, military, and artistic achievements.

The French crown acquired the duchy* of Burgundy in 1361 when its duke, Philip of Rouvres, died without an heir. The king of France named

* **duchy** territory ruled by a duke or duchess

Philip the Good of Burgundy expanded and strengthened his state through a series of shrewd political maneuvers that briefly turned Burgundy into a significant European power. Known as a great patron of the arts, Philip made his court into the artistic center of northern Europe.

his youngest son, Philip the Bold (1363–1404), the first duke of Burgundy in the VALOIS line. Philip added to his realm when he married Margaret of Flanders, the heir to a wealthy county along the North Sea. Philip the Bold's grandson, Philip the Good (1419–1467), expanded the territory again. Through marital alliances, he gained various regions and duchies, including Holland, Zeeland, Brabant, and Luxembourg.

Both Philip the Good and his successor, Charles the Bold, worked to centralize rule in Burgundy, but the region lacked a sense of political unity. The various counties, duchies, and lordships that made up Burgundy were distinct parts of a larger whole. The regions had different languages, cultures, economies, and political systems. Geographically, however, the state of Burgundy served as a useful buffer* between France and the Holy Roman Empire*.

During the Hundred Years' War (1337–1453) between England and France, the dukes of Burgundy took advantage of the conflicts between those two countries to promote their own interests. In 1415 John the Fearless sided with England against France, contributing to the French defeat at the famous battle of Agincourt in that year. John's son, Philip the Good, switched sides and supported France. The result was a French victory that largely expelled the English from France. Through such actions, the dukes of Burgundy turned their patchwork state into a significant European power.

Culturally, the Burgundian court came to rival the courts of Renaissance Italy in splendor and artistic display. The dukes of Burgundy actually maintained two courts: a Flemish* one in BRUSSELS (now part of Belgium) and a French one in Dijon (in eastern France). Both cities became centers of artistic achievement, promoting the works of such artists as Jan van EYCK and Rogier van der WEYDEN. In 1430 Philip the Good founded the Order of the Golden Fleece, a select group of nobles who served as great patrons* of the arts. The Burgundian court became the greatest source of artistic patronage in northern Europe.

Burgundy came to a sudden end in the same way as it was founded. In January 1477, Charles the Bold, the last Valois duke of Burgundy, died in battle. His only heir was his daughter Mary. Louis XI of France, who had been at war with Burgundy, took the opportunity to seize control of Dijon. Mary sought support from the ruler of Austria, who later became Holy Roman Emperor as MAXIMILIAN I. The two powers became involved in a tug of war over the fate of Burgundy and eventually divided the state between them. (*See also* **Dynastic Rivalry; England; France; Holy Roman Empire; Patronage.**)

* **buffer** neutral area between two rival powers
* **Holy Roman Empire** political body in central Europe composed of several states; existed until 1806
* **Flemish** referring to Flanders, a region along the coasts of present-day Belgium, France, and the Netherlands
* **patron** supporter or financial sponsor of an artist or writer

Byrd, William

ca. 1542–1623
English composer

William Byrd was the leading English composer of the Renaissance. His development of the English madrigal, among other musical accomplishments, earned him the title "father of British music."

As a young man, Byrd held the positions of organist and choirmaster at Lincoln Cathedral. By the age of 30, he had moved to London to join the Chapel Royal, a group of musicians and clergy members who

arranged and performed religious music for English royalty. Byrd sang and played the organ with the Chapel Royal until 1594. After retiring from these duties, he continued to compose music.

* **secular** nonreligious; connected with everyday life

* **madrigal** piece of nonreligious vocal music involving complex harmonies, usually for several voices without instrumental accompaniment

Byrd's work includes nearly every type of Renaissance music, both sacred and secular*. Of his sacred works, the best known are his three Masses, published during the 1590s. He earned his fame, however, for his work with secular vocal music. Byrd developed a new form of madrigal* that featured a solo voice accompanied by stringed instruments, rather than many voices. He also broke new ground by composing purely instrumental works at a time when most English music featured the voice. (*See also* **Music; Music, Instrumental; Music, Vocal.**)

Calderón de la Barca, Pedro

1600–1681
Spanish playwright

Pedro Calderón de la Barca of Madrid was one of the greatest Spanish playwrights of the Renaissance. During his career Calderón wrote several poems and approximately 120 three-act plays. His later work with musical theater contributed to the development of OPERA in Spain.

As a young man, Calderón respected his father's dying wish for him to study to become a priest. After four years of studying church law, he changed his focus to literature, writing plays and poems. In 1621, Calderón took a position at the royal court in Castile, and two years later he produced his first play for the court. This production, *Love, Honor, and Power,* revolved around the conflicts between desire, honor, and the demands of those in authority. These themes reappear in many of his later works.

Calderón wrote most of his well-known works early in his career, including comedies such as *The Phantom Lady* and murderous tragedies like *The Surgeon of His Honor.* Father-son conflicts appeared frequently in Calderón's work. They formed the basis for his most celebrated play, *Life Is a Dream,* written in 1630. In this drama, Calderón questioned faith, knowledge, freedom, and political power.

In 1637 Calderón became a knight. Between 1640 and 1642 he served in two campaigns to crush a revolt in the community of Catalonia. The Catalonian revolt closed Spanish theaters for several years, possibly influencing Calderón's decision to join the priesthood in 1651. Afterward he wrote less for the public theater, but he composed several elaborate "spectacle-plays" for the court. These pieces were tragicomedies based on mythological themes that used music, dance, scenery, and stage effects lavishly. Such works contributed to the beginnings of opera in Spain.

Translations of Calderón's works and adaptations of his plots spread his influence throughout Europe. In Germany, especially, they helped create a renewed appreciation of Spanish drama. As his work spread, Calderón gained a reputation as Spain's master playwright. (*See also* **Drama, Spanish; Spanish Language and Literature.**)

Calendars

Throughout history, people have used various systems to organize the year into units such as days, weeks, and months. One of the most significant reforms of the calendar system occurred during the Renaissance. It resulted in the creation of the Gregorian calendar, which still serves as the worldwide standard today.

The Julian Calendar. Calendars are based on ASTRONOMY. The rising and setting of the Sun determine the length of a day. Each day the Sun rises to a slightly different point in the sky than it did the day before. The time it takes the Sun to return to a specific noontime height is equal to one year. Originally, the month also related to astronomy—it depended on the phases of the Moon. However, calendars did away with this relationship around 2,000 years ago.

The main difficulty in creating a calendar is that the year contains approximately 365.25 days. The odd quarter day means that calendars based on whole days sooner or later fall out of step with the solar year. In 45 B.C., the Roman leader Julius Caesar introduced the Julian calendar. Adopted in A.D. 8, the calendar solved the problem of the odd quarter day by adding an entire extra day to the calendar every fourth year, or leap year.

The early Christian church used the Julian calendar to determine the dates of many religious holidays. Easter, however, had no fixed date in the calendar. In the late 400s a church scholar named Dionysius Exiguus developed a method for determining the date of Easter based on the phases of the Moon. He also began the practice of dating the modern or Christian era from the birth of Christ, although he erred by four to seven years in calculating the date of that event.

The Julian calendar made January 1 the official start of the year. However, countries that used the calendar chose a variety of dates to mark the new year. In Florence, Italy, the year began on March 25, while in nearby Pisa it began on March 24. In England the start of a new year fell on Christmas Day, December 25, until the 1300s, when it shifted to March 25. Not until the 1700s did January 1 become the accepted start of a new year in England.

The Gregorian Reform. The Julian calendar was an improvement on older calendars, but it was based on a length for the year that was 11 minutes and 14 seconds too long. As a result, the vernal equinox, one of the two times each year that the day and night are of equal length, moved ahead about one calendar day every 314 years. By the 1500s the astronomical or seasonal equinox was ten days ahead of the calendar's equinox, which fell on March 21.

The fact that the calendar was out of step with nature concerned church officials because the vernal equinox determined when Easter was celebrated. In the 1570s Pope Gregory XIII appointed a commission to study the matter and suggest reforms. The result was the Gregorian calendar, put into use in 1582. Ten days were dropped from the calendar to bring the vernal equinox back to where it had been in Julius Caesar's time. This meant that in 1582, October 15 directly followed October 4.

The Gregorian calendar was based on a year of 365.2425 days. It continued to use leap years but dropped three of them from the calendar in each 400-year period.

Most Catholic countries immediately accepted the Gregorian calendar. But because the calendar came from Rome, center of the Catholic world, most Protestant countries resisted it for political and religious reasons. Eventually, however, they accepted the reform. England introduced the Gregorian calendar in 1752 and, at the same time, changed the beginning of the year to January 1. Simple, easy to use, and reasonably accurate, the Gregorian calendar is still the standard—although astronomers now know that it is off by about one day for every 2,500 years.

Calligraphy

See *Writing.*

Calvin, John

1509–1564
Protestant reformer

* **Protestant Reformation** religious movement that began in the 1500s as a protest against certain practices of the Roman Catholic Church and eventually led to the establishment of a variety of Protestant churches

* **humanism** Renaissance cultural movement promoting the study of the humanities (the languages, literature, and history of ancient Greece and Rome) as a guide to living

* **theology** study of the nature of God and of religion

* **rhetoric** art of speaking or writing effectively

The leading intellectual spokesman for the Protestant Reformation* was John Calvin (born Jean Chauvin in Noyon, France). More than any other reformer, Calvin brought Renaissance humanism* to the study of Protestant religion.

While still in his teens, Calvin moved to Paris to study theology*. However, at his father's urging, he later switched to the field of law. His studies brought him into contact with several of the royal lecturers the king had appointed to promote humanist learning in Paris. Calvin became a young humanist and, in 1532, produced his first major publication, a study of the ancient Greek writer Seneca. Calvin's work displayed his mastery of both Latin and rhetoric*. His abilities as a speaker and a writer proved to be the key to his power as a reformer.

In the early 1530s Calvin became a Protestant and began associating with other Protestants in Paris. He fled Paris in 1533 after the government took a firm stand against the Protestant Reformation. For the next few years he privately studied a number of Protestant theologies, especially the works of Martin LUTHER.

In 1536 Calvin published his most important book, *Institutes of the Christian Religion.* In it, Calvin explained the essentials of Protestant Christianity to common readers and promoted his vision of the Christian faith. *Institutes* became the most widely read book on theology published during the Reformation. While other reformers produced a variety of texts, Calvin spent much of his life adjusting, translating, and expanding this single book. Final versions appeared in 1559 in Latin and in 1560 in French.

Because of the strength of *Institutes,* reformer Guillaume Farel invited Calvin to join him as a teacher in Geneva. The city expelled both men in 1538 but invited Calvin back in 1541—this time as both a teacher and a pastor. From Geneva, he spread his new version of Christianity throughout Europe. His Reformed Church became the chief Protestant alternative to Lutheranism.

Some of the most important reforms that Calvin introduced in Geneva were his efforts to promote humanist education. He reformed the elementary school system and created an academy to teach advanced humanist studies and theology. The academy, established in 1559 to train Protestant pastors, is now the University of Geneva. (*See also* **Humanism; Protestant Reformation; Religious Thought; Rhetoric.**)

Camões, Luíz Vaz de

ca. 1524–1580
Portuguese poet

* **epic** long poem about the adventures of a hero

* **satire** literary or artistic work ridiculing human wickedness and foolishness

The Portuguese poet Luíz Vaz de Camões is best known as the author of *The Lusiads,* an epic* glorifying his homeland. Born in Lisbon to a family of lower nobility, Camões served as a soldier in North Africa, where he lost an eye. After returning to Portugal in 1549, he became involved in a street fight, for which he was jailed and later deported. He spent the next 17 years as a soldier in India and China.

During his exile, Camões wrote plays, satires*, and his masterpiece, *The Lusiads.* Shipwrecked off the coast of Cambodia in 1559, he barely managed to save the manuscript of his epic. After many struggles, he finally returned to Lisbon in 1570. The boy-king Sebastião was on the throne at that time, and Camões dedicated *The Lusiads* to him. Camões received a modest pension for the work, but not enough to relieve his poverty.

In 1578, Sebastião died in battle. Camões did not live to see PHILIP II of Spain invade Portugal, but he knew that his country was in danger. On his deathbed he wrote: "All will see that so dear to me was my country that I was content to die not only in it but with it."

In *The Lusiads,* Camões not only relates the history of Portugal, but also links his country to the greatness of ancient Rome. The epic centers on Portuguese explorer Vasco da GAMA's historic journey to India (1497–1498). Around this point, Camões weaves past and present together to include both his country's mythical origins and events after Gama's journey. He likens Portugal to ancient Rome by modeling his work on the Roman poet VIRGIL's famous epic, the *Aeneid.* Both epics include the theme of a divine plan behind the events of human history. Camões uses his country's history to present the idea that human beings are flawed, capable of both good and evil.

The first English translation of Camões's work was an English diplomat's version of *The Lusiads* in 1655. Since then, others have produced new English translations of *The Lusiads* and the rest of Camões's works. Camões's poetry was popular among such American writers of the 1800s as Edgar Allan Poe, Henry Wadsworth Longfellow, and Herman Melville. (*See also* **Portuguese Language and Literature.**)

Campanella, Tommaso

1568–1639
Italian philosopher and writer

Tommaso Campanella was one of the great writers and thinkers in Italy in the early 1600s. He spent much of his life in jail because of his unusual religious views and his plots against the government.

However, while imprisoned, he produced some of his most noted works, including his vision of the ideal society.

Dangerous Ideas. Giovanni Dominico Campanella adopted the name Tommaso when he entered the Dominican* religious order in 1583. A gifted scholar, he soon became dissatisfied with the works of Aristotle, the philosopher whose writings dominated the schools. He decided to create his own system of philosophy based on Christian sources. Campanella presented his ideas in *Philosophy Proven by the Senses* (1591).

* **Dominican** religious order of brothers and priests founded by St. Dominic

In Campanella's system, everything that exists contains three parts that he calls primalities: power, knowledge, and love. He linked these three primalities to God the Father, God the Son, and God the Holy Spirit. This philosophy ran against the popular view that people were made of body and spirit. It also suggested that God was part of everything, including humans—a belief contrary to traditional Christian ideas.

Campanella's writings made him a target of the Spanish Inquisition*. For several years, he was in and out of jail. In 1595, the Inquisition brought him to Rome and forced him to deny what he had written. Two years later he was arrested again and ordered to return to his home in southern Italy. There Campanella became the leader of a political conspiracy* to end Spanish control of the kingdom of Naples. His goal was to found a new state based on the ideals of knowledge, shared wealth, and freedom of conscience.

* **Spanish Inquisition** court established by the Spanish monarchs that investigated Christians accused of straying from the official doctrine of the Roman Catholic Church, particularly during the period 1480–1530

* **conspiracy** plotting with others to commit a crime

In 1599 one of Campanella's co-conspirators betrayed him. He was arrested for both heresy* and conspiracy against the Spanish state. The authorities sent him to Naples, where he was tortured, forced to confess, and condemned to death. Campanella knew that it was illegal to execute an insane person, so he pretended to be mad. He escaped the death penalty but remained in jail for nearly 30 years.

* **heresy** belief that is contrary to the doctrine of an established church

Prison Writings. During his imprisonment, Campanella wrote many works of poetry and philosophy. The best known of these is *The City of the Sun,* written in 1602 and published in 1623. In this work, Campanella described his idea of the perfect society. He saw the government and the Catholic Church uniting to rule a perfect society that promoted education, science, and technology. All people, male and female, would be equal. They would wear white clothing and share property. There would be no marriage, but the community as a whole would raise children.

Campanella believed that the citizens of this ideal state would not need most of the Catholic Church's teachings. Being made of the three primalities, they would be able to understand the nature of God on their own. When he wrote *The City of the Sun,* Campanella believed that such a society could exist in the real world. At the same time, the same organizations that he expected to rule his ideal state—the government and the church—were keeping him in prison.

Even after a charge of heresy, Campanella had a strong reputation as a theologian*. In 1616 a cardinal asked Campanella to offer his view on the trial of the astronomer Galileo Galilei. Galileo had been accused of heresy for contradicting church teachings about the solar system. Campanella disagreed with Galileo's ideas, but in *A Defense of Galileo* (published 1622) he argued strongly for the astronomer's right to express his views. This courageous work has become famous as an appeal for freedom of thought.

* **theologian** person who studies religion and the nature of God

With the help of Pope Urban VIII, Campanella was released from prison in 1626. After his release, he spent eight years in Rome. When he realized that the pope's protection was weakening, he fled to France, where he was already famous. King Louis XIII granted him a pension, and he continued writing until his death in Paris in 1639. (*See also* **Aristotle and Aristotelianism; Inquisition.**)

Caravaggio, Michelangelo Merisi da

1571–1610
Italian painter

The Italian artist Caravaggio is best known for his powerful and emotional paintings of saints and other religious figures. He worked in a naturalistic* style and used chiaroscuro (the contrast of light and darkness) to create dramatic effects and give his figures a sense of solidity and weight.

* **naturalistic** realistic, showing the world as it is without idealization

* **apprenticeship** system under which a person is bound by legal agreement to work for another for a specified period of time in return for instruction in a trade or craft

Early Works. Probably born in Milan, Michelangelo Merisi grew up in the town of Caravaggio and adopted its name as part of his own. After completing an apprenticeship*, he moved to Rome in 1592. However, his work continued to reflect the style of northern Italy, particularly its naturalism and dramatic use of light. Unlike many Renaissance painters, he did not imitate the work of ancient artists.

Caravaggio's earliest works are all similar in style. Each canvas shows a youth, in a style of dress typical of ancient Greece or Rome, looking toward the viewer. Caravaggio painted the figures in a highly realistic style, yet their poses and surroundings have an artificial quality. He focused on the central figure's gestures, expressions, and emotions, leaving the background flat and undefined. He also painted objects with exaggerated realism, often making them appear very close to the viewer.

See color plate 8, vol. 2

In later pieces, Caravaggio presented groups of figures in a way that hints at a story. Rather than focusing on aristocrats, he created scenes from the everyday life of common people. For example, his *Cardsharps* shows a pair of rogues cheating an inexperienced young player at cards.

Religious Works. Caravaggio's religious paintings show a change in mood and style from his secular* works. Landscapes replace the stark, blank backgrounds of his early paintings. In these works, the artist employed chiaroscuro to add interest, make forms seem more solid, and indicate God's presence. In *St. Francis in Ecstasy,* for example, the use of light is the only sign of the subject's divine nature. In *Judith and Holofernes* and *Conversion of the Magdalene,* Caravaggio used lighting effects to increase the sense of drama.

* **secular** nonreligious; connected with everyday life

Painter Michelangelo Merisi da Caravaggio created realistic works with a vivid use of light. His *Cardsharps* (1594), which shows two experienced card players cheating a newcomer, reflects his fondness for scenes of everyday life.

* **patron** supporter or financial sponsor of an artist or writer

In 1599 Caravaggio received his first public commission: a pair of paintings on the life of St. Matthew for the Contarelli Chapel of San Luigi dei Francesi in Rome. These highly praised pieces show two different sources of light: sunlight entering through a window at an angle and overhead light from a lamp. This lighting gives the figures a three-dimensional quality and hints at a divine presence. The sacred figures in the paintings appear as realistic, not idealized, humans. Nonetheless, they contrast with the secular figures, who are dressed in modern costumes of exaggerated high style. Caravaggio eventually had to redesign the pieces, which were too dramatic for his patrons*.

In 1601 Caravaggio began work on two canvases for the Cerasi Chapel of Santa Maria del Popolo in Rome. Once again the patrons rejected his original designs, but he quickly produced two excellent replacements. From this point on, Caravaggio's religious works were very serious, a mood expressed by the use of dark shadowing. Some of his pieces, such as *Death of the Virgin,* were too dark and realistic for his patrons' tastes. However, Caravaggio had no shortage of supporters.

Later Life. Caravaggio committed a murder in 1606 and fled from Rome to escape arrest. He moved to Naples, which was under Spanish control and out of the pope's reach. Caravaggio also spent a year in Malta, where he was knighted and later imprisoned. He escaped to Sicily and made his way back to Naples.

During his exile from Rome, Caravaggio continued to receive commissions from important members of Italian society. His style became less natural and more expressive, using broader brush strokes that reveal more of the reddish-brown background. The figures in these late works are smaller and their gestures less dramatic. The use of dark open spaces and massive buildings in the paintings creates a solemn mood and makes the figures seem more human. The overall atmosphere is humble, sober, and even tragic.

The dark mood of Caravaggio's late works oddly hints at the artist's own doom. In July of 1610, as he was on his way to Rome to receive a pardon from the pope, Caravaggio fell ill and died of a fever. However, his work had a great influence on the developing style of the Baroque* period, with its powerful appeal to the senses. (*See also* **Art in Italy; Patronage.**)

* **Baroque** artistic style of the 1600s characterized by movement, drama, and grandness of scale

Carpaccio, Vittore

ca. 1465–ca. 1525
Italian painter

Vittore Carpaccio was one of the most celebrated artists of Renaissance Venice, but little is known of his life or early work. Carpaccio's first major project, between 1490 and 1500, involved a series of nine large canvases for the School of St. Ursula in Venice. These works, which tell the story of the saint's life, made Carpaccio's reputation as a painter.

Following this success, Carpaccio painted narrative* works for other schools in the city. These schools, or *scuole,* were Venetian organizations dedicated to charity and devotional exercises that spent lavishly to decorate their churches and meeting halls. For the School of St. John the Baptist, Carpaccio created *Healing of the Possessed Man,* which presents a richly detailed scene of Venetian city life. The painting shows his talent for blending sacred events into the realities of everyday life.

* **narrative** storytelling

Carpaccio had a gift for presenting large numbers of people in his paintings by organizing them into groups. His works combine liveliness and variety with a sense of balance and order. For inspiration, he drew from the architecture and spectacle of Venice, as well as from books illustrating the geography and costumes of different parts of the world.

In addition to his work for schools, Carpaccio painted various works for the city of Venice and for churches within and outside the city. Although best known for his narrative scenes, he also achieved fame as a portrait painter. Later generations regarded Carpaccio as the most important contemporary of the great Venetian painter Giovanni Bellini. (*See also* **Art; Art in Italy; Venice.**)

Carracci Family

Italian painters

The Carracci were a family of artists from the city of Bologna who played a key role in developing the style now known as Baroque*. Working in the late 1500s and early 1600s, they rejected the artistic tendency of their day toward Mannerism* with its exaggeration and distortion. They favored a naturalistic* approach to painting. The Carracci established an important academy, or art school, to train young artists in their new style.

* **Baroque** artistic style of the 1600s characterized by movement, drama, and grandness of scale

* **Mannerism** artistic style of the 1500s characterized by vivid colors and exaggeration, such as elongated figures in complex poses

* **naturalistic** realistic, showing the world as it is without idealization

* **guild** association of craft and trade owners and workers that set standards for and represented the interests of its members

* **humanist** referring to a Renaissance cultural movement promoting the study of the humanities (the languages, literature, and history of ancient Greece and Rome) as a guide to living

Education and Influences. The three most famous Carracci painters were Ludovico (1555–1619) and his cousins Agostino (1557–1602) and Annibale (1560–1609). Ludovico, the son of a butcher, studied under local artists and joined the painter's guild* of Bologna in 1578. His cousins attended a Latin school before deciding, with Ludovico's encouragement, to become artists. Both received training from Ludovico and other Bolognese artists. However, their early exposure to humanist* learning influenced their ideas about art.

After joining the painter's guild, Ludovico traveled throughout northern Italy and studied the artistic traditions of cities such as Florence and Venice. He probably met painters from Florence's Accademia del Disegno, who were already turning away from Mannerism and toward the more naturalistic style of artists such as CORREGGIO and Federico BAROCCI. These artists, as well as the noted Venetians VERONESE and TITIAN, inspired Ludovico. He later sent his cousins on a similar tour to study the works of Correggio and the Venetians.

* **perspective** artistic technique for creating the illusion of three-dimensional space on a flat surface

The Carracci Academy. In 1582 the Carracci founded an academy in Bologna, modeled after the Accademia del Disegno. Its program was similar to the one in Florence, with courses in such topics as anatomy, proportion, perspective*, and life drawing. These subjects reflected the teachings of noted humanists such as Leon Battista ALBERTI on the theory of art.

The Carracci stressed the importance of drawing from real life as well as from models. They encouraged their students to keep sketchbooks with them at all times and to record things they observed in daily life. However, they urged students not to simply copy what they saw, but to analyze it and find its essence. Annibale Carracci is said to have invented the art of caricature, in which an artist greatly exaggerates some feature of the subject's anatomy.

The Carracci accused the Mannerists of painting by routine, rather than looking deeper to discover the universal truths of nature. They particularly disliked the ideas of Mannerist artist Giorgio Vasari, who wrote a history of the lives of leading artists of the Renaissance. Vasari preferred central Italian artists such as MICHELANGELO to the northern Italian artists favored by the Carracci. Their copy of Vasari's book contains sharp criticisms written in the margins.

* **fresco** mural painted on a plaster wall

Artistic Achievements. In the early 1580s the Carracci painted a series of frescoes* on subjects from ancient mythology in the Palazzo

Fava at Bologna. They expanded this work in 1586. Three years later they traveled to Rome to create another series portraying the myth of the city's founding. None took individual credit for this work, stating: "It is by the Carracci; we all made it."

In 1593 Ludovico and Agostino entered the service of the duke of Parma, Ranuccio I Farnese. The duke's younger brother, a cardinal in Rome, hired Annibale. Agostino soon joined his brother in Rome, where they achieved fame with their decoration of two rooms in the Farnese Palace. Their work on this project shows the influence of Michelangelo and Raphael. However, the Carracci adapted these artists' methods to their own more naturalistic style, creating a striking new blend of forms.

The brothers argued frequently over the work, and in 1599 Agostino left Rome to work for the duke of Parma. Annibale stayed in Rome but came down with a mysterious illness that claimed his life in 1609. Meanwhile, Ludovico remained in Bologna, running the academy. His late artistic projects included decorating the cloister* of San Michele in Bosco and creating several frescoes for the Cathedral of Piacenza. *(See also* **Art, Education and Training; Art in Italy; Baroque; Bologna; Florence; Guilds; Patronage; Venice.**)

* **cloister** covered passageway around a courtyard in a convent or monastery

Castiglione, Baldassare

1478–1529
Italian writer and diplomat

Baldassare Castiglione served as a diplomat to Italian rulers and the pope in the early 1500s. However, he is best known for *The Book of the Courtier,* which became the leading guide for social behavior and remained influential for centuries after its publication. This work places Castiglione among the most important literary figures of the Renaissance.

Life and Work. Castiglione was the son of a professional soldier who served the marquis of Mantua. Baldassare attended school in Milan but returned to Mantua in 1499 when his father died. For the next five years he traveled about Italy as a military officer and diplomat for the marquis. In 1504 he entered the service of the duke of Urbino.

Castiglione worked for the duke and his successor until 1516. Then the Medici family captured Urbino and forced the duke into exile. Castiglione returned to Mantua and entered the service of the ruling Gonzaga family. He accompanied Francesco Gonzaga II to Venice and acted as Mantua's ambassador to the papal* court in Rome. In 1524 Pope Clement VII named Castiglione his ambassador to the court of Charles V in Spain. Castiglione moved to Spain the following year and remained there until his death.

* **papal** referring to the office and authority of the pope

Castiglione wrote poetry, biography, letters, and even a prologue for a play. However, his most famous work is *The Book of the Courtier,* which he began by 1513 or 1514. In 1518 he began sending copies to his close friends for suggestions and corrections as he revised his manuscript. The book appeared in 1528.

The Book of the Courtier. Castiglione called his masterpiece a "portrait of the court of Urbino." He sets his scene at the court during a visit

The Italian diplomat Baldassare Castiglione was a major Renaissance author whose work ranged from letters to poetry. His most famous work, *The Book of the Courtier,* served as a guide to proper social behavior for centuries. The Italian artist Raphael painted this portrait of Castiglione around 1515.

from Pope JULIUS II in 1506. Castiglione's characters—the courtiers and ladies of the court—play a game in which they "portray in words a perfect courtier." As they discuss the perfect courtier, they also argue current issues such as the merits of different forms of government and types of art. Castiglione uses his own friends from court as characters, carefully portraying them to reflect their real-life points of view.

Castiglione patterned *The Courtier* on classical* writings. In the tradition of Roman writer CICERO and the Greek philosopher PLATO, he described a model character, someone for his readers to try to imitate. Like the classical writers, Castiglione structured his work as a dialogue.

* **classical** in the tradition of ancient Greece and Rome

The first book outlines the physical and moral qualities of the ideal courtier. He must, of course, be a nobleman. His first role should be as a soldier, but he must also appreciate and practice arts and scholarship. He must never do things to excess and must always move naturally,

with grace and ease. Above all else he must present an attractive physical appearance. Book two discusses how the courtier should demonstrate these qualities, especially through his skill at conversation. He must be able to talk seriously and to use language to entertain.

The subject of book three is the courtier's ideal female companion. The characters discuss the merits and faults of women, a favorite topic of debate at the time. The ideal woman has much the same qualities as the ideal courtier, though physical beauty plays a larger role than in a man. A lady must also be careful to protect her good reputation.

The final book examines how the courtier can best serve his prince or nobleman. He must earn favor so he can speak honestly and even correct his lord if necessary. This book also discusses how the aging courtier should love. It describes platonic love, which moves from human beauty to an understanding of the idea of beauty and finally to an understanding of God.

Some modern observers criticize *The Courtier* for focusing on image and physical appearance and for devoting too little attention to the courtier's main duty of serving the prince. Nevertheless, *The Courtier* was brilliantly original and widely imitated. The work enjoyed enormous success throughout the 1500s, and by 1571 translations were available in Spanish, French, English, and even Latin. (*See also* **Literature; Mantua; Princes and Princedoms; Urbino.**)

Catalan Language and Literature

See *Spanish Language and Literature.*

Catherine de Médicis

1519–1589
French queen and regent

Daughter of the powerful Lorenzo de' Medici of Italy, Catherine de Médicis was the wife of one French king and the mother of three others. She played a key role in the religious wars between Roman Catholics and Huguenots (French Protestants) that tore France apart in the late 1500s.

Catherine's uncle, Pope Clement VII, arranged for her to marry Henry, Duke of Orléans in 1533. Fourteen years later the duke became Henry II, king of France. Catherine did not become involved in politics until Henry's death in 1559. Her oldest son, then 15 years of age, inherited the throne as Francis II. He was strongly influenced by the Guise family, Roman Catholics dedicated to stamping out Protestant heresy*. Catherine attempted to restrict the Guise's power and steer France on a middle path between Catholics and Huguenots.

After the death of Francis in 1560, Catherine become regent* for her son Charles IX. She continued her efforts to resolve the growing religious conflict in France and issued an order, the Edict of January (1562), that allowed Protestants limited religious rights. Outright rejection of the edict by Catholics eventually led the country into a series of civil wars, often called the Wars of Religion (1562–1598).

In August 1572, between two of these conflicts, Catherine married her daughter Margaret of Valois to a Protestant leader, Henry of Navarre.

* **heresy** belief that is contrary to the doctrine of an established church

* **regent** person who acts on behalf of a monarch who is too young or unable to rule

He later ruled France as HENRY IV. Tragically, this effort to bring the two sides together was followed by the worst atrocity of the religious wars. An attempt on the life of a Huguenot leader had raised fears of a Protestant counterattack. To avoid a renewal of violence, Catherine decided to have some key Huguenots killed. But the plan turned into a bloodbath as French Catholics slaughtered thousands of Huguenots. This grim episode, known as the St. Bartholomew's Day massacre, gave Catherine a lasting reputation as a wicked queen.

After Charles's death in 1574, Catherine served as regent to her youngest son, Henry III. By then, however, her political power was in decline. Catherine's influence in politics was matched by her lasting impact on French culture. By commissioning architects to build several large palaces, Catherine launched the development of Paris as a city of grand monuments. She also brought a new Italian art form, the ballet, to France and collected rare manuscripts that eventually became part of France's national library. (*See also* **Guise-Lorraine Family; Valois Dynasty.**)

Catherine of Aragon

1485–1536
Queen of England

Catherine of Aragon was the first wife of HENRY VIII of England. The daughter of Spanish monarchs ISABELLA OF CASTILE and FERDINAND OF ARAGON, Catherine had received a typical female education in domestic arts. But she had also learned to read and write in Spanish and Latin. In 1501 she married Arthur, prince of Wales, who died a few months after the wedding. The young widow remained in England and was promised to Arthur's brother, Henry.

In 1509, in a double coronation ceremony, Henry wed Catherine and took the English throne. The first decade of their marriage was a happy one. During Henry's reign, Catherine represented Spanish interests in England as her father's unofficial ambassador. She was also a patron* of the arts. Their marriage began to falter, however, when Catherine failed to produce a male heir to the throne. In 1516, after several miscarriages, she gave birth to a daughter named Mary. However, Henry did not believe that Mary would be accepted as his successor and still wanted a son. In 1527 the king sought to annul* his marriage to Catherine and marry again in the hopes that a new wife would provide him with a male heir.

* **patron** supporter or financial sponsor of an artist or writer

* **annul** to declare legally invalid

Catherine wanted to protect her daughter's inheritance, and protested Henry's actions. Even after the annulment had been approved and she was no longer queen, Catherine continued to fight the decision. Henry eventually had a son, who ruled England as Edward VI. But on Edward's death in 1553, Catherine's daughter took the throne as MARY I. (*See also* **England; Queens and Queenship.**)

Catholic Church

See *Catholic Reformation and Counter-Reformation; Christianity; Clergy; Popes and Papacy.*

Catholic Reformation and Counter-Reformation

Scholars use the terms *Catholic Reformation* and *Counter-Reformation* to identify the changes in the Roman Catholic Church that occurred in the 1400s and 1500s. The phrase *Catholic Reformation* generally refers to the efforts at reform that began in the late Middle Ages and continued throughout the Renaissance. *Counter-Reformation* means the steps the Catholic Church took to oppose the growth of Protestantism in the 1500s.

See color plate 10, vol. 2

CATHOLIC REFORMATION

Toward the end of the Middle Ages, many people became unhappy with the behavior of high-ranking officials in the Catholic Church. At the same time, many Christians were searching for new ways to express their devotion to God. Their concerns triggered a movement for reform.

Complaints about church officials were widespread in the 1400s. Some of the most common charges were that church officials ignored church laws; that popes were corrupt; that cardinals lived in luxury; and that bishops did not reside within their dioceses*. Several councils in the 1400s and early 1500s attempted to address these problems. However, many officials—especially the popes—did not support reforms.

* **diocese** geographical area under the authority of a bishop

Meanwhile, many Christians craved better ways of expressing their faith. In the Netherlands, a movement called the DEVOTIO MODERNA encouraged people to form religious communities like those within the early Christian church. Mystics* recorded their experiences of an intimate union with God. Humanists* like Desiderius ERASMUS called for changes in the way the Catholic faith was taught, studied, and practiced.

* **mystic** believer in the idea of a direct, personal union with the divine

* **humanist** Renaissance expert in the humanities (the languages, literature, history, and speech and writing techniques of ancient Greece and Rome)

COUNTER-REFORMATION

In 1517 a German monk named Martin LUTHER challenged the Roman Catholic Church on many points of doctrine. For example, he argued that only the grace of God could save people from punishment after death and that human actions could not lead to salvation. He also based his theology* on the Bible rather than on the traditions and practices of the church. Luther's actions marked the beginning of the Protestant Reformation*. The rapid growth of Protestantism alarmed Catholics, and they demanded that church leaders deal with the situation.

* **theology** study of the nature of God and of religion

* **Protestant Reformation** religious movement that began in the 1500s as a protest against certain practices of the Roman Catholic Church and eventually led to the establishment of a variety of Protestant churches

The Council of Trent. After many delays, Pope Paul III called bishops and religious scholars together at the Council of Trent. The council, which held three sessions between 1545 and 1563, had two central tasks. The first was to address Protestant teachings that questioned the Roman Catholic Church. The pope considered this issue the council's highest priority. The second was to reform the church, especially the papacy*. The council's internal conflicts made these difficult tasks nearly impossible.

* **papacy** office and authority of the pope

In the painting *Fishing for Souls,* Adriaen van de Venne illustrated the divisions among Christians during the Renaissance. In the picture, Protestants on the left bank of the river and Catholics on the right side vie for the souls in the middle.

The council responded to Protestant teachings by affirming traditional Catholic beliefs. It addressed Luther's Bible-based theology by stating that Christians should base their religious views both on the Bible and on the spiritual authority of the Catholic Church. After discussing Luther's teachings on salvation, the council announced that God's grace was the most important factor, but that humans have some responsibility for their own salvation. The council also defended the Catholic position on other questions of theology.

The council also made efforts to reform church offices. It passed new laws requiring bishops to live in their dioceses and pastors to live in their parishes. In addition, it required each bishop to operate a seminary, a school to train future priests, in his diocese. However, the pope's representatives in the council blocked any attempts to reform the papacy. In fact, the papacy ended up with even more power when it became responsible for interpreting and enforcing the council's new laws.

The Papacy. Popes continued to take the lead in fighting the spread of Protestantism throughout the 1500s. In 1559 Pope Paul IV became the first pope to publish an Index of Prohibited Books, a list of books Catholics were not allowed to read without the permission of a bishop. When religious wars broke out in Europe in the mid-1500s, popes began to supply Catholic armies with troops and weapons, as well as spiritual support, in their battles against Protestant states. Realizing that the Protestants challenged their power, many Catholics stopped criticizing the pope in a show of unity. Pope Sixtus V (ruled 1585–1590) took this opportunity to strengthen his curia, the body that helped him govern the church.

The papacy also became more visible in Catholic teachings. Before the Reformation, Catholic catechisms* did not mention the papacy. Most European Christians probably had no idea that the pope was an important part of their religion. When Protestants began to challenge the pope's authority, the Catholic Church quickly reformed its catechisms to make the pope part of the definition of the church. Catholics began to define themselves as papists, followers of the pope.

* **catechism** handbook of religious teachings

Local Authorities. Important as the pope was, local authorities had a much greater effect on individual Catholics. By the end of the 1500s, high church officials had formed partnerships with the monarchs in Catholic countries. Local bishops also assumed stronger roles in their religious communities. The most important of these men was Carlo Borromeo, the archbishop of Milan. Borromeo studied the decrees of the Council of Trent and published his own set of rules and regulations, known as *Acts of the Church of Milan* (1582). This influential book established codes of conduct for both Catholic clergy and laypeople*.

* **laypeople** those who are not members of the clergy

Keeping the Faith. Reform-minded Catholics were committed to fighting ignorance and superstition among their members. This battle took many forms. During the late 1500s, bishops and pastors began to give more attention to their sermons than ever before. Humanism* played a strong role in this golden age of Catholic preaching, promoting a belief in the power of the spoken word. Religious orders such as the Jesuits* established networks of schools for boys, which taught both Catholicism and humanist studies.

* **humanism** Renaissance cultural movement promoting the study of the humanities (the languages, literature, and history of ancient Greece and Rome) as a guide to living

* **Jesuit** belonging to a Roman Catholic religious order founded by St. Ignatius Loyola and approved in 1540

Catholics worked to spread their beliefs in the 1500s. In new "Schools of Christian Doctrine," Catholic laypeople used the catechism to teach boys and girls the basics of their religion. Before the Protestant Reformation, the schools' goal was to instruct students about how to practice their religion. By the end of the 1500s, however, the schools were teaching students how to understand and defend their Catholic beliefs. Overseas, large numbers of Catholic missionaries tried to bring their faith to cultures in newly discovered lands—by force if necessary.

The Catholic Church strengthened its identity by showing a renewed interest in its traditions, especially those that Protestants did not share. Some religious orders doubled in size between 1540 and 1700, and new orders sprang up at the same time. The new male orders built some of Europe's most beautiful Catholic churches. Church officials and Catholic royalty commissioned religious artworks. Catholic scholars revived scholasticism, a movement that blended Christian teachings with ancient philosophy. Devotion to the saints regained popularity, and more Catholics took up the old practice of making pilgrimages, or journeys to sacred places.

Power of the Pen

Biographies of saints and books that praised devout lifestyles were powerful tools in the Catholic Reformation. Spain produced some of the most popular Catholic writers, including Francisco de Osuna and the great Christian mystics Teresa of Ávila and John of the Cross. During the 1600s France became the major source of books on devotion. The best known among these are Francis de Sale's *Introduction to the Devout Life* (1609) and *Treatise on the Love of God* (1616).

Women and the Church. In the late 1500s, women took increasingly active roles in the church. One of the most important was TERESA OF ÁVILA, who founded many convents and reformed the Carmelite order of nuns. Another was Barbe-Jeanne Acarie, who helped bring the

Carmelites to France and who used her house as a religious meeting place.

French nuns began to minister to the public in the 1600s. One of their most important activities was the organization of schools for girls. Other nuns worked outside their convents nursing the sick and running hospitals. (*See also* **Censorship; Councils; Popes and Papacy; Protestant Reformation; Religious Literature; Religious Orders; Religious Thought; Trent, Council of.**)

Cavendish, Margaret

ca. 1624–1673
English writer

* **humanist** referring to a Renaissance cultural movement promoting the study of the humanities (the languages, literature, and history of ancient Greece and Rome) as a guide to living

* **genre** literary form

Englishwoman Margaret Cavendish, the first Duchess of Newcastle, was one of the most notable women writers of her time. During her lifetime she received both praise and criticism for her writings, which focused largely on the role of women in society. However, her work did not gain serious scholarly attention until the late 1900s.

Born into a wealthy family in southeastern England, Cavendish never received any humanist* education. As a young woman she served at the court of Queen Henrietta Maria. When the English Civil War (1642–1646) threatened to destroy the English monarchy, Cavendish fled to Paris with the queen. There she married and began her writing career. Her first book, *Poems and Fancies,* appeared in 1653. In the years that followed, Cavendish produced many works, including plays, poetry, essays, and letters. Her writing spanned more genres* than that of any other female, and most male, writers of her time.

Cavendish held complex and sometimes contradictory opinions on the role of women in society. She criticized their inferior social and legal position and the fact that they seldom received serious education. However, she also portrayed women as weak and overemotional. She held similarly opposing views about the English monarchy, which she supported yet criticized in her letters and essays.

Cavendish had many critics, both during her lifetime and afterward. Many considered her writings unpolished. They also noted that she often wrote on subjects that she had little knowledge of, notably science. Many critics objected strongly to her views on the education of women. People of her own time often mocked her work, calling her "Mad Madge." However, supporters of Cavendish have pointed to the originality and quality of some of her work and her strong support for women's rights. (*See also* **English Language and Literature.**)

Cellini, Benvenuto

1500–1571
Italian goldsmith, sculptor, and writer

* **patron** supporter or financial sponsor of an artist or writer

Benvenuto Cellini's life was filled with conflict and controversy and included two artistic careers. His first career as a goldsmith and sculptor ended when he fell out of favor with his patron*, Cosimo I de' MEDICI. This withdrawal of support led the artist to lay down his chisel and start a new career as a writer.

Early Artistic Career. Cellini came from a family of respected arti-

Benvenuto Cellini's gold salt dish is considered a masterpiece of Renaissance gold work. Despite its small scale, the piece clearly shows the mythological characters of Earth and Neptune along with figures representing Morning, Day, Evening, Night, and the four seasons.

* **artisan** skilled worker or craftsperson

sans* in FLORENCE. At age 13 he began training with Florentine goldsmiths, but three years later was forced to flee the city because of his involvement in a brawl. He worked in Bologna, Pisa, and ROME before moving back to Florence in the early 1520s. After a violent conflict with other goldsmiths in 1523, he left once again for Rome. There he worked for many important nobles and members of the clergy until the city was invaded in 1527.

After another period of wandering, Cellini returned to Rome in 1529 and entered the service of Pope Clement VII. Among the pieces he created for his new patron were two silver medals. After Clement VII died, Cellini was accused of murdering a fellow goldsmith. The new pope, Paul III, pardoned Cellini and hired him to work on a gold coin of St. Paul. Despite the pope's support, Cellini had to leave Rome in 1535 to avoid arrest. Over the next two years he traveled in Italy and France, returning to Rome only briefly. During this time he created a portrait medal for an Italian nobleman and perhaps one for the king of France. He went back to Rome in 1537, where he was arrested and jailed the next year. He soon escaped. By 1540 he had returned to France.

* **relief** type of sculpture in which figures are raised slightly from a flat surface

* **Mannerist** referring to an artistic style of the 1500s characterized by vivid colors and exaggeration, such as elongated figures in complex poses

Work in France and Florence. During his stay in France, Cellini took on many projects for the French king FRANCIS I. One of the first pieces was a bas-relief* for the king's chateau in Fontainebleau, based on a local legend involving a hunting dog and a water nymph. In the bas-relief, Cellini gave the water nymph long, elegant arms and legs in the Mannerist* style. However, the other figures—dogs, boars, and a stag—are extremely realistic and show a goldsmith's eye for detail.

While in France, Cellini created a sculpted saltcellar (salt dish), the most celebrated work in gold from the Renaissance. In this piece, the main characters of Earth and Neptune are joined by figures representing Morning, Day, Evening, Night, the four seasons, and animal figures.

Despite their reduced scale, the figures have the power of much larger monumental sculpture.

Cellini had to leave Paris in 1545 when he was accused of stealing from the king. He returned again to Florence, where he found a patron in Duke Cosimo I. The duke commissioned him to create a bronze statue of the Greek hero Perseus holding the head of the monster Medusa. Cellini created a powerful statue of *Perseus,* who symbolizes Florence's civic pride and Cosimo's leadership. The figure's graceful pose shows the influence of Mannerism. The base of the statue includes fine detailing that reflects Cellini's experience as a goldsmith.

During the same period, Cellini began a bronze bust of Cosimo that captured the duke's personality. With its deep-set eyes and windswept locks of hair, the work conveyed a sense of Cosimo's nervous energy. Cellini wanted this piece to outshine a marble bust by Bandinelli, a rival artist. In the end, the duke chose the more traditional image by Bandinelli.

Cellini took on a number of other projects in the following years, but the completion of the *Perseus* in 1533 marked the high point of his career as an artist. However, after falling out of favor with Cosimo in the late 1550s, he abandoned the fine arts. Today, experts view Cellini as one of Italy's greatest Mannerist artists.

Cellini the Writer. In the late 1550s, Cellini claimed that "everyone who has to his credit ... great achievements ... ought to write the story of his own life." He decided to take his own advice, though he worried that others might view his efforts as excess pride.

In his autobiography, Cellini presents himself as the leading artistic figure of the 1500s. He describes how kings honored and favored him and discusses rival artists as uncultured, talentless fools. Cellini boasts, "I outdo many rivals and can equal the ones who outdid me." Although harsh with his critics, Cellini writes honestly about his crimes, murders, and affairs.

Cellini's autobiography was not published until 1728. Called *Vita,* meaning "life" or "autobiography," it was a huge success. It presents the author as a talented hero forced to work for a petty nobleman who is "more like a businessman than a duke." With its lively prose and its focus on the struggles of the hero to find meaning in life, some critics have called it the forerunner to the modern novel.

Besides *Vita,* Cellini published two technical books, *On Goldsmithing* and *On Sculpting.* They mix discussions of artistic techniques with details of the author's life. Cellini also wrote a collection of unremarkable poetry and some songs. (*See also* **Art; Art in Italy; Biography and Autobiography; Coins and Medals; Decorative Arts; Italian Language and Literature; Medici, House of; Patronage; Popes and Papacy.**)

Celtis, Conrad

1459–1508
German poet

* **humanist** Renaissance expert in the humanities (the languages, literature, history, and speech and writing techniques of ancient Greece and Rome)

Poet and scholar Conrad Celtis was one of the most important German humanists* of the Renaissance. As a young man, he received a degree in liberal arts at the University of Cologne. He then moved to the University of Heidelberg, drawn there by the presence of noted humanist Rudolf AGRICOLA. He went on to teach poetry at several universities. In 1486 he published his first work, *The Art of Making Verses and of Poems.*

In 1487 Celtis began a ten-year period of travel. He visited several cities in Italy, where he had contact with other humanists, and studied science in Cracow, Poland. Eventually he settled in Vienna, Austria. There he persuaded ruler MAXIMILIAN I to establish a new college that would promote humanist studies. He also founded several humanist societies. Modeled after the ACADEMIES of Italy, these groups gave members a sense of belonging to the larger humanist movement.

Celtis's most important work, and the only major one published during his lifetime, was *Four Books of Love Poetry* (1502). Written in Latin, the books were not only a collection of love poems, but also a geographical description of Germany. Many critics called them the most original contribution of German humanism to Renaissance literature. Celtis also edited and published several texts about German history and culture. (*See also* **German Language and Literature; Humanism; Poetry.**)

Censorship

* **Protestant Reformation** religious movement that began in the 1500s as a protest against certain practices of the Roman Catholic Church and eventually led to the establishment of a variety of Protestant churches

* **dissent** to oppose or disagree with established belief

* **classical** in the tradition of ancient Greece and Rome

* **pagan** referring to ancient religions that worshiped many gods, or more generally, to any non-Christian religion

* **humanist** Renaissance expert in the humanities (the languages, literature, history, and speech and writing techniques of ancient Greece and Rome)

At various times in history, the church and the state have tried to suppress ideas they considered dangerous. In early Renaissance Europe, most censorship was political. Government officials often punished those who criticized them. However, rulers and churches did not usually censor works on the basis of their religious or moral content until the 1500s, when the Protestant Reformation* divided Europe politically and religiously. By 1600, religious and political censorship in Europe was stronger than it had been a century earlier. However, it never totally stopped the spread of dissenting* views.

Censorship in the Early Renaissance. During the 1400s, the main question of censorship involved classical* literature. Many people wondered whether readers should be exposed to stories that praised the pagan* gods and glorified their immoral behavior. Humanists* argued that everyone should read the classics. They believed that the immoral behavior in the stories was not to be taken literally. In fact, they thought that the stories would inspire readers to be more virtuous. Aside from removing some racy passages from books for children, the humanists did not see a reason for censorship.

Humanists and other readers took a similar, hands-off approach to more modern works that people might read for pleasure. Books such as the *Decameron,* a collection of stories by Italian writer Giovanni BOCCACCIO, contained a great deal of improper behavior, including open sex and adultery. In some texts, nuns and monks also ignored their

*** chastity** purity or virginity

vows of chastity*. There was even some pornographic literature at this time. No one made attempts to censor these books until the late 1500s.

At the same time, political censorship was widespread. People did not dare to criticize their rulers openly. Even if the government did not specifically forbid such criticism, it might view such writings as treason and punish their authors. In order to speak out against their own leaders, people had to publish their work anonymously or leave the territory that their government controlled. Political censorship grew stronger in the late 1500s, as governments tried to stop the spread of pamphlets attacking rulers and promoting rebellion.

Philosophical Differences. Around 1500 some Italian philosophers set off a debate about whether the church should censor certain philosophical ideas. The Roman Catholic Church taught that the soul was immortal, but these thinkers claimed that reason alone could not prove this idea. In 1513 the Catholic Church declared that the soul was immortal and set up its own guidelines for any teachings on the subject. The church left philosophers to discuss other ideas freely, as long as they did not claim that their views disproved church teachings.

The trial of astronomer Galileo GALILEI in 1633 is a famous example of philosophical censorship during the Renaissance. Galileo had stated that the Earth revolved around the Sun, contradicting church teachings that held that the Sun traveled around the Earth. The church brought Galileo to trial for teaching that his Sun-centered system was a physical truth. As part of his defense, Galileo claimed that his system was only a theory, not a physical truth. However, the religious leaders were not satisfied with his argument. They made him give up his system, they forbade him to write about it, and they banned his existing writings on the subject.

Religious Censorship. After the Protestant Reformation, both Protestants and Catholics used the printing press as a means to spread their views. Therefore, both sides tried to control the press. In 1559 the pope established the INDEX OF PROHIBITED BOOKS, the main tool of censorship in the Catholic Church. The index was a list of authors and titles that Catholics could not print, read, or even keep. It also listed books that contained some errors but were still mostly acceptable. Catholics could own and read these books if the offensive parts were removed. The index included rules for publishing new books and for judging books from foreign presses. It banned books with ideas the church considered heretical* or counter to Christian morality.

*** heretical** contrary to the doctrine of an established church

Although Protestants did not publish one list of forbidden books, each Protestant state created its own censorship policies. They banned the publication, importing, and ownership of Catholic works—and sometimes the works of other Protestants. Protestant censors also prohibited works that they considered immoral.

Both Protestant and Catholic churches and states also censored the material that was taught in their universities and preached in their churches. Scholars often had to accept changes from censors before they

could publish their works. However, although Catholic and Protestant states could block the publication of forbidden works, they had less success preventing people from reading and owning them. Book smuggling became widespread during the Renaissance.

The Play's the Thing

In Elizabethan England, some Protestants viewed plays as a threat to peace and moral order. In 1559 Elizabeth I required all plays to be licensed by town officials. Plays could not receive licenses if they dealt with matters of religion or the government. Eventually, the crown created the office of the Master of Revels to control drama in England. The master had the authority to license acting companies, to censor and license plays, and to charge a fee for his services. He generally blocked plays that contained offensive language and those that presented living rulers on stage.

Censorship in England. In the 1500s, power in England shifted back and forth between Protestant and Catholic rulers. When HENRY VIII formed a new English church in the 1530s, Parliament outlawed writings by European Protestants, whose views contradicted Henry's traditional religious doctrines. It also required that books printed in England be approved and licensed by the government. When EDWARD VI took the throne in 1547, he called a halt to censorship. The result was a brief explosion of all kinds of printing in England. However, Edward became concerned about immorality in printed material. In 1551, he proclaimed that all texts needed to have the approval of the government before printing.

When MARY I came to power in 1553, she ended Protestant reforms and brought Catholicism back to England. In 1555 she issued a proclamation forbidding Protestant writings. It gave bishops and local officials the authority "to enter into the house or houses, closets, and secret places of every person" to find Protestant texts. Many people opposed Mary's policies. In response, Parliament expanded existing laws against treason to forbid all writings that threatened or criticized the monarchy.

During the reign of ELIZABETH I (1558–1603), Parliament established a national Protestant church in England and placed it under the control of the monarch. Under Elizabeth, the government continued to censor all criticism of the monarchy. Elizabeth used the Court of High Commission to control opposition to her religious policies, including printed criticism. The court became responsible for approving works before they went to press. It also had the authority to approve requests for establishing new printing presses. However, another organization—the London Company of Stationers—did the real work of licensing presses.

A royal charter created the London Company of Stationers in 1557 and made it the only legal printing company in England. The company had the authority to shut down illegal printers. It benefited enormously from this monopoly*. In return, it agreed not to print texts that attacked the government. It also required official approval before printing texts, especially religious, political, and foreign works. By stopping other presses in England and by allowing itself to be censored, the London Company of Stationers helped the government keep unwanted works out of print. (*See also* **Catholic Reformation and Counter-Reformation; Drama, English; Inquisition; Printing and Publishing; Protestant Reformation.**)

* **monopoly** exclusive right to engage in a particular type of business

Ceramics

See *Decorative Arts.*

Cervantes Saavedra, Miguel de

1547–1616
Spanish author

Miguel de Cervantes, one of the most celebrated writers of the Renaissance, led a life of danger and intrigue. On more than one occasion Cervantes almost lost his life, but he lived to turn his often hair-raising escapades into literary achievements. The most famous of these is his novel *Don Quixote,* a classic of world literature.

A Troubled Life. Cervantes was born in the university town of Alcalá de Henares. His father, a surgeon, suffered from money troubles, and the family moved constantly in search of a decent living. As a result, Cervantes received no formal university training. However, his family's frequent travels exposed him to all parts of Spanish society.

When Cervantes was in his early 20s, a late-night fight led to a warrant for his arrest and for the removal of his right hand. In 1569 Cervantes fled to Italy, the center of Renaissance culture. His experience of Italy greatly influenced his growth as an artist. Cervantes enlisted in the Spanish army in 1570 and lost the use of his left hand in the battle of Lepanto a year later.

Traveling from Italy to Spain in 1575, Cervantes was kidnapped by Muslim pirates and sold into captivity in Algiers. The pirates mistakenly thought Cervantes was a person of some importance, and they set his ransom so high that it took five years before he could return to Spain. Cervantes described his ordeal in *The Commerce of Algiers,* his first literary work. This document, written shortly before he left Algiers, describes his heroic behavior and loyalty to Christianity during his captivity. It also relates his four unsuccessful attempts to escape and his astonishing ability to avoid punishment for them.

Back in Spain, Cervantes tried to use his heroic experiences to secure a comfortable position in the Spanish government. When this effort failed, he took a job collecting supplies for the Spanish ARMADA, a fleet of ships sent to attack England in 1588. He also worked as a tax collector. His duties took him all over Spain and brought him into contact with people from all levels of Spanish society. He made little money, however, and twice he was sent to prison for irregularities in his accounts.

In 1584 Cervantes married Catalina Salazar Palacios, who came from an area known as La Mancha. He continued to seek out government positions, usually without success. In 1601 King PHILIP II moved the Spanish court from Madrid to Valladolid, and Cervantes set up a household there with his wife, his two sisters, his illegitimate* daughter, and his niece. At one point the entire family was jailed after the murder of a man in the street outside their house. When the king moved Spain's capital back to Madrid in 1606, Cervantes followed. He spent the rest of his life living and writing in Madrid.

* **illegitimate** refers to a child born outside of marriage

Literary Accomplishments. During the 1580s Cervantes began writing for the theater. He hoped to create an official form of Spanish drama, but instead that accomplishment fell to the writer Lope de VEGA. However, Cervantes did produce several notable plays, including *The Siege of Numantia* and *The Business of Algiers,* both written in the 1580s.

Miguel de Cervantes used his own adventures as a basis for his writings. His most famous work, *Don Quixote,* is the tale of a madman who decides to imitate the life of a heroic knight. This piece has become a classic for generations of readers.

* **romance** adventure story of the Middle Ages, the forerunner of the modern novel

* **epic** long poem about the adventures of a hero

Cervantes's greatest achievements are his works of fiction. In his major writings Cervantes challenged the accepted literary and cultural standards of his day. For example, two of his *Exemplary Tales,* a collection of short stories published in 1613, are told from more than one point of view, forcing readers to question their own relationship with reality. He also broke with tradition by portraying strong female characters, showing respect for Muslim societies, and mocking certain practices of the Roman Catholic Church.

Cervantes's masterpiece, *Don Quixote,* tells the story of an unknown nobleman who, at the age of 50, suddenly decides to pattern his life after the romances* of the Middle Ages. The novel appeared in two parts. In part one, published in 1605, Quixote creates a new existence for himself as an adventurous knight. Accompanied by his sidekick, Sancho Panza, he commits himself to fighting evil and saving women in a modern world far removed from the Middle Ages. The first half of *Don Quixote* established its author as a literary success. In part two, published ten years later, Quixote suffers many defeats and is forced to face the real world. Eventually he returns to his village and dies a loyal Christian.

Cervantes combined an astonishing variety of literary forms in *Don Quixote,* including the epic*, the romance, and the Spanish ballad tradition. The book also blurred the line between history and fiction. For centuries literary critics have puzzled over how to interpret the novel. Some have described the title character as a threat to society, while others have viewed him as a misunderstood genius. Most readers see the novel as contrasting an ideal world with reality. The many different interpretations of the book reveal how complex and enduring a work it is. The novel also inspired the well-known musical *Man of La Mancha* (1965).

Cervantes was one of only a few Spaniards who followed the ideals and values of the Renaissance. In many ways, he was a man ahead of his time. His highly original writings question traditional values and point the way toward modern Western culture. (*See also* **Chivalry; Spanish Language and Literature.**)

Charles I

1600–1649
King of Great Britain

* **authoritarian** referring to strong leadership with unrestricted powers

Charles I was the second king to rule the united kingdoms of Scotland and England. However, his authoritarian* policies resulted in a break with Parliament, the nation's elected government. This division ultimately led to a revolution that toppled the English monarchy.

Early Life. Charles I was the second son of King James VI of Scotland and Anne, princess of Denmark. When his father assumed the English throne in 1603 as JAMES I, young Charles was left behind in Scotland. A sickly child, Charles never received much attention from his parents, and his older brother, Henry, teased him mercilessly. When Henry died of typhoid fever in 1612, Charles became the heir to the throne. However, his father continued to ignore him, and his mother died in

1619. His only close friend was George Villiers, one of the king's gentleman companions.

In 1623 Charles went to Spain to propose marriage to Donna Maria, sister of the Spanish king. The offer was pointedly refused, and Charles angrily returned to England. The trip, however, had a lasting influence on the English prince. It exposed him to the work of many noted artists, such as TITIAN, MICHELANGELO, and RAPHAEL. It also left him bitter toward Spain.

King and Parliament. Charles succeeded to the throne on March 27, 1625. For the next three years, his friend George Villiers, now duke of Buckingham, dominated English politics. Together they planned a number of military expeditions against Spain and France. In 1625 they attacked a fleet of Spanish treasure ships, seeking revenge for the humiliation they had experienced in Spain two years earlier. In 1627 Buckingham led an expedition against France. Both campaigns ended in failure.

To pay for these military adventures, the king asked Parliament to vote for new taxes. The House of Commons refused to do so unless Charles dismissed Buckingham. Charles responded by breaking up Parliament and collecting the taxes anyway, triggering a constitutional crisis. In July 1628 Parliament passed the Petition of Right, a statement of grievances against the king. Charles grudgingly accepted the petition, but relations between the king and Parliament continued to decline.

In August 1628 an insane army officer assassinated Buckingham, who was about to lead a fleet against the French. The loss devastated Charles. Moreover, the fleet was soundly defeated, further poisoning the relationship between the king and Parliament. In March 1629 the House of Commons defied Charles's order to adjourn and passed several resolutions opposing decisions that the king had made. Outraged by this open resistance to his authority, Charles became determined to rule on his own.

Personal Rule. The years from 1629 to 1640 formed Charles's so-called Personal Rule. In many ways, the king retreated from political life during this period. He became deeply attached to his wife, the former French princess Henrietta Maria, and the couple produced several children.

Charles also used this time to build one of the finest art collections the English court had ever seen. A collector from an early age, Charles amassed a superb collection of paintings by Italian Renaissance artists, including Titian, CORREGGIO, Raphael, and Andrea MANTEGNA. Charles often used diplomats, artists, and agents to obtain pieces of art for him. Foreign rulers and diplomats, as well politicians and people attached to the English court, often gave the king artworks to win his favor.

Charles's collection not only revealed his fine taste in art, it also shed light on his personality and policies. The glory and power of English monarchs are common themes in the works. Charles appears as a hero in several pieces. Paintings by Peter Paul RUBENS and Anthony van Dyck reinforce the ideas of divine right* and absolute rule.

* **divine right** idea that a monarch receives the right to rule directly from God

Civil War. By 1639 Charles's hold on his kingdom was weakening. He imposed several new taxes, which were unpopular, but it was his religious policies that truly infuriated his subjects. In 1637 Charles introduced a new prayer book into Scotland, which was largely Calvinist*. The book, which most viewed as close to Roman Catholicism, led to riots. Hundreds of thousands of Scots vowed to fight to keep their own religion and resist the power of English bishops.

* **Calvinist** member of a Protestant church founded by John Calvin

Charles became convinced that the Scots were determined to fight not only the Church of England but also the crown. Vowing not to give in to their demands, the king fought two wars against the Scots. The First Bishops' War of 1639 forced Charles to call the "Short Parliament," which lasted from April to May of 1640. After his defeat in the Second Bishops' War that same year, he called the "Long Parliament," which opened that November.

For over a year, the king and Parliament tried to compromise. Parliament wanted to control the crown, but the king would accept no limits on his power. In January 1642, Charles led soldiers to the House of Commons to arrest the leaders of his opposition. The members escaped, but the king's action badly damaged his relations with Parliament. Both sides began arming for war.

Charles declared war against his rebellious subjects in August 1642. The two sides clashed several times between 1642 and 1644, and Charles won several victories. However, the rebel forces—led by parliamentary statesman Oliver Cromwell—decisively defeated the king's army at the Battle of Naseby in June 1645. The fighting continued for a year, but in May 1646 Charles surrendered to the Scots.

For several years Charles bargained with the Scots, the army, and Parliament, hoping to gain control by dividing them. Instead he produced a second civil war, more brutal than the first. In December 1648, the army arrested Charles and brought him to London. Found guilty of treason, Charles was executed on January 30, 1649. (*See also* **England; Monarchy; Scotland.**)

Charles V

1500–1558
King of Spain and Holy Roman Emperor

Charles V became the most powerful monarch of his day, ruling over an empire that included what is now Spain, Germany, the Netherlands, parts of Italy and central Europe, and large areas in the Americas. He spent much of his reign trying to reform the Roman Catholic Church and fighting the two greatest threats to its power: Islam and Protestantism.

Rise to Power. Charles's father was Archduke Philip I of Austria, son of Holy Roman Emperor* MAXIMILIAN I. His mother, Joanna of Castile, was the daughter of Spanish monarchs Ferdinand and Isabella. From his illustrious family, Charles inherited a large number of titles and lands—a legacy that would bring him both power and frustration during his reign.

* **Holy Roman Emperor** ruler of the Holy Roman Empire, a political body in central Europe composed of several states that existed until 1806

Charles had little contact with his parents. His father died when Charles was six, and his mother suffered from mental illness. The young

prince grew up at the court in Brussels, then part of BURGUNDY, under the guidance of his aunt, MARGARET OF AUSTRIA. One of his tutors later became Pope Adrian VI.

Charles inherited the Netherlands and other territories in Burgundy upon his father's death in 1506. When his grandfather FERDINAND OF ARAGON died ten years later, Charles also acquired the throne of Spain and the Spanish lands in Italy. In 1519 Maximilian I died, and Charles saw the chance to add Holy Roman Emperor to his titles. Despite opposition from the kings of France and England, Charles won election as emperor unanimously—due in part to large bribes to the electors. These combined titles placed Charles in control of an enormous European empire.

Charles saw himself as the leader of the Christian world. He hoped to drive Muslim invaders from Europe and crush the Protestant challenge to Catholicism. However, his Spanish subjects wanted him to focus on their problems rather than spending time and money crusading far from home. In 1520 the towns of Castile revolted, leading Charles to put down the uprising by force. This rebellion was only the first of many social and military conflicts the young ruler would face.

Struggles for Control. Charles's rise to power occurred at the same time that Martin LUTHER was leading the Protestant Reformation* in Europe. Although strongly opposed to Luther, Charles supported reforms within the Catholic Church. But the papacy* resisted the emperor's calls for reform and feared his political power. Pope Clement VII struck back at Charles by signing an alliance with France's king FRANCIS I, who hoped to acquire Spanish territories in Italy. Charles responded by supporting an English invasion of France and a rebellion by the French nobleman Charles de BOURBON.

* **Protestant Reformation** religious movement that began in the 1500s as a protest against certain practices of the Roman Catholic Church and eventually led to the establishment of a variety of Protestant churches

* **papacy** office and authority of the pope

Both the invasion and the rebellion failed, but Charles's forces captured the French king at the Battle of Pavia in 1525. Charles forced Francis to give up French claims to Naples and Milan as well as its holdings in Burgundy. Once released, however, Francis refused to honor the terms of the surrender and the war resumed. Charles's troops sacked* Rome in 1527, taking Pope Clement VII prisoner. Since Charles was not there, it is not clear how responsible he was for the brutal destruction of the city. Charles and the pope finally signed a truce in 1530.

* **sack** to loot a captured city

Charles had also hoped to use his military might against German princes who had become Protestants. However, the forces of the Ottoman Turks* were putting pressure on Austria, and Charles needed the Protestant princes to help him fight the Turks. After defeating Turkish attempts to seize Vienna in 1532, Charles attacked and captured the Ottoman port of Tunis in North Africa. However, he and his Christian allies were unable to take the city of Algiers or to stop Turkish pirates operating in the Mediterranean. To make matters worse, the French were helping the Ottoman cause. In 1544 Charles finally convinced France to make peace and end its support to the Turks. A truce with the Ottomans came soon afterward.

* **Ottoman Turks** Turkish followers of Islam who founded the Ottoman Empire in the 1300s; the empire eventually included large areas of eastern Europe, the Middle East, and northern Africa

Charles V ruled both Spain and the Holy Roman Empire, making him perhaps the most powerful ruler of his day. This painting by the Venetian master Titian shows the emperor in full armor, riding into battle against Protestant forces in Germany.

The break in fighting provided an opportunity for a council to reform church practices. The Council of TRENT in 1545 addressed many of the abuses that had caused Protestants to reject the Catholic Church. Meanwhile, Charles took this chance to attack the Schmalkaldic League, an alliance of Protestant princes in Germany. He defeated the league in 1547 and compelled them to accept the Interim of Augsburg, a religious compromise between Catholic and Protestant practices.

Unfortunately for Charles, his victory was short lived. The Turks, the French, and the Protestant princes all went to war against the emperor again. In 1552 he had to flee from the city of Innsbruck to avoid being captured by the new French king Henry II. The French also seized several cities of the Holy Roman Empire in Germany. Charles tried to put his son PHILIP II on the English throne by marrying him to England's queen MARY I. The English accepted the marriage, but they refused to crown Philip as king.

Building an Empire

Although he failed to achieve many of his goals in Europe, Charles V oversaw great Spanish ventures overseas. He encouraged the Spanish explorers who conquered large portions of the Americas and sponsored the plans of Ferdinand Magellan to sail around the world. Magellan and many of his crew died along the way, but one of his ships managed to complete the first round-the-world voyage. Charles helped build a global empire for Spain, and under the rule of his son Philip II the country was a major world power.

Frustrated by setbacks on all sides, Charles decided to abdicate*. He gave the Netherlands and Spain to his son Philip and yielded the title of Holy Roman Emperor to his brother Frederick. He assembled a group of close friends and courtiers and retired to a villa* in Spain, where he died in 1558. During his life Charles had successfully kept the Ottoman Turks out of western Europe and protected Spain's interests in Italy. However, he was unable to pass his empire intact to his son or to stop the spread of Protestantism in Europe.

Artistic Patronage. Charles was a great patron* of the arts, especially music. His chapel singers accompanied him on all his travels and stayed with him in his retirement. Charles also formed a chapel choir for his wife, Isabella of Portugal, and gave his son Philip a suite of musicians and composers for his twelfth birthday. The excellence of Charles's singers upheld the reputation of Flemish* music throughout the 1500s. His court also employed such famous composers as JOSQUIN DES PREZ.

Artists also benefited from Charles's patronage. He was a great admirer of the Venetian painter TITIAN, to whom he awarded a knighthood. Some of Titian's greatest works were produced for Charles, including his famous portrait of the emperor, *Charles V at the Battle of Mühlberg*. Charles also supported sculptors and brought a poet and a painter along on his campaign against Tunis.

Interestingly, Charles may have had the greatest impact on the course of Renaissance art with his troops' sack of Rome in 1527. At the time, Rome was the center of artistic activity and patronage in Italy. After the attack, the focus of patronage moved to Venice and other northern Italian cities. (*See also* **Austria; Catholic Reformation and Counter-Reformation; Councils; Habsburg Dynasty; Holy Roman Empire; Isabella of Castile; Music; Netherlands; Patronage; Popes and Papacy; Protestant Reformation; Revolts.**)

* **abdicate** to give up the throne voluntarily or under pressure
* **villa** luxurious country home and the land surrounding it
* **patron** supporter or financial sponsor of an artist or writer
* **Flemish** relating to Flanders, a region along the coasts of present-day Belgium, France, and the Netherlands

Châteaus and Villas

The terms *château* and *villa* refer to two different kinds of country residences built by European nobles and prominent citizens during the Renaissance. The château was a type of French castle dating from the Middle Ages. The early ones were fortresses, designed to withstand an armed attack, and Renaissance châteaus had traces of this military function. Villas, by contrast, served as rural retreats from the pressures of city living. They reflected a new appreciation for country life among the urban aristocracy*.

* **aristocracy** privileged upper classes of society; nobles or the nobility

Châteaus. Even the earliest châteaus combined a practical emphasis on defense with touches of comfort and elegance. By the Renaissance the military role of these buildings had declined, and many earlier castles were redesigned as country retreats.

Several wars between 1494 and 1559 brought French culture into close contact with Italy. The French court employed Italian artists and architects, whose ideas influenced the design of châteaus. The châteaus

built during the 1500s blended French Gothic* architecture with the styles of the Italian Renaissance. Francis I, who ruled France from 1515 to 1547, erected several important châteaus, including those at Blois and Chambord. Other French nobles also built impressive châteaus that combined elements of medieval* castle architecture, such as towers and moats, with Renaissance forms such as classical* columns and Italian staircases.

* **Gothic** style of architecture characterized by pointed arches and high, thin walls supported by flying buttresses

* **medieval** referring to the Middle Ages, a period that began around A.D. 400 and ended around 1400 in Italy and 1500 in the rest of Europe

* **classical** in the tradition of ancient Greece and Rome

Even without a military function, châteaus symbolized political power. During the 1600s, Cardinal Richelieu of France led a campaign to destroy fortified castles, which he saw as a threat to the authority of the French crown. However, French nobles continued to build new châteaus throughout the 1600s.

See color plate 10, vol. 1

Villas. The oldest Italian villas date from the 1400s. Early ones, such as the villas of the MEDICI family at Trebbio and Cafaggiolo, served as centers for collecting farm products to be transported to the city. These country estates ensured that the Medici urban palaces and their inhabitants would have a secure supply of food even during times of unrest or famine. A villa also served as a place of escape when disease broke out in the city.

The designs of early Italian villas often borrowed from older castles and forts. By the 1500s, however, villas began to reflect the Renaissance passion for classical style. Architects such as RAPHAEL and Donato BRAMANTE created designs based on ancient Roman models, such as the villa of the emperor Hadrian near Rome. This ancient structure influenced Raphael's Villa Madama and Bramante's addition to the Vatican Palace. Landscape and gardens also played an important role in villa design. The buildings were often laid out in a way that called attention to beautiful outside views.

Architect Andrea PALLADIO gained renown for his villa designs. His work joined elements of commonplace buildings with classical features. His designs varied widely according to the villa's function and its owner's social status. Palladio paid attention not only to the villa itself, but also to the design of stables, sheds, and other outer buildings. His designs remained extremely popular long past his lifetime. (*See also* **Architecture; Fortifications; Gardens; Palaces and Townhouses.**)

Childhood

Young people were important in the Renaissance primarily because there were so many of them. During that period, more than half the population of Europe was under age 25. Children were dependent on adults, who controlled their behavior and taught them the skills they would need in later life.

The Meaning of Childhood. Renaissance life before adulthood had three stages—infancy, childhood, and youth. Infants—children under seven years old—were the responsibility of women. After age seven, children were ready to begin learning from instruction. People general-

Renaissance children usually played in groups, as shown in the painting *Children's Games* (1560) by Pieter Brueghel the Elder. Games and horseplay were common, as were toys such as balls, sticks, and hoops.

ly saw age 14 as the end of childhood, but this age limit was not clear-cut. Some laws considered young people under age 14 to be capable of committing adult crimes. Many children started to work before age 14, and boys of 9 or even younger could be required to bear arms. Therefore, the line between childhood and youth was blurry. Youth ended with an event that changed a person's legal status, such as marriage.

Bringing Up Children. Renaissance children were powerless, completely under the control of adults. Adults believed that such control was necessary to tame children's natural wildness. To them, dealing with children was a battle of wills, and the only good outcome was for a child to submit to authority.

Renaissance adults also believed that children needed protection from the forces of evil, which usually meant sexuality. Except for the home, most institutions kept boys and girls apart. Yet children were often exposed to other undesirable behavior—such as coarse language, gambling, and excessive drinking—in their towns, villages, and homes.

Some historians see the strict control of children as a sign that their lives lacked warmth and affection. Others argue that most Renaissance parents loved and cared for their children. Many children had only one living parent. Others were orphans and lived under the care of sometimes reluctant relatives. Guardians sometimes took advantage of rich orphans. Children without relatives went to foundling homes, or orphanages.

Play was a common part of children's lives during the Renaissance. Toys from this period included balls, sticks, hoops, dolls, and marbles. Children also played games and engaged in horseplay. Most children played in groups rather than alone. Children from poor families, who lived in small houses, probably did most of their playing outdoors.

Education. Boys and girls started learning about religion in the

household at a very early age, often from women. In peasant families, children under seven might also learn to help around the house or look after younger children. In wealthy households, children usually had governesses* or tutors who saw to their early training and education. As in peasant households, a child's gender determined what he or she would learn. Girls studied needlework and household management, while boys learned horsemanship and hunting.

* **governess** woman employed to take charge of a child's upbringing and education

Between the ages of five and seven, fortunate children began formal schooling either inside or outside the home. The type and amount of education varied according to the family's economic and social status, the child's gender, the parents' expectations, and the availability of schooling. Children of the lower classes often became apprentices* to learn a trade. Parents made all the necessary arrangements with apprentice masters regarding their children's training.

* **apprentice** person bound by legal agreement to work for another for a specified period of time in return for instruction in a trade or craft

In Italy, most children continued to live with their parents during their education. Even apprentices usually worked for their own fathers or for artisans* in their hometowns. In northwestern Europe, by contrast, children of both town and country commonly left home for training or an education. The age at which children left home and the length of time they stayed away varied. Peasant children might leave for a year or two, spend some time working at home, and then leave again. Apprenticeships usually lasted for several years and permanently separated children from their homes. Those who took in children assumed the educational and disciplinary role of parents.

* **artisan** skilled worker or craftsperson

Apprenticeships could take several forms. Peasant children went to other peasant households or, less frequently, to wealthy households. Many children of higher social rank trained with merchants or with professionals such as physicians or lawyers. At the highest levels of society, children served in nobles' homes. These children had to master elaborate codes of social behavior. Serving in a noble household provided valuable contacts for these children and for their families.

Youth. Youth was, in many ways, an extension of childhood. There was no clear transition between the two, although the signs of physical development made a significant difference. These signs—such as voice change and menstruation—seem to have appeared fairly late, after age 14.

Like children, young people had little freedom, and they often behaved irresponsibly. Sports and games might become wild, especially when combined with drinking and gambling. Some old village traditions were open to youth without adult supervision. Groups of young people organized seasonal celebrations and supervised courtship behavior.

Many youths, both boys and girls, spent time as SERVANTS. Their period of service began around age 14 and could last for many years, especially in the countryside. Servants moved frequently from place to place, serving many different masters. Such wandering was not a sign of independence—servants moved from depending on one master to depending on another. Some highborn youths served in noble houses until they were in their 20s. Apprenticeships could also last that long.

The end of youth came only with a change in legal status. Youth was the time for courtship, and marriage usually marked the start of adult-

hood. Most people married around the same time their apprenticeships or periods of service ended. Marriage brought more independence to young men than it did to young women, who became legally dependent on their husbands. Males could also end their youth by joining monasteries. Some young men who did not marry became responsible for themselves as adults when their fathers chose to "emancipate" them (legally set them free). (*See also* **Daily Life; Education; Family and Kinship; Literacy; Motherhood; Orphans and Foundlings; Peasantry.**)

Chivalry

* **medieval** referring to the Middle Ages, a period that began around A.D. 400 and ended around 1400 in Italy and 1500 in the rest of Europe

* **ethics** branch of philosophy concerned with questions of right and wrong

* **feudal** relating to an economic and political system in which individuals gave services to a lord in return for protection and use of the land

Chivalry refers to the lifestyle and moral code followed by medieval* knights. It takes its name from *chevalier,* the French word for knight. Chivalry included the values of honor, valor, courtesy, and purity, as well as loyalty to a lord, a cause, or a noblewoman. Its basis was a blend of military, social, and Christian ethics*. Although chivalry began as a code of conduct for medieval warriors, it adapted to the changing social conditions of the Renaissance.

The Tradition of Chivalry. In the feudal* system of the Middle Ages, knights pledged their loyalty and service to their lords. This relationship became part of the code of chivalry. Literary works also contributed to ideas about "knightly" behavior. They portrayed knights as both courageous warriors and refined men. Knights drew on books to develop standards for etiquette, style, and even the proper way to conduct a love affair. Handbooks from the 1200s laid out the rules of behavior for knights, and pageants and tournaments celebrated chivalric honor. Because knights were part of the culture of feudal courts, their behavior inspired terms such as *courtly, courtship,* and *courtesy.*

The culture of chivalry remained popular in the late Middle Ages and well into the Renaissance. Wealthy Renaissance nobles continued to promote military traditions and to show off their strength in tournaments and in war. However, unlike knights of the Middle Ages, who often acted on their own, they tended to form knightly orders and brotherhoods supported by the ruling government. By 1469 such orders had formed in almost every major court in Europe.

During the late Middle Ages and the Renaissance, the definition of nobility came to depend on family history, rather than military might. For a would-be noble, an ancestor who had worked in a trade or done manual labor was an embarrassment. One way to straighten a crooked limb on an otherwise noble family tree was to adopt the symbols and manners of chivalry. Men who had never spent a day in battle sought the title of knight and created their own coats of arms*.

* **coat of arms** set of symbols used to represent a noble family

Early Chivalric Literature. The literary concept of chivalry dates back to the romances of the Middle Ages. Early romances were not love stories but tales of war. Most were French translations and adaptations of ancient Latin works. Chivalry was the code of behavior that the knights in these medieval romances followed.

Dueling for Honor

During the Renaissance, people were extremely concerned with honor. If one person questioned another's honor, they settled the matter with a duel of honor, a practice that became extremely popular in the 1500s. People followed the elaborate rules of dueling to the letter. Whether or not they actually crossed swords, wealthy men published their messages to each other to prove to "the world" that they had followed the proper code of honor. The shoot-outs of America's Old West and the violent codes of honor of urban street gangs echo the tradition of chivalric duels.

The first—and greatest—of the French romances was *The Song of Roland* (1098), which tells the story of Roland, a brave warrior who died protecting the French army. However, the most influential chivalric romance was the story of the Welsh king Arthur and his Knights of the Round Table. This legend developed from the writings of the French author Chrétien de Troyes. It includes such familiar characters as Lancelot, Guinevere, Percival, and Sir Gawain.

The tales of Arthur's knights provided a pattern of action that appears in most romances. First, a knight sets out on a quest: he must save a lady, right a wrong, complete a task, slay a dragon, break a spell, or find the way to heaven. Along the way he has adventures that test his strength, and he must behave according to a code of conduct. Sometimes he is strong enough, but his luck (or Fortune) may be bad. Good knights try to do the right thing, but they often find themselves in difficult situations. The plots of chivalric romances include many common elements, such as jousts, tournaments, strange customs, giants, enchantments, and flying horses. Some critics argue that readers can interpret these elements as symbols that have moral meanings.

Chivalry in Renaissance Literature. During the 1300s and 1400s, medieval French romances were expanded, altered, and translated into English, Spanish, and Italian. Many included elements that Chrétien created. Their heroes are completely good and their villains are completely evil. These works also echo the rigid pride and codes of honor of military elites*.

* **elite** privileged group; upper class

Italy was home to the most popular romances during the Renaissance. There, writers combined the romance of chivalry with the epic*. Italian poet Ludovico ARIOSTO's *Orlando Furioso* (*Mad Roland,* 1516) is particularly notable because its narrator is both self-conscious and mocking. *Orlando Furioso* had enormous influence on Renaissance literature and literary criticism. The story was so popular that it touched off an explosion of romances based on its minor characters. *Jerusalem Delivered* (1580), by poet Torquato TASSO, is the other Italian masterpiece of the 1500s.

* **epic** long poem about the adventures of a hero

During the years of discovery and conquest in North America in the late 1500s, Spain saw a vast outpouring of chivalric romances. By 1575, more romances were translated from Spanish than from French. Spain's Miguel de CERVANTES wrote one of the most enduring works inspired by the code of chivalry, *Don Quixote* (1605). It tells the story of a gentleman from La Mancha whose mind has been seriously affected by reading romances.

In England, chivalric romances were the most popular form of fiction after the introduction of printing. In 1485 William Caxton, the first English printer, printed Thomas Malory's *Le Morte d'Arthur* (*The Death of Arthur*), a version of the King Arthur legend. English poets of the late 1500s, such as Philip SIDNEY and Edmund SPENSER, created works inspired by the romance tradition.

Influence on Renaissance Culture. The legend of King Arthur became an important source of inspiration in England. Like Arthur, the

ruling Tudor family was Welsh. In the 1490s, Henry VII named his first-born son Arthur and created the title "Prince of Wales" for him. Elizabeth I used Arthur's Knights of the Round Table as a model for her Order of the Garter (a knightly order).

The chivalric legends also appeared in Renaissance art, especially in decorations. Images of King Arthur and the Knights of the Round Table appeared on such personal items as small boxes, combs, mirror cases, writing tablets, and decks of cards. Arthurian legends and other romance stories also inspired tapestries and frescoes* on the walls of Renaissance castles and manor houses.

* **fresco** mural painted on a plaster wall

The tradition of chivalry did not survive the changing political climate of Europe following the Renaissance. Materialism and self-interest soon replaced the knightly code of honor. The values of old nobility gave way to the democracies of France and America and to the Industrial Revolution. (*See also* **English Language and Literature; French Language and Literature; Literature; Spanish Language and Literature.**)

Christianity

The Renaissance was a time of significant change in Christian thought and practice. Christian theology* and philosophy evolved in response to the spread of humanism* and the reexamination of religious texts. When the period began, the Roman Catholic Church had hopes of reuniting with the Orthodox churches of the east, which had broken away from Rome centuries earlier. Instead, new divisions arose within the Catholic Church, which led to the Protestant Reformation*.

* **theology** study of the nature of God and of religion

* **humanism** Renaissance cultural movement promoting the study of the humanities (the languages, literature, and history of ancient Greece and Rome) as a guide to living

* **Protestant Reformation** religious movement that began in the 1500s as a protest against certain practices of the Roman Catholic Church and eventually led to the establishment of a variety of Protestant churches

THE ROMAN CATHOLIC CHURCH

The Catholic Church had a long-standing tradition of religious scholarship. Early Christian writers such as St. AUGUSTINE (354–430) and Boethius (ca. 480–524) had explored the relationship between Christianity and the traditions of ancient Greece and Rome. Writers and preachers of the Middle Ages, such as Dante Alighieri and St. Francis of Assisi, had also raised ideas and concerns that became central to Renaissance thought. However, during the Renaissance many Christians took a fresh look at traditional religious beliefs. Scholars began to read the Bible and other basic Christian writings in their original languages. At the same time, reformers were reconsidering the traditions and institutions of the church.

Biblical Studies. Humanist scholars in the Renaissance were fascinated by classical* culture. Many of them tried to recover ancient texts in their original languages, including copies of the New Testament—the second part of the Christian Bible—in the original Greek. For hundreds of years the Catholic Church had used a Latin translation of the Bible called the Vulgate. But study of the Greek original revealed many errors and mistranslations in the Vulgate. Scholars began to reexamine the Bible and to question the church's interpretation of certain passages.

* **classical** in the tradition of ancient Greece and Rome

See color plate 10, vol. 2

During the Renaissance, when disputes over doctrine threatened the unity of the Roman Catholic Church, many popes undertook projects to enhance the beauty and splendor of the Vatican, the traditional center of Catholicism. St. Peter's Church (shown here) and the Vatican Palace (at right) were both rebuilt during this period.

Some even learned to read Hebrew, which few Christians knew at the time. This enabled them to study the text of the Old Testament in its original language.

Division and Calls for Reform. During the Renaissance, divisions threatened the Catholic Church. It was not the first time. In 1054 differences in beliefs had caused a schism—a formal split—between the Roman Catholic Church and the Orthodox churches in the east. Another schism occurred in the 1300s. In 1309 the papacy* had moved from Rome to Avignon, France, where it remained for decades. In 1377 a second pope was elected in Rome, and for the next 40 years popes in both cities struggled for control of the church. The split ended in 1417 when a church council deposed* the sitting popes and elected a new one who was accepted as the legitimate leader.

* **papacy** office and authority of the pope

* **depose** to remove from high office, often by force

However, concern about widespread abuses within the church continued, leading to calls for reform. Practices such as the sale of church offices and the immoral behavior of clergy members worried many Christians. In the late 1300s and early 1400s, reform movements developed, led by individuals such as John Wycliffe in England and Jan Hus in Prague. The followers of Hus eventually broke away from the church altogether.

During the 1400s church leaders held a series of councils to address issues such as reform of the Catholic Church and the split between east and west. These efforts enjoyed some short-lived successes. The Roman Catholic Church reached a temporary agreement with the Hussites in 1433, but it did not last. In 1439 the Council of Florence produced a plan to reunite the Catholic and Orthodox churches. However, many Orthodox churches rejected it, and these two branches of Christianity remained separate.

The movement for reform continued. In the Netherlands, the humanist scholar Desiderius ERASMUS wrote a number of works deeply critical of church practices. Erasmus used biting satire* to portray corruption among members of the clergy, from monks to the pope. He and other scholars also urged Christians to read the Bible for themselves, rather than depending on the church's interpretation of Scripture. Many of them believed that better translations of the Bible were the key to reform. In 1516 Erasmus contributed to this movement by producing a version of the New Testament in Greek.

* **satire** literary or artistic work ridiculing human wickedness and foolishness

Protestant Reformation and Counter-Reformation. Eventually some religious reformers, such as Martin LUTHER and John CALVIN, broke away from the Catholic Church altogether. Luther believed that the pope had abused his power and that many Catholic beliefs and practices were flawed. He rejected the authority of the pope and declared that salvation came through faith in God and a proper understanding of the Bible.

To help promote his cause, Luther prepared a new translation of the New Testament in German in 1522. This version translated key passages in new ways. Although some editions of the Bible in vernacular* languages had been available before the 1500s, new translations such as Luther's proved to be a great aid to the cause of the Protestant reformers. Protestant scholars also published commentaries on the Bible and spread their ideas through persuasive preaching.

* **vernacular** native language or dialect of a region or country

Many critics of the church felt that Luther had gone too far. His break with the Catholic Church triggered a reaction within the church known as the Counter-Reformation. This movement aimed to restore order and authority in the church and to combat the spread of Protestantism. Catholic officials banned the works of writers whom they considered too critical of the church. However, these efforts did not succeed in preventing Protestant beliefs from spreading.

ORTHODOX CHRISTIANITY

At the beginning of the Renaissance, the Christian church had two main branches: the Roman Catholic Church and the Orthodox churches. These two churches had originally been one. The separation between them began in 330, when the emperor Constantine established a new capital at Byzantium (present-day Istanbul, Turkey). In his honor, the city was renamed CONSTANTINOPLE. The new capital became a major center of Christianity.

In the 500s Constantinople became one of five cities recognized as sees, seats of religious authority. The others were Rome, Alexandria (in Egypt), Antioch (Turkey), and Jerusalem (in present-day Israel). Each see was headed by a bishop with the title *patriarch.* Over time the clergy in Constantinople came to challenge the leadership of the pope, whom they called the patriarch of Rome. This conflict, as well as certain differences in theology, ultimately led to a schism—a formal split—in the church. In 1054 the eastern sees broke away from the Catholic Church and developed into the Orthodox churches. However, they continued to share many basic beliefs with the Roman Catholic Church.

The Church in Constantinople. After the split with Rome, the patriarch of Constantinople became recognized as the leader of the Orthodox churches. However, throughout the Middle Ages the Orthodox leadership faced a series of problems. Invasions by Islamic forces into the Byzantine Empire* threatened the survival of many eastern churches. In addition, Orthodox churches in Alexandria and Ethiopia broke away from Constantinople's control after Arabs occupied those areas.

* **Byzantine Empire** Eastern Christian Empire based in Constantinople (A.D. 476–1453)

In the mid-1200s the church in Constantinople experienced a revival. Although some internal struggles remained, the patriarchs of Constantinople reestablished control over the Orthodox churches. The main issues facing the Orthodox leadership were the movement to reunite with the Catholic Church and the threat of further Muslim invasion. Plans to reunite with Rome collapsed when the patriarchs of the major eastern churches in Jerusalem, Alexandria, and Antioch rejected the settlement at the Council of Florence. Then, in 1453, the Muslim threat became a reality when Turkish invaders from the OTTOMAN EMPIRE captured Constantinople.

After the Ottoman conquest the Orthodox churches declined in size and authority. Members of the clergy could carry out religious duties only with the approval of the local Ottoman leader. The Ottomans influenced the selection of the patriarch in Constantinople and kept tight control over the church. Many Orthodox Christians fled to the west, bringing with them the Greek language and classical Greek culture. They helped promote the revival of classical scholarship that shaped Renaissance thinking.

Ancient Hebrew Wisdom

German scholar Johann Reuchlin (1455–1522) was a Christian pioneer in the study of Hebrew. He believed that ancient Hebrew religious writings contained a hidden treasury of wisdom revealed by God to sages of old. He claimed that if Christian scholars understood these books, they would discover that the Jewish and Christian faiths were compatible. In 1510 Reuchlin persuaded Emperor Maximilan I against a plan to seize and destroy Jewish religious texts, claiming that such an act would harm biblical scholarship. Critics responded by claiming that wealthy Jews must have bribed him.

Other Orthodox Churches. Five years before the Ottoman conquest, a council of Russian bishops had elected a bishop of Moscow without the approval of the patriarch of Constantinople. This move established an independent Russian Orthodox Church. In 1589 Russia also established its own patriarchate, which lasted for about 100 years. Other territories, such as Bulgaria and Serbia, tried to do the same. Such attempts weakened the power of the patriarchs in Constantinople, who were already grappling with the problems of leading a church spread over a vast region with many different languages.

The cultural traditions of Russia and eastern Europe led the Orthodox churches in these areas to grow apart from the church in Constantinople in their beliefs. These eastern European churches

emphasized the mystery of religious ritual, whereas the leadership in Constantinople tended to focus on theology and moral philosophy.

CHRISTIAN THEOLOGY

Christian thinkers in western Europe debated various issues of theology throughout the late Middle Ages and the Renaissance. Renaissance ideas affected Christian theology by promoting a new critical spirit and a better understanding of the ancient languages of Greek, Latin, and Hebrew. As scholars applied these ideas to traditional beliefs and writings, many became Protestants and broke with Rome. But the new critical ideas also profoundly shaped the beliefs of faithful Catholics.

Scholasticism. By the 1200s Christian theology had become amazingly varied. Disputes about the authority of the pope and matters of faith were widespread. Medieval* Christian thought owed much to St. Thomas Aquinas, who saw theology as a "sacred science" and argued that to understand Scripture one must apply human reason. He based his idea of reason on the teachings of the Greek philosopher ARISTOTLE. This approach to Scripture was called Scholasticism.

* **medieval** referring to the Middle Ages, a period that began around A.D. 400 and ended around 1400 in Italy and 1500 in the rest of Europe

Religious thinkers of the Renaissance criticized Scholasticism for its reliance on formal rules and definitions. Critics such as Erasmus claimed that following the example and teaching of Christ was more important than arguing about the fine points of theology. Protestants also attacked Scholasticism because many of its doctrines, such as the freedom of the human will in relation to God, conflicted with theirs. During the Counter-Reformation, the Catholic Church responded to these criticisms by defending the views of Scholastic thinkers on certain key points in Catholic thought.

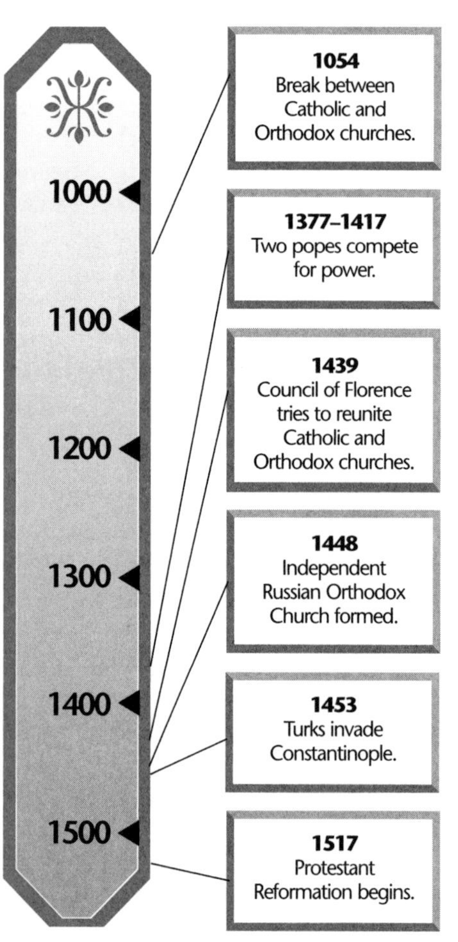

Other Influences. During the Renaissance, the Greek-speaking Orthodox Christians who fled to the west made a major contribution to the rediscovery of classical scholarship. They brought with them not only knowledge of Greek, but also the writings of Greek philosophers and early church fathers, many of whose works had been lost to the west. The invention of the printing press around 1455 made it possible to publish copies of these works for wide distribution.

One of the ancient writers whose work was rediscovered during the Renaissance was the Greek philosopher PLATO. Renaissance scholars such as George Gemistus (ca. 1355–1452) and Marsilio FICINO (1433–1499) noted the influence of Plato's philosophy on the early church fathers. According to these scholars, theologians should study Plato's works, rather than those of Aristotle, in order to understand the ideas of early Christian writers.

Another important aspect of Renaissance theology was an interest in mysticism, the belief in a direct personal union with the divine. Mystics focused less on theological ideas than on understanding the significance of figures and events in the history of Israel and the life of Christ. They sought spiritual knowledge through experience and through inter-

pretations of symbols. One example of a mystical belief system was the Jewish Kabbalah. According to this system, Biblical symbols, such as the letters in the Hebrew name of God, held deep meaning. Some Renaissance philosophers studied the Kabbalah for keys to understanding certain Christian beliefs.

Lasting Influence. The ideas of the Renaissance had a lasting influence on the history of Christianity. Some scholars have argued that the modern trend of secularization, in which the church plays a less important role in society, began during the Renaissance. They claim that the critical spirit of humanism encouraged people to think for themselves and to challenge authority—including the authority of the church. These scholars portray the Christian church as a force for tradition that worked against the Renaissance spirit of free inquiry.

However, if the church sometimes resisted the new ideas of the Renaissance, it was also influenced by them. Since the 1500s, many Protestant thinkers have drawn on Renaissance ideas, urging people to read the Bible with a critical eye and not to rely on church teachings. Renaissance ideas also inspired many later developments in the Roman Catholic Church. For example, in the 1960s the Second Vatican Council made many changes that promoted greater openness within the church, encouraged laypeople* to participate more in worship, and stressed the importance of freedom of conscience. In short, it is clear that the ideas of the Renaissance had a major impact on the development of modern Christianity. (*See also* **Catholic Reformation and Counter-Reformation; Classical Scholarship; Clergy; Councils; Greek Émigrés; Nicholas of Cusa; Popes and Papacy; Protestant Reformation; Religious Orders; Religious Thought; Trent, Council of.**)

* **laypeople** those who are not members of the clergy

Christina of Sweden

1626–1689
Queen of Sweden

Crowned queen in 1644, Christina of Sweden was a patron* of the arts and a lifelong scholar. She became heir to the throne at the age of six after her father, King Gustavus Adolphus, died in battle. The education arranged for the young princess included traditional male subjects such as politics, mathematics, and science to prepare her to rule.

* **patron** supporter or financial sponsor of an artist or writer

Christina took the throne at the age of 18. Early in her reign, she oversaw the peace talks that ended the THIRTY YEARS' WAR (1618–1648). She also gained control over Sweden's political structure, previously dominated by an unruly noble class. She was an effective ruler, and within five years had gained unlimited authority. It was at this point that Christina announced she would never marry, making the issue of succession* a problem. Christina's cousin Charles was named as her heir.

* **succession** determination of person who will inherit the throne

Christina presided over a brilliant court, surrounding herself with artists, musicians, and scholars. She dedicated her life to the pursuit of knowledge and regularly studied in her library, one of the largest in Europe. In 1654, at the height of her power, Christina abandoned the Lutheran church of Sweden and converted to Roman Catholicism. As a

result, she had to give up the throne. She spent the rest of her life in Rome, where she maintained an influential court and continued to support the arts. (*See also* **Scandinavian Kingdoms; Women.**)

Cicero

106–43 B.C.
Roman statesman and orator

* **rhetoric** art of speaking or writing effectively

* **humanist** Renaissance expert in the humanities (the languages, literature, history, and speech and writing techniques of ancient Greece and Rome)

* **classical** in the tradition of ancient Greece and Rome

* **pagan** referring to ancient religions that worshiped many gods, or more generally, to any non-Christian religion

Cicero was an ancient Roman statesman whose writings had a significant impact on Renaissance thought and literature. Scholars of the Middle Ages had known Cicero mainly for his philosophical works, including *On Duties* and *On the Nature of the Gods*. They were also familiar with some of his works on rhetoric*, such as *On Invention*. However, in the mid-1300s, Italian scholar and poet PETRARCH discovered many of Cicero's letters and formal speeches, or orations. Over the course of the next 100 years, scholars recovered nearly all of Cicero's works.

Many Renaissance humanists* admired and imitated Cicero's writing style. They saw him as the best of all ancient writers. By the mid-1400s all the leading teachers of classical* style were modeling their use of Latin after his. However, some intellectuals of the time criticized these "Ciceronians." The Dutch scholar Desiderius ERASMUS mocked them in several writings, most notably *The Ciceronian* (1528). He thought it was foolish to copy the style of ancient pagan* Rome to write about Christian Europe in the 1500s. However, he did express his respect for Cicero as a philosopher.

Scholars continued to draw on Cicero's ideas throughout the Renaissance. Printers published thousands of editions of and commentaries on Cicero's works. By the year 1600, Cicero was one of the most published authors of the time. His works also dominated Latin education and the study of rhetoric for centuries after the Renaissance. (*See also* **Classical Antiquity; Classical Scholarship; Humanism; Latin Language and Literature; Rhetoric.**)

Cities and Urban Life

See color plate 1, vol. 3

Cities in western Europe experienced significant growth and change during the Renaissance. About a quarter of the population lived in urban areas, and the percentage was even higher in northern Italy, southern Germany, and the Netherlands. By 1600 Venice had 190,000 inhabitants and Paris had 220,000. This urban growth led to changes in the nature of city life and the challenges of city government.

Characteristics of Urban Life. Renaissance cities varied a great deal. While some cities were surrounded by walls or FORTIFICATIONS, others no longer had walls or had developed suburbs beyond them. Cities served mainly as centers for the exchange and production of goods, but agriculture often remained an important element. Farmers made up a large part of the population of many towns and sometimes raised crops inside city walls. People from different backgrounds and social classes mixed in the shops and marketplaces, and women moved about with considerable freedom. Urban areas also attracted a wide variety of visitors.

As European cities grew during the Renaissance, governing them became a challenge. This street scene from the 1300s shows the clean, orderly city that some believed was possible with good government.

See color plate 2, vol. 3

Cities enjoyed a lively, often hectic, street life. Religious and other processions featuring music, dancing, and elaborate costumes were common. Pedestrians frequently had to share the streets with pigs and geese. Crowding and traffic became serious problems in some urban areas, especially as the use of carriages increased among the wealthy. During one traffic jam in Paris in 1610, HENRY IV of France was assassinated in his coach. Some cities made attempts to control the traffic problem. Amsterdam developed a system of one-way streets, and London licensed carriages for hire. In both cases, the situation became more complex as the use of carriages grew.

A significant development in urban society during the Renaissance was the popularity of indoor entertainment. Wealthy residents began to take part in invitation-only dances, private gambling, and new forms of diversion such as OPERA, theater, and poetry readings. These urban elites*

* **elite** privileged group; upper class

sought entertainment that excluded the ordinary people and reinforced their own sense of social superiority.

Religion and Education in Cities. Religion was a major force in urban life throughout the Renaissance. In most cities religious buildings dominated the skyline, and parish churches served as cultural and social centers. Churches also had their own laws and courts separate from those of civil authorities.

* **Protestant Reformation** religious movement that began in the 1500s as a protest against certain practices of the Roman Catholic Church and eventually led to the establishment of a variety of Protestant churches

* **Counter-Reformation** actions taken by the Roman Catholic Church after 1540 to oppose Protestantism

The role of city churches changed after the Protestant Reformation*. In northern Europe the church lost its separate legal status, and many Catholic religious buildings were destroyed or converted to other uses. Education and relief for the poor, once largely provided by the church, fell to other groups and institutions. In southern Europe, the Catholic Counter-Reformation* strengthened the church's role. New churches were built to emphasize the importance of faith in daily life. Urban authorities worked with church leaders to impose accepted political and religious beliefs.

* **apprenticeship** system under which a person is bound by legal agreement to work for another for a specified period of time in return for instruction in a trade or craft

Towns and cities were the educational centers of the Renaissance. Instruction aimed at different levels of achievement. Dame schools (small classes conducted by women in their homes) provided only enough learning to allow their pupils to attend to business and understand religious principles. Vocational schools and trade apprenticeships* prepared young people for various crafts and professions. Latin grammar schools and universities offered more advanced education. Schooling and training were available for both boys and girls, but the education of girls usually ended at a much earlier age.

City Government. The organization of city government remained largely unchanged from the Middle Ages to the Renaissance. However, traditional government structures were unable to deal with the growing complexity of city life. Issues such as immigration, public health, fire prevention, defense, and maintaining order required more specialized expertise than most town councils possessed. Civic officials set up committees to deal with these types of issues. These committees created new opportunities for corruption, but bribery and gifts often helped urban services function more smoothly.

* **guild** association of craft and trade owners and workers that set standards for and represented the interests of its members

Although many residents of cities were counted as citizens, the term had little practical political significance. Most cities contained too many citizens to call together at one time to make decisions or choose local leaders. In any event, only those who were financially independent had any voice in local government. Women and the poor had little political influence. This led many urban dwellers to identify as strongly with neighborhoods, parishes, guilds*, or other associations as with the city.

During the Renaissance most cities lost their political independence to rulers of larger territories and states. These rulers often enforced their policies by maintaining their own courts, troops, and tax collectors in cities. In some cases, rulers used their power to appoint city officials who would follow their policies.

New Glory for Old Rome

During the Renaissance, Rome went through extensive changes at the hands of urban planners, as a series of popes decided to transform the face of the city. Many straight new streets were cut through the city's maze of twisting, narrow lanes. Major plazas were updated and connected to important avenues. A new water supply system featured fountains at prominent intersections and urban squares. Most importantly, the city's churches of pilgrimage were linked to a network of streets. This large-scale renewal reflected Rome's evolution during the Renaissance from a rather shabby town of less than 20,000 people in 1420 to the capital of Catholic Christianity with a population of 100,000 by 1600.

The Urban Economy. Guilds and market authorities regulated economic activity in cities. However, many merchants and peddlers conducted business in places outside official control, such as inns and taverns. Homes and shops often shared the same buildings, and business typically spilled out into the sidewalk and streets. But long-standing city regulations limited the size of most manufacturing enterprises. Urban craft production thus remained small in scale.

The level of economic activity and prosperity varied considerably in Renaissance cities. The number of residents changed unpredictably as rapid increases in population were interrupted by outbreaks of disease that caused sharp declines. Nevertheless, most city economies continued to expand until the late 1500s. At that time Mediterranean cities experienced a slowdown as trade and shipping shifted from Italy to England and the Netherlands.

City economies were based on production, trade, and services that supported these activities, such as innkeeping, domestic work, and transporting goods. Professionals such as lawyers and doctors also formed an important part of the urban economy. However, the prosperity of a town more often depended on other sources of income. Rents from houses and income from properties outside the city were as important to urban dwellers as the money they made in the marketplace. Increases in the size of government accounted for much of the growth in many cities.

Urban Design and Planning. The rediscovery of ancient Greek and Roman writings on the arts and ARCHITECTURE brought a new sense of urban design to Renaissance Europe. Reports from ancient Rome explained how rulers could express ideas of power and authority through monumental architecture and city design. Renaissance architects and urban planners embraced these ideas, studying classical* design principles such as the use of ideal geometric figures (the circle and square) and building proportions based on the measurements of the human body. They attempted to find a balance between firmness, beauty, and utility in construction.

* **classical** in the tradition of ancient Greece and Rome

Yet few cities were built or restructured according to classical principles because it was difficult to make major changes in existing urban centers. However, the design of one new town of the 1400s, Pienza, did follow the principles of Renaissance urban planning. Pope Pius II made this village in Tuscany into an urban monument to himself and his family. Exposure to classical influences led to a more refined architectural style and planned town additions and improvements in northern Europe. Classical models of urban planning were eventually adopted to appeal to local tastes and needs. (*See also* **City-States; Economy and Trade; Education; Government, Forms of; Guilds; Industry; Population; Taxation and Public Finance.**)

See color plate 3, vol. 3

City-States

City-states emerged as a form of political organization in Europe during the Middle Ages. The city-state was a largely independent city that extended its authority over the surrounding territory. In some cases, this authority also included other cities, creating a larger territorial state. City-states adopted different forms of government; some were organized as republics*, while others were ruled by an individual such as a prince*.

* **republic** form of Renaissance government dominated by leading merchants with limited participation by others
* **prince** Renaissance term for the ruler of an independent state
* **Holy Roman Empire** political body in central Europe composed of several states; existed until 1806
* **papacy** office and authority of the pope

Independent Sovereign States. City-states were most common in northern Italy in the regions of Lombardy, Tuscany, and the Veneto. They fell under the loose authority of the Holy Roman Empire*. Notable examples of these northern city-states include FLORENCE, SIENA, and VENICE. City-states such as FERRARA and URBINO emerged in the Papal States, the area in central Italy controlled by the papacy*.

During the Middle Ages both the Holy Roman Empire and the papacy claimed to be the successor to ancient Rome. The city-state emerged out of the struggle for power between these two great authorities. Owing allegiance to neither, the city-state depended on its own resources rather than on privileges granted by a higher power. Authority and legitimacy in the city-state came from the commune (community) and the idea and practice of popular sovereignty*.

* **sovereignty** supreme power or authority

Some city-states sought to extend their frontiers well beyond the surrounding territory. Between the late 1300s and early 1500s, the Republic of Venice took over other city-states in northern Italy. Florence did the same in central Italy.

City-states in Italy formed a new social and economic order. Status and citizenship were determined by the community itself, rather than by medieval* ideas of wealth, power, and feudal* obligations. The Italian city-state drew on sources of wealth more familiar to the modern world. Employment and wealth depended increasingly on trade, industry, and financial activities such as banking and insurance. Furthermore, the scope of commerce expanded beyond local or regional activities to international trade.

* **medieval** referring to the Middle Ages, a period that began around A.D. 400 and ended around 1400 in Italy and 1500 in the rest of Europe
* **feudal** relating to an economic and political system in which individuals gave services to a lord in return for protection and use of the land

Emerging city-states sought to defend their authority while reducing the power of their opponents. Urban governments constructed walls, gates, and other FORTIFICATIONS while taking steps to destroy private fortresses within the city and its territory. City-states also made their own laws, established their own courts, and appointed their own judges and officials. They signed treaties, declared war and peace, and raised taxes. City-states even challenged the power of the Roman Catholic Church, influencing church appointments and taxing the clergy.

See color plate 7, vol. 3

Medieval Origins of City-States. Italian city-states were not truly a product of the Renaissance. Some of them—including MILAN, Verona, Siena, and Florence—traced their origin to the days of ancient Rome, or even earlier. Moreover, the cities experienced their greatest economic and population growth during the Middle Ages. Their physical boundaries and layouts were also established at this time.

From the 1000s to the 1200s, an intense rivalry existed between the Holy Roman Empire and the papacy, providing an opportunity for the cities of northern and central Italy to develop. By the time of the Renaissance, the two great power centers had grown somewhat weaker. But the papacy began to recover its political authority in the Papal States in the mid-1400s. As it did, it limited the liberties of cities under its control. The Holy Roman Empire also regained authority and influence when it became part of the HABSBURG empire in the 1500s.

These developments meant that during the Renaissance the number of independent city-states was actually in decline. The large representative bodies of citizens lost influence and citizenship became more strictly defined. In some cases, the right to participate in government was limited to people of noble birth. Increasingly, a privileged class of landowners, lawyers, and merchants controlled access to public office.

The social and economic changes often associated with city-states were not that significant. Although new areas of economic activity developed, land remained the basis of the economy. Even in the urban areas of northern Italy, the majority of the population had no rights to citizenship and lived and worked on the land. In most instances, the power of the noble families had not been destroyed. In fact, in some places, their influence increased.

The wealth and opportunities for political power offered by city-states attracted ambitious nobles. From the 1200s onward, many cities in northern and central Italy surrendered authority to the *signoria,* the lordship of a powerful noble family. This occurred in Milan and Padua. Venice was the only major city-state with the resources and political stability to keep its independence and status as a republic throughout the Renaissance. Although Florence remained a republic, after 1434 its government was increasingly controlled by the MEDICI family.

Public Health

During the 1300s many Italian city-states took on new responsibilities, as the range of government activities expanded beyond the basic tasks of making and enforcing laws and defending the city. Numerous cities began to manage the supply of food and to take steps to control disease. After a deadly outbreak of plague ravaged Italian cities in 1348, the need to control disease took on new urgency. Preventing further outbreaks of the plague prompted government actions to improve sanitation, to prevent sick people from entering the city, and to isolate infected citizens.

Contributions. Scholars now assert that Renaissance city-states were not as numerous, independent, republican, and powerful as was generally assumed. Nevertheless, the cities made significant contributions to Renaissance culture, and they had sufficient wealth to serve as patrons* of the arts. Individuals, families, guilds*, and other organizations also played an important role in supporting the arts. Economic conditions in the cities provided money, skills, and materials to undertake massive public projects, such as construction of the cathedral of Milan. These projects, in turn, increased economic activity. The rapid development of printing was another result of the resources and patronage of city-states.

City-states and their universities also contributed to law, literacy*, and other aspects of culture. The cities needed literate and trained administrators to write laws, preside over courts, keep records of legal proceedings, conduct diplomacy and correspondence, and manage accounts. The basis of laws and legal procedures in most city-states was Roman law. The need for professionals who could master ancient Roman law encouraged the study of Latin and Roman history. This produced a number of political thinkers and humanists* who were familiar with classical* ideas.

* **patron** supporter or financial sponsor of an artist or writer

* **guild** association of craft and trade owners and workers that set standards for and represented the interests of its members

* **literacy** ability to read

* **humanist** Renaissance expert in the humanities (the languages, literature, history, and speech and writing techniques of ancient Greece and Rome)

* **classical** in the tradition of ancient Greece and Rome

The Republic of Venice had a long tradition of native and foreign political thinkers. Other city-states produced political writers who used ancient ideas to justify the authority of their rulers. Much of this writing took the form of histories. The Medici family, for example, employed many talented writers to praise their greatness and the benefits that their rule brought to Florence. (*See also* **Cities and Urban Life; Government, Forms of; Holy Roman Empire; Nation-state; Popes and Papacy; Princes and Princedoms; Representative Institutions.**)

Classical Antiquity

Scholars and artists of the Renaissance were fascinated by the great cultures of ancient Greece and Rome. They believed that studying the achievements of the past was the key to creating a glorious future. They pored over ancient texts and sifted through ruins to unearth objects such as monuments, coins, and statues. Growing awareness of this era known as classical antiquity influenced Renaissance architecture, art, and city planning. It also transformed the study of history and formed the basis of the cultural movement called humanism*.

* **humanism** Renaissance cultural movement promoting the study of the humanities (the languages, literature, and history of ancient Greece and Rome) as a guide to living

DISCOVERING THE PAST

The study of ancient cultures began in Italy, particularly in Rome, where citizens lived among the crumbling remains of a long-dead civilization. Scholars of the ancient world, known as antiquarians, searched these ruins for clues to life in lost civilizations. Meanwhile, historians in Britain and other parts of Europe worked to uncover their own countries' distant past.

Greece and Rome. At the beginning of the Renaissance, the ruins of ancient theaters, temples, columns, and arches dotted the landscape of Italy and other Mediterranean regions. However, maps and city guides from the Middle Ages reveal that citizens no longer understood the significance of these ancient monuments. Even in Rome, the ruins had become little more than landmarks in a Christian city. Although residents knew the names of such grand structures as the Pantheon and the Colosseum, they often knew little of their original functions. Nor did the Romans of 1400 have any idea of the full size and spread of the ancient city.

The works of scholars and historians of ancient Greece and Rome suffered much the same fate. The writings had survived, but no one truly understood their meaning. Knowledge of the great poets of the classical* world was even murkier. Medieval* legends had mislabeled the Roman poet VIRGIL as either a sorcerer or a prophet of Christianity. The Greek poet Homer had become little more than a name, his epics* unread. The dust and debris of centuries lay not only on the ancient cities but on nearly all that their cultures had produced.

* **classical** in the tradition of ancient Greece and Rome

* **medieval** referring to the Middle Ages, a period that began around A.D. 400 and ended around 1400 in Italy and 1500 in the rest of Europe

* **epic** long poem about the adventures of a hero

The study of ancient cultures influenced art, architecture, city planning, history, and many other fields of knowledge during the Renaissance. Antiquity provided the inspiration for Raphael's fresco *School of Athens,* created around 1510. The piece features Plato, Aristotle, and several other ancient Greek philosophers.

Renaissance scholars devoted themselves to finding, unearthing, and collecting relics of the distant past. The ancient world lay closest to the surface in Rome. Residents of the city turned up many long-buried marvels simply by digging in their suburban vineyards or excavating the foundations for new buildings. An immense statue discovered in 1506, for example, proved to be a piece of art mentioned in the works of the ancient Roman writer Pliny.

From these fragments, scholars tried to piece together the societies that had created them. As antiquarians learned more about the values and practices of the ancient world, they began to adopt them as part of their own culture. For example, Renaissance architects such as Filippo Brunelleschi and Leon Battista Alberti examined, measured, and sketched the spectacular ruins of ancient buildings, seeking to understand how they had been built and used. They then adapted these classical forms in the designs of their own buildings, linking their own world with the great cultures of the past.

At first, students of the ancient world focused on gathering as many relics and texts as possible. During the 1400s, however, historians developed a concern for the quality of evidence. They began comparing sources, trying to determine which were original and which drew on older works. They also developed standards for judging the value and authenticity of material. This newfound concern with the usefulness of sources formed the basis of the modern approach to history.

Ancient Britain. While scholars in Italy sought to uncover the ancient glories of Rome, researchers in England were busy delving into their own country's past. They pursued knowledge both for its own sake and to serve practical goals. Henry VIII hired the antiquarian John

Leland to examine English relics for evidence that would support the king's claims to be the legitimate head of the English church.

An entire field of English antiquarianism focused on King Arthur and other legendary monarchs. Geoffrey of Monmouth had chronicled the reigns of several such rulers in the 1100s in *History of the Kings of Britain.* Throughout the 1500s scholars and poets debated the accuracy of Geoffrey's history. English patriots saw Geoffrey's accounts of King Arthur and the Round Table as proof of an ancient British history as glorious as that of Rome. Legal historians used them to support their view that English law was even older than Roman law. In the 1600s, however, a younger generation of antiquarians began disproving this legal myth, showing that English law had its origins in European feudal* law.

Some English antiquarians focused on specific regions of Britain. Richard Carew, for example, published a *Survey of Cornwall* in the 1580s. Others turned their attention to genealogy*, church history, and heraldry*. Explorers of the past shared their findings through groups such as the Society of Antiquaries, formed around 1586 in London. Its leading figure, William Camden, published a detailed survey of British geography and history in Latin. Another member, Robert Cotton, assembled a mass of books and manuscripts dealing with ancient Britain. This assortment later became the core collection of the modern British Library.

* **feudal** referring to an economic and political system in which individuals gave services to a lord in return for protection and use of the land

* **genealogy** study of family origins and relationships

* **heraldry** design and use of coats of arms for military purposes and as family symbols

RENAISSANCE IMAGES OF ANTIQUITY

Many Renaissance artists portrayed the ancient world in their paintings and sculptures. However, they viewed antiquity through the lens of Christianity and often blended images of antiquity with Christian themes. Artists gathered ideas about the ancient world from their Bibles as well as from the writings of classical authors. Italian artists could also seek inspiration in the ruins that surrounded them and in other relics of the ancient world.

Renaissance artists often portrayed the Virgin Mary, Christ, and other Christian figures wearing Roman clothing, set among crumbling Roman ruins. This choice not only indicated that Christ had appeared on earth in Roman times but also suggested Christianity's triumph over pagan* Rome. Creating backgrounds for these paintings presented a challenge for artists, as no European landscape resembled the ancient Near East where Christianity had been born. When Sandro BOTTICELLI painted *Scenes from the Life of Moses* on the walls on Rome's Sistine Chapel in the 1480s, he used the lush countryside of north-central Italy to represent Egypt.

Greek culture played a significant role in the ideas of Renaissance artists and thinkers. This role increased in the mid-1400s, when the fall of CONSTANTINOPLE drove many Greek scholars to Italy. Renaissance artists and scholars tended to view Greek art in terms of the Byzantine Empire* rather than that of ancient Greece. RAPHAEL was one of the first artists to seek out drawings of ancient Greek monuments, according to Renaissance historian Giorgio Vasari, in an effort to gain a sense of their special qualities.

* **pagan** referring to ancient religions that worshiped many gods, or more generally, to any non-Christian religion

* **Byzantine Empire** Eastern Christian Empire based in Constantinople (A.D. 476–1453)

Links to Rome

Renaissance historians developed a great interest in the origins of cities. They traced the beginnings of many European cities back to ancient Rome, placing local histories within the grand framework of the Roman Empire. They carefully studied local ruins, seeking hints of Roman influence. The people of Florence proudly pointed to the baptistery of their cathedral as a Roman monument—though later scholars showed that this claim had no basis in fact.

Scenes of ancient Egypt posed a particular problem for Renaissance artists. Controlled at the time by Turks, Egypt was almost impossible for Europeans to visit. They could gain glimpses of Egyptian antiquity from artifacts such as sphinxes and obelisks (pillars inscribed with Egyptian letters) collected by ancient Romans. But many Renaissance images of ancient Egypt—including the frescoes* of Egyptian gods painted for Pope ALEXANDER VI—drew almost entirely on imagination.

* **fresco** mural painted on a plaster wall

Some ambitious Renaissance artists did more than use classical antiquity as a background for their own creations. They tried to re-create long-lost works of art from descriptions left by ancient authors. For example, the painting *Venus Rising from the Sea* was TITIAN's version of a painting by the ancient artist Apelles.

Antiquity supplied the subject matter for history painting, one of the most highly regarded types of Renaissance art. Artists used their knowledge of the ancient world to make their works more realistic. In *The Triumph of Caesar,* artist Andrea MANTEGNA drew on his careful studies of ancient Roman carvings, especially those on the Roman monument known as Trajan's Column. Paintings in the Vatican, the seat of the Roman Catholic Church, also repeat designs from Trajan's Column and other Roman relics. Through such works, artists transformed the Roman Empire into a backdrop for the Christian story, creating a link between their own time and the classical world. (*See also* **Architecture; Art; Chivalry; Classical Scholarship; Greek Émigrés; Heraldry; History, Writing of; Humanism.**)

Classical Scholarship

A defining feature of Renaissance culture was its fascination with the ancient world. Scholars of the period devoted themselves to the study of ancient Greek and Roman writings. Humanists* dreamed of discovering and preserving classical* works and making them available to society as a whole.

* **humanist** Renaissance expert in the humanities (the languages, literature, history, and speech and writing techniques of ancient Greece and Rome)
* **classical** in the tradition of ancient Greece and Rome

Classical scholarship began in northern Italy in the late 1200s when a small group of learned people developed a passion for Roman literature and history. In the 1300s, the Italian poet PETRARCH turned these early glimmerings of scholarship into a complete program. He discovered lost works of Latin literature, including the letters of the Roman orator CICERO. He also made efforts to improve classical texts, comparing different versions to find and correct errors. He even attempted to learn Greek so that he could study the literature of ancient Greece in its original form. Finally, he used his knowledge of ancient writings in his own works of poetry, history, and ethics (or moral philosophy). Petrarch's approach to classical learning became a model for generations of humanists in Italy and elsewhere.

Recovering Lost Works. During the Renaissance, classical scholars unearthed many copies of ancient works. Some of these writings were completely unknown. Others were more complete versions of known texts. In the early 1400s a scholar named Poggio Bracciolini discovered a large number of Latin manuscripts while traveling through northern

Europe. His finds included new speeches by Cicero and a poem about the universe by the philosopher Lucretius. Other scholars discovered works by Roman historians such as Tacitus. Many of these ended up in the Vatican Library.

In the early Renaissance, European scholars brought manuscripts to Italy, recognized as the home of classical studies. Later, however, leadership in this field shifted toward northern Europe. In 1527 a German scholar found lost works by the Roman historian Livy in a German monastery. Instead of traveling to Italy like past discoveries, this new manuscript was published in Switzerland.

The rediscovery of Greek literature was even more dramatic. Latin translations of a few ancient Greek authors, such as ARISTOTLE, had existed in the Middle Ages. Manuscripts in Greek, however, were rare, and few scholars could read the language. Petrarch owned Greek texts of works by the poet Homer and the philosopher PLATO but was unable to read them. During the 1400s, large numbers of Greek texts entered western Europe. Some of these were brought by Greek-speaking scholars from the Byzantine Empire*, who fled to Italy to escape the invading Turks. Western Europeans recovered many previously unknown works, such as the influential *Outline of Geography* by the ancient scholar PTOLEMY. By the end of the 1400s, nearly all the classical Greek literature that survives today had reached Italy.

* **Byzantine Empire** Eastern Christian Empire based in Constantinople (A.D. 476–1453)

To share their discoveries, Renaissance scholars began translating these Greek works into Latin. Patrons* such as the MEDICI family in Florence supported this work. They also encouraged the spread of scholarship by founding libraries where scholars could study manuscripts and books. One of the finest Renaissance libraries occupied four specially designed rooms in the Vatican, the pope's official seat in Rome. Scholars were free to use this collection, which included many classical texts, as long as they followed certain rules. For example, they had to put books back in their places and avoid quarreling with other readers.

* **patron** supporter or financial sponsor of an artist or writer

Improving the Texts. During the Middle Ages, scribes* copied and recopied ancient texts by hand. In the process, they introduced many errors that later scribes picked up. By the Renaissance, many different versions of these texts existed. Scholars of the Renaissance attempted to untangle the web of errors and identify the true text through a process called textual criticism. Textual critics collated, or compared, the variations found in different manuscripts to determine which was the original. They also used their own imagination and knowledge to make conjectures—educated guesses—as to what the original text might have been.

* **scribe** person who copies manuscripts

Early textual critics, including Petrarch, did not explain the reasons for their changes to the text. In the late 1400s, Angelo POLIZIANO of Italy transformed the field of textual criticism. A master of both Greek and Latin, Poliziano took a systematic approach to each text. He carefully recorded all his alterations to the text and noted whether they were based on collation or on conjecture. When he compared texts, he noted which reading came from which manuscript, identifying it by its owner, appearance, and history.

The Power of the Press

The invention of the printing press around 1455 was a blessing to classical scholars. Until then, the only way to copy a newly discovered text had been to write it out by hand—a time-consuming process with countless possibilities for error. The press made it possible to print hundreds, even thousands, of identical copies of works. By the end of the 1400s most classical Latin literature was available in a variety of printed editions, at prices virtually any scholar could afford.

By analyzing the errors found in all copies of a given text, Poliziano was sometimes able to identify the original version from which the others had descended. For example, he realized that many manuscripts of Cicero's letters had the pages in the wrong order. He traced this problem back to a specific copy and identified it as the original source. His careful methods set a new standard for textual criticism.

Textual studies also involved explaining and interpreting ancient works. Poliziano excelled in this field, largely because of his exceptional knowledge of Greek literature. For example, he was able to explain an obscure line in a Roman poem as a reference to a myth mentioned in an ancient Greek song.

In the 1500s France replaced Italy as the most important center of classical studies. French editors tended to avoid the drudgery of collation in favor of changes based on conjecture. They also commented at length on the texts. One French scholar's editions of Roman works were notable chiefly for the long-winded notes in which he compared the Latin texts to earlier Greek models. Scholars in the Netherlands and Germany also produced important editions of classical materials in the late 1500s and early 1600s. Their creations included the first edition of the *Meditations* of the Roman emperor Marcus Aurelius, a work that influenced later movements in ethics. Many of them applied material from ancient writings to the problems of modern life in their own works.

Study of Classical Languages. Latin had been taught and studied throughout the Middle Ages. Over the years, the language had gradually changed. In the 1300s Petrarch began a trend toward returning the Latin language to its ancient roots. Other early humanists revised existing textbooks and methods for Latin study, placing more stress on classical models and forms.

A new era in Latin studies began in 1471, with the printing of a guide to the Latin language written by the Italian humanist Lorenzo VALLA. Valla had based this work on a careful study of Roman literature. He believed that the return to the classical style of writing Latin was helping to renew all fields of study, from law and medicine to philosophy and art. His book reformed the study of Latin, teaching Renaissance writers to imitate the great Roman authors in their poetry and prose. Other scholars also worked to restore the Latin of ancient Rome, removing from it every trace of medieval* vocabulary and style.

* **medieval** referring to the Middle Ages, a period that began around A.D. 400 and ended around 1400 in Italy and 1500 in the rest of Europe

Until the late 1400s the teaching of Greek was largely in the hands of scholars who had moved to Italy after the fall of the Byzantine Empire. One of them, Manuel Chrysoloras, taught Greek in Florence to a generation of young Italian humanists. Byzantine scholars published textbooks and dictionaries, some in Greek and some in both Greek and Latin. Western scholars began producing their own Greek dictionaries in the 1500s. In 1572 two scholarly printers, Robert and Henri Estienne, published the *Treasure-House of the Greek Language,* the greatest monument of Greek scholarship in the Renaissance.

Influences of Classical Scholarship. Advances in classical scholarship during the Renaissance had important effects on the fields of theology*, philosophy, and medicine, which were based on ancient texts. Scholars transformed theology by applying the new techniques of textual criticism to the BIBLE. Valla, for example, approached the New Testament much as he had approached other ancient works, attempting to restore the true meaning of the text by undoing the errors scribes had made over the years. Humanists such as Desiderius ERASMUS hailed this new approach to the sacred text. Erasmus discovered, however, that the Bible required special treatment. An uproar broke out when he removed a passage from the New Testament on the grounds that it could not be found in any of the Greek versions and must have been added later. He restored the passage in later editions.

* **theology** study of the nature of God and of religion

Meanwhile, other humanists devoted their attention to the works of ancient philosophers, especially Aristotle. Throughout the 1400s and 1500s they produced new editions of Aristotle's writings. Their translations were both more accurate and more readable than earlier versions. Classical scholars further expanded the study of philosophy by editing and translating the works of other Greek thinkers, such as Plato. They also uncovered important Latin works of philosophy.

In the same way, new critical editions of classical works reshaped the study of medicine. Poliziano spent the last years of his life studying Greek medical texts and translating the technical terms they contained into Latin. In 1492 physician Niccolò Lenoniceno wrote a treatise* on the medical errors in an ancient Roman work. He showed that the author had misunderstood the Greek terms for various plants and herbs. Other doctors of the 1500s made new translations of works by GALEN and HIPPOCRATES, two Greek physicians whose works formed the basis of medicine. Overall, classical scholarship affected nearly every aspect of intellectual and cultural life in the Renaissance. (*See also* **Books and Manuscripts; Classical Antiquity; Geography and Cartography; Greek Émigrés; History, Writing of; Humanism; Latin Language and Literature; Libraries; Medicine; Philosophy; Religious Thought.**)

* **treatise** long, detailed essay

Clement VII

See *Popes and Papacy.*

Clergy

Members of the clergy played a large role in everyday life during the Renaissance. They performed certain religious activities and duties within Christian churches and provided leadership and guidance for laypeople*. During the Renaissance, Catholics and Protestants had very different ideas about the structure of the clergy, their duties, and their relationships with laypeople.

* **laypeople** those who are not members of the clergy

The Catholic Clergy. The Roman Catholic Church maintained a sharp distinction between clergy and laypeople. Catholic theology*

* **theology** study of the nature of God and of religion

taught that members of the clergy had been called by God to serve the church. They had the power to bless church members and to help them achieve salvation. Clergy members were easy to identify because they wore special clothing and hairstyles. When a man entered the service of the church, a bishop ceremonially removed some of his hair, marking him as a clergyman.

Clergy members were entitled to respect from laypeople, and they also enjoyed legal privileges. For example, they could not be tried in regular courts, but only in special church courts. They also did not have to pay taxes or perform military service. However, clergy members also had restrictions on their behavior. Most notably, they were not permitted to marry or have children.

Some clergy members belonged to RELIGIOUS ORDERS, such as the Franciscans and the Dominicans. These people, known as "regulars" (meaning "those who live according to a religious rule") often lived in communal houses, known as monasteries or convents. Within these houses, the regulars remained apart from everyday life. They also took vows of poverty, chastity*, and obedience. The secular* clergy, by contrast, lived in the community. This group included local priests and bishops.

* **chastity** purity or virginity

* **secular** nonreligious; connected with everyday life

At the lowest levels of the clergy were the men in minor orders, which served the church in lesser ways. For example, lectors read from the Bible during services. Minor orders were not permanent positions. Those who held them could give them up and reenter secular life.

Members of the minor orders could enter the major orders, becoming subdeacons, deacons, priests, or bishops. Subdeacons and deacons assisted bishops during services, but the positions served mainly as steppingstones to the priesthood. Priests had the authority to preach, lead services, and perform marriages and other rituals. Bishops oversaw the priests and directed and controlled religious activity in their dioceses*. The supreme authority in the church was the pope. Elected by the College of Cardinals—a select body of bishops, priests, and deacons who advised the pope—he had the final say over matters of church policy, appointments, beliefs, and morals.

* **diocese** geographical area under the authority of a bishop

The Protestant Clergy. The German religious reformer Martin LUTHER rejected the idea that the clergy should be separate from and have authority over laypeople. Luther believed that the church as a whole, not certain chosen individuals, had the power to forgive sin. He saw the congregation as a "priesthood of all believers." Although he saw the need for certain people to perform official religious functions, he believed that local congregations or their secular leaders should elect their own clergy members.

Luther did not support the idea of having ranks within the clergy. His follower Philipp MELANCHTHON, however, believed that God had established the ministry and that only those chosen for it had the authority to perform religious functions. In the late 1500s Lutherans took the first steps toward creating a church hierarchy*. They created the office of superintendent to supervise pastors and established a governing body, called the consistory, to oversee the clergy.

* **hierarchy** organization of a group into higher and lower levels

Different Protestant faiths had other views of the clergy. Swiss reformer Huldrych ZWINGLI (1484–1531) believed only those with a mission could teach or preach the word of God. John CALVIN of France, by contrast, established a rigid system of ranks within the clergy. Pastors counseled believers, while teachers explained the Bible. Above them were church elders, or presbyters, and deacons, who cared for the poor. In the late 1500s Calvin's system became standard practice in the churches of the Netherlands, Switzerland, and parts of the Holy Roman Empire*. England, meanwhile, maintained a church structure similar to that of the Roman Catholic Church. However, the monarch replaced the pope as the supreme head of the church. (*See also* **Christianity; Confraternities; Popes and Papacy; Protestant Reformation.**)

* **Holy Roman Empire** political body in central Europe composed of several states; existed until 1806

Clocks

Throughout history, people have worked to build more accurate clocks. At the beginning of the Renaissance, clocks used hanging weights as a source of power, making them large and heavy. Renaissance clock makers produced timepieces powered by springs, which were smaller and more portable. Improvements to the clock continued throughout the Renaissance, leading up to the invention of the pendulum clock, pioneered by astronomer Galileo GALILEI.

Weight-driven clocks, used during the Middle Ages, worked by suspending a weight from a cord wound around the main gear of the clock. As gravity pulled the weight down, the gear turned, powering the clock. An early weight-driven clock, built in the mid-1300s, charted the positions of the Sun, Moon, and planets. Later weight-powered clocks were heavy metal-framed structures that kept poor time and required continuous care and adjustment.

In the mid-1400s, engineers developed the first spring-powered clocks. These timepieces had a coiled spring inside. As it unwound, it drove the main gear, which in turn powered the clock. Spring-powered clocks were smaller and lighter, allowing people to display them in their homes. Their small size also made them suitable for use as pocket watches. The oldest surviving models of the spring-driven clock date from around 1500 and are the work of Peter Henlein, a German locksmith. Early spring-driven clocks did not keep accurate time, however. Not until the 1600s did scientists discover ways of making spring-driven clocks dependable.

In the early 1600s Galileo experimented with the pendulum, a weight suspended from a fixed point that swings back and forth due to gravity. He thought that a pendulum could regulate a clock. Late in his life, he began work on such a clock, but he was unable to complete it before his death in 1642. Fourteen years later, Dutch astronomer Christiaan Huygens perfected Galileo's idea and built the first successful pendulum clock. With the use of the pendulum, clocks could reliably count minutes and seconds for the first time. (*See also* **Scientific Instruments.**)

Clothing

Clothing took on great importance during the Renaissance. It not only protected people from the elements, but also proclaimed their social status. The cut, color, and fabric of a person's garments held clues to the wearer's place in society. The changing styles of the Renaissance reflected new ideas about beauty, luxury, and the importance of class distinctions.

The Clothing Trade. In the late 1300s, the clothing trade grew dramatically in Italy and other parts of Europe. A period of political stability and growing prosperity gave rise to new industries based on the production and trade of fine cloth and other luxury goods. Although wool and linen remained the main fabrics of the time, luxury fabrics became increasingly popular. The weaving of silk, satin, and velvet expanded, and greater quantities of silks were imported from the East through Venice and other ports.

During the 1500s, new centers of cloth manufacturing and trade emerged in northern Europe. Knitting machines and other new manufacturing equipment, which had formerly been banned by the textile guilds*, began to appear. New technology also improved methods of weaving and dyeing cloth. In England, landowners increased wool production by turning farmland into sheep pasture—displacing farm populations in the process.

* **guild** association of craft and trade owners and workers that set standards for and represented the interests of its members

As fine fabrics became more popular, governments began passing laws to restrict their use. The main goal of these "sumptuary laws" was to limit the consumption of luxury goods. However, they also attempted to keep people from dressing above their social status. Specific guidelines explained which classes could wear particular kinds of garments and ornaments, right down to details of shape and style. Through sumptuary laws, authorities tried to maintain control in a world that increasingly defined itself by dress.

See color plate 4, vol. 2

Styles of Dress. Male and female clothing styles changed significantly during the Renaissance. In the Middle Ages, both men and women had worn long, loose-fitting garments called tunics. A sleeveless outer coat or cloak called a surcoat often topped the tunic. Beginning in the late 1300s, these simple styles gave way to more complex garments tailored to show off the shape of the body. Men and women of the upper classes became highly concerned with clothing and adornment.

During the Renaissance, men's garments became much shorter. Men abandoned the surcoat in favor of the pourpoint, a close-fitting jacket, worn with tight-fitting trousers, almost like stockings, called hose. Only the clergy and university scholars continued to wear the long garments of the Middle Ages. Men's clothing became a tool for projecting masculinity and power. Jackets were puffed or padded to broaden the shoulders, and pouches called codpieces encased the male organs. A fashionable man required the help of a servant each morning to tie up his points (the pieces of lace that held garments together), fasten his frilled shirt, and help with other aspects of dressing and grooming.

Renaissance nobles took pride in their appearance and usually wore the latest styles. This painting by Lucas Cranach the Elder shows three princesses dressed in the luxurious fabrics, fitted tops, and low necklines popular during the 1500s.

While men's garments became shorter, women's grew longer. The most common female garments were the gown and the surcoat. Both fitted tightly to the upper body, then extended into flowing skirts that swept along the ground. Gowns featured long, trailing sleeves. Women's fashions often provoked criticism from churchmen who considered them too revealing or luxurious. Sumptuary laws attempted to regulate every aspect of women's dress, from the number of jewels to the depth of necklines.

In the late 1500s, the upper classes throughout Europe began to copy the Spanish style of dress, which featured stiff outlines, dark colors, and narrow waistlines. Men wore tight jackets called doublets that exaggerated the slimness of the waist. Women adopted tight-fitting bodices* that pinched in their waists and compressed their breasts. They also draped their skirts over farthingales, elaborate garments that circled the lower part of a woman's body with a series of hoops. Women in these huge skirts required special high chairs in order to sit down. Both men and women wore high, stiff collars called ruffs, which were often so large that wearers could scarcely turn their heads.

* **bodice** upper part of a woman's dress

Military Styles

Renaissance dress borrowed many elements from the military. One example is the slashed, puffed sleeves that became fashionable in the 1500s. According to legend, this style was modeled on the tattered garments of Swiss soldiers returning from war. The soldiers had donned the clothes of their defeated opponents, but finding them too tight, they slashed the seams, causing the layer below to puff out. In the 1600s the general population also adopted the soldier's soft, broad-brimmed hat, wide collar, and rows of trouser buttons.

Accessories took on new importance for both men and women. Earrings, which had disappeared in the Middle Ages, became popular once again. Handkerchiefs, fans, and fancy gloves were also fashionable, and women used cosmetics. The English queen ELIZABETH I, in her attempts to project a youthful, virginal complexion, regularly applied half an inch of makeup to her face.

Among the lower classes, clothing was simple and varied little. Women wore skirts and aprons tucked up for work, topped by tight bodices and cloaks. Men wore buttoned jackets, short breeches, and wide-brimmed hats. Most clothing was made out of coarse wool or unbleached linen in a limited range of colors—black (in women's clothing), dull brown, and gray. Those who could afford extra frills dressed up these drab clothes with silver buttons or scarves of finer material. Not until the late 1600s did improvements in textile manufacturing offer the lower classes more choices of fabric and color.

Specialized Clothing. The Renaissance also affected the clothing styles of those in specific fields, such as the military, the clergy, and performers. Military dress began to change after the 1500s in response to changes in the nature of warfare. Battles tended to involve large numbers of foot soldiers, creating a need for uniforms to distinguish members of the same army. For example, English soldiers fighting under the duke of Norfolk in the mid-1500s wore blue suits with red trim. However, their clothes did not resemble the basic, practical garments of modern armies.

Many high-ranking clergy members yielded to the allure of splendid clothing. In one extreme case, a cardinal of the mid-1400s fell into debt buying floor-length, Turkish-style robes of rich crimson and green fabric and other garments of velvet, silk, and fur. In 1464 Pope Paul II issued laws to curb extravagant dressing by the clergy. The Italian monk Girolamo SAVONAROLA responded to these lavish displays by organizing "bonfires of vanities" to burn garments, ornaments, and other items he considered dangerous to the soul. The Protestant Reformation* had an important effect on clothing, as churchmen of the new faith adopted white gowns, plain white capes, and black scarves. Members of strict Protestant sects, such as Calvinists and Puritans, scorned any form of luxury or fashion in favor of plain black garments.

Festivals, processions, and other special events were plentiful during the Renaissance. New and creative types of clothing developed for such occasions, especially in the 1600s, when the masque* emerged as a form of court theater. Performers sported elaborate costumes adorned with tinsel, beads, sequins, tassels, bells, and lace. Masks were usually made of velvet and lavishly decorated. During the 1600s, the French court became particularly well known for the richness of the costumes worn at special events. (*See also* **Arms and Armor; Jewelry; Luxury.**)

* **Protestant Reformation** religious movement that began in the 1500s as a protest against certain practices of the Roman Catholic Church and eventually led to the establishment of a variety of Protestant churches

* **masque** dramatic entertainment performed by masked actors, or a ball or party at which all guests wear masks or costumes

Coins and Medals

During the Renaissance, many people collected coins and medals with portraits on them. For example, the poet PETRARCH collected antique Roman coins, and his interest influenced other intellectuals. Although coins were units of currency and medals served mostly as decorations, both were valued as works of art.

Coins. Renaissance coins were made from gold, silver, and various copper mixtures. In 1252 Florence, Italy, introduced a gold coin called the florin. The florin displayed a lily on one side and a portrait of John the Baptist, the city's patron saint, on the other. The florin, along with a Venetian coin called the ducat, dominated western European currency for most of the 1300s and 1400s. As a result, it influenced the design of coins throughout the continent.

From the mid-1450s through the 1500s, much of Europe returned to the ancient Roman practice of displaying portraits on coins. Displaying a ruler's portrait on a coin helped spread his or her fame. In some areas a coat of arms* appeared on the reverse side of the coin. In other places, such as Spain and Portugal, it took the place of the portrait.

* **coat of arms** set of symbols used to represent a noble family

Medals. Portrait medals were double-sided, palm-sized disks that displayed a person's image. The medals of the Renaissance were based on medallions and coins created in honor of ancient Roman emperors. However, they were available to anyone who could afford to commission them.

The basic design of a medal included a portrait of a man or woman on one side, surrounded by a Latin inscription of the subject's name and position. The other side of the medal showed a symbol of the subject's personality. Medals served to court distant brides and to celebrate building projects and patrons*. People collected them, traded them with friends, and wore them around their necks. They even buried medals in the foundations of buildings.

* **patron** supporter or financial sponsor of an artist or writer

Painter Antonio di Puccio PISANO, or PISANELLO, created the first portrait medals in the early 1400s. Some earlier objects resemble medals, but Pisanello established their standard form. The artist's first medal commemorated the visit of John VIII Palaeologus, ruler of the Byzantine Empire*, to the council of Ferrara-Florence in the 1430s. During the next 22 years, Pisanello created more than 26 medals for many important Italian clients.

* **Byzantine Empire** Eastern Christian Empire based in Constantinople (A.D. 476–1453)

During the 1400s, most medal designers cast their creations—that is, poured liquid metal into a mold created from a wax model. In the 1500s, metalworkers adopted the "striking" method, which involved hammering a hard metal mold against a softer (usually heated) metal to create an impression. They might also create medals by using the screw-press, invented by Benvenuto CELLINI. This large, screwlike machine pressed the mold against the softer metal. Although the striking and pressing methods allowed for greater detail and larger production than casting, they limited the depth and size of the portraits.

During the 1500s Milan, Italy, became a center for medal work. Italian artists produced medals for many of the leading courts of Europe,

and their work profoundly influenced the style of medals throughout the continent. Talented medal artists also appeared in Germany, France, the Netherlands, and England. (*See also* **Councils.**)

Columbus, Christopher

1451–1506
Italian explorer

* **exploitation** relationship in which one side benefits at the other's expense

Explorer Christopher Columbus set world history on a new course with a series of voyages across the Atlantic Ocean. Pioneering what he hoped would be a new sea route to Asia, Columbus instead reached some islands in the Caribbean Sea. His discovery led in due course to the European exploration, exploitation*, and settlement of the Americas.

Westward to the East. Born in the Italian republic of Genoa, Columbus had little schooling and went to sea at an early age. He did, however, read widely as an adult. In the mid-1470s Columbus joined a colony of Italian merchants living in Lisbon, then the center of Portuguese seafaring in the Atlantic. Sailing on Portuguese vessels, he traveled north to England and Ireland, south along the African coast, and west to the Canary Islands. These voyages taught him much about Atlantic winds and currents.

Columbus married a Portuguese noblewoman, with whom he had a son named Diego. The marriage improved Columbus's connections to the Portuguese court, where he hoped to find backing for an ambitious project—a voyage to Asia.

For centuries the spices, silks, and other goods from Asia had been prized in Europe. In the 1400s, however, European merchants found it almost impossible to travel overland to Asia. They could buy Asian goods from Muslim dealers in Mediterranean ports, but they sought a sea route that would allow them to buy these products directly at their source. In the 1480s the Portuguese were trying to find a passage to Asia around the southern tip of Africa. Columbus had a different idea. He became convinced that he could reach Asia, the easternmost part of the known world, by sailing west from Europe.

Columbus probably based his idea on several sources—rumors of islands in the distant Atlantic and his reading of works on geography, such as those by the ancient scholar Ptolemy. In addition, he knew that objects often drifted in from the western ocean, suggesting lands beyond the horizon. Like other well-read Europeans of his time, Columbus understood that the world was round. He reasoned that by sailing westward he would reach the other side of the world. But he underestimated the size of the earth. He believed that Japan lay only 2,400 sailing miles from the Canary Islands, when in fact it was 10,600 miles away. Neither Columbus nor anyone else in Europe suspected that two large continents stood in the way of a westward passage to Asia.

Unable to interest the Portuguese court in financing his voyage, Columbus went to Spain around 1485. The Spanish monarchs Ferdinand of Aragon and Isabella of Castile eventually agreed to sponsor him, in the hopes that a sea route would lead to trade with Asia and great riches. They promised Columbus titles, nobility, and the right to govern any lands he might discover.

When Christopher Columbus arrived in the New World, he called the people he encountered "Indians," believing that he had reached the East Indies islands in Asia. This etching shows Indians greeting Columbus with gifts.

The Voyages. In September of 1492 Columbus left the Canary Islands with three ships, sailing west into unknown waters. About five weeks later they reached an island that Columbus called San Salvador. This was probably the island in the Bahamas once know as Watlings and now called San Salvador. Here the explorer made an error with lasting consequences. Convinced that he had arrived in the Indies, as Europeans referred to southeastern Asia, he called the local people "Indians." After visiting several other islands, Columbus took seven Indians back to Spain with him as proof that he had reached a distant land.

Upon reaching Spain in March of 1493, Columbus assured Ferdinand and Isabella that the rich Asian mainland lay close to the islands he had discovered. Soon he left on a second, larger voyage, this time planting a colony on the island of Hispaniola. If the native people yielded peace-

Shipwrecked in the New World

Sea exploration was a perilous venture. Mariners risked drowning or being cast away on a distant shore. The largest ship on Christopher Columbus's first voyage, the *Santa Maria,* ran aground and wrecked, forcing Columbus to leave 39 men on Hispaniola. Returning a year later, he found that most had died fighting with the Indians. Columbus himself was shipwrecked on his fourth and final voyage when his last two ships became unseaworthy. He beached them on Jamaica, turned them into strongholds for himself and his crew, and spent a miserable year before he was rescued.

fully to Spanish authority, they would be protected. However, those who resisted could be enslaved according to European law. Because many Indians fought with the Spanish, Columbus felt justified in conquering and enslaving them. He then set sail for Cuba, leaving Hispaniola under the control of his brother Diego. During his absence, the colony fell into chaos. An investigator sent by the Spanish crown found that Indians and settlers alike had died in great numbers.

Meanwhile, Columbus explored the coast of Cuba, thinking it was part of the Asian mainland. To avoid disappointing his royal backers, he made his crew sign a document saying that they had reached Asia. However, they had failed to locate any known Asian cities. By the time Columbus returned to Spain, Ferdinand and Isabella had given up hope of any short-term profits from his ventures. Nonetheless, they let him make a third voyage.

In 1498 Columbus explored the coast of Venezuela, which he thought might be near the Garden of Eden described in the Bible. Further problems with the administration of Hispaniola, however, caused a royal investigator to send Columbus back to Spain in chains. Ferdinand and Isabella freed the explorer but stripped him of his right to govern the colony. In 1501 the Spanish crown began organizing a new system to govern its American colonies.

The following year Columbus set out on his fourth and final voyage, which he spent mostly exploring the coast of Central America. He returned to Spain in 1504, never again to visit the lands that other Europeans would call the New World. Unable to regain his titles and land grants, Columbus died wealthy but disappointed in Valladolid, Spain.

Myths and Realities. Although one of history's most famous figures, Columbus is the subject of many myths and misunderstandings. Some have portrayed Columbus as a hero who fought to convince others that the world was round, struggled against traditional religious views, and in the end died poor and alone. None of this is true. More recently, some historians have painted Columbus as a villain who set in motion the European destruction of the nature and cultures of the Americas.

In reality, Columbus was neither a hero nor a monster. He was, above all, a man of his time, shaped by the religious beliefs, customs, and laws of his age. He sought to enslave the native people of the Caribbean, especially those who practiced cannibalism, partly because slavery would allow them to be converted to Christianity. Far from being an example of the new scientific thinking of the Renaissance, Columbus followed well-established patterns of the time in his obsession with Asia and his devotion to Christianity.

Christopher Columbus was a complex person who embodied both the virtues and the vices of his age. Although he failed to find a sea route to Asia, his voyages profoundly shaped the modern world, with its global networks of trade and its many connections between different societies. (*See also* **Americas; Exploration.**)

Commedia dell'Arte

*** elite** privileged group; upper class

Commedia dell'arte is a term that came into use after the Renaissance to describe a type of theatrical entertainment that began in Italy in the mid-1500s. It was best known for its improvised, or unscripted, performances. The shows employed familiar characters and situations, often involving acrobatics and slapstick comedy.

The earliest written evidence of commedia dell'arte is a contract signed by eight men at Padua, Italy, in 1545. The signers agreed to travel together and earn money by performing comedies. By the 1560s, commedia dell'arte performers, or *comici,* were setting up stages in city squares and collecting money from passersby. At the same time, more prosperous and organized troupes appeared with popular leading ladies. These troupes, such as the Gelosi and the Accesi, performed before elite* audiences. In addition to improvising comedies, they also performed scripted pieces. In 1589 the Gelosi company performed at the wedding of a member of the MEDICI family. An account of the show describes the female star playing a scene as a madwoman, raving in Spanish, Greek, French, and Italian to mimic the characters played by her fellow actors. She also sang French songs in honor of the bride, who was French.

Commedia dell'arte performances were three acts long, shorter than the five acts that were customary for serious drama at the time. The plots changed constantly but usually revolved around a core of standard or stock characters. Actors often specialized in performing specific roles. For example, every company included female servants and a pair of young lovers who spoke in poetic language. Other important characters included a doctor, a wealthy and pompous gentleman named Pantalone (sometimes called Pantaloon), and clowns. These characters usually wore masks or other accessories on their faces. To accommodate the many minor parts, such as innkeepers, peasants, policemen, magicians, and gypsies, actors often played more than one character. Music and dance were also essential to commedia dell'arte. The *comici* sang, danced, and played instruments.

As acting was not a respected profession, the *comici* lived on the margins of society. Hungry for any material they could sell onstage, they often borrowed stories from other comedies. Common plots included conflicts within families and love affairs aided by clever servants, all ending happily in marriages and family reunions. Many educated writers looked down upon improvised comedies because the plots were often stolen and the material tended to be obscene. However, some literary playwrights learned from the *comici* how to enliven their plays with variety, physical action, and fuller roles for women.

In the late 1500s the *comici* began touring abroad. They went to France, Spain, England, and as far east as Poland. Commedia dell'arte was popular with French audiences, creating an image of Italian comedy that later influenced the style of the famous French actor and playwright Molière. By the late 1600s, however, commedia dell'arte had become somewhat mechanical and routine. A more realistic form of comedy replaced it for some time. Scholars rediscovered commedia dell'arte in the 1800s, and performers revived it in the 1900s. (*See also* **Humor; Italian Language and Literature; Popular Culture.**)

Communication

See *Transportation and Communication.*

Comuneros, Revolt of the

See *Revolts.*

Confraternities

* **laypeople** those who are not members of the clergy

During the Renaissance, the most important religious groups for laypeople* in the Roman Catholic Church were spiritual brotherhoods called confraternities. Members of these groups worshiped together, both privately and publicly, and performed acts of charity and service to the public. Between 10 and 20 percent of adults in European cities belonged to confraternities. This figure was even larger in rural areas and in northern parts of Europe.

* **penance** act performed to show sorrow or repentance for sin

* **artisan** skilled worker or craftsperson

Roles of Confraternities. The earliest confraternities arose during the 1200s as extensions of RELIGIOUS ORDERS. Members of these groups engaged in public acts of worship and penance*, as well as performing works of charity. They drew their members mainly from the ranks of artisans*, merchants, and professionals.

The smallest confraternities modeled themselves after the disciples of Jesus in the Bible. These groups had only a few dozen members and devoted themselves to private prayer and moral guidance. Larger groups, with several hundred members, engaged in more public activities. They wrote songs for religious services, led public processions, and performed acts of charity. Members of confraternities joined together based on their neighborhood, profession, or nationality.

Confraternities adopted many of the practices of religious orders such as the Franciscans. These included daily prayer, confession, and regular meetings for religious services. Many groups had their own priests who delivered sermons and performed sacred rituals. In some areas, these activities challenged local churches. In many parts of northern Europe, however, confraternities and churches worked together.

Confraternities performed a great deal of charitable work. They aided orphans and prisoners, helped to house and educate the poor, and cared for the sick and dying. Many towns and cities relied heavily on confraternities to provide these types of public services. The groups also developed extensive aid schemes for their own members. The dues they collected went into a fund to provide early forms of health insurance and pensions for families struck by sickness or death.

* **patronage** support or financial sponsorship

* **mystery play** early form of drama based on biblical stories

Another function of confraternities was patronage* of the arts and culture. They sponsored the creation of many early hymns and mystery plays* that laid the foundations for later, more complex forms of music and drama. At first, members called for works that they could perform themselves in private or in public. Later, the groups began hiring professional actors and musicians to perform for them. Confraternities also sponsored works of art and architecture.

* **Protestant Reformation** religious movement that began in the 1500s as a protest against certain practices of the Roman Catholic Church and eventually led to the establishment of a variety of Protestant churches

Confraternities and Reform. The Protestant Reformation* dealt a serious blow to confraternities in northern Europe and England. The groups' goal of helping Catholics achieve salvation though good works and religious rituals was at odds with the Protestant belief in salvation through faith alone. In many German cities, the government suppressed confraternities and took their assets. In England, however, many confraternities survived in a changed form. Some became parish councils, while others became the new local government in towns that had once been controlled by Catholic monasteries.

The Counter-Reformation, the Catholic Church's response to the Protestant challenge, also struck at the strength and independence of confraternities. The church sought to give bishops greater control over the actions of these groups. It also developed new confraternities to promote specific rituals. In addition, the church extended special privileges to certain confraternities in Rome, which came to be known as archconfraternities. These groups offered other confraternities the chance to share in their privileges by agreeing to follow their rules. In this way, the church gained greater control over many confraternities.

In many places, Catholic rulers took over confraternities. In other areas, wealthy citizens joined the groups and effectively gained control of many of their functions. Sponsoring religious activities and public works gave these individuals prestige and power in the community. It also provided them with an edge in dealing with religious and political leaders. By 1600 political and religious figures had stripped confraternities of much of their independence, making the groups tools to achieve their own goals. (*See also* **Catholic Reformation and Counter-Reformation; Christianity; Drama; Music; Patronage; Poverty and Charity; Protestant Reformation.**)

Constantinople, Fall of

* **Byzantine Empire** Eastern Christian empire based in Constantinople (A.D. 476–1453)

* **Mongol** member of a central Asian tribe that controlled much of Asia and eastern Europe during the Middle Ages

* **siege** prolonged effort to force a surrender by surrounding a fortress or town with armed troops, cutting the area off from aid

On May 29, 1453, Turkish invaders captured the city of Constantinople, capital of the Byzantine Empire*. The fall of the city was a significant turning point in history, marking the end of more than 1,000 years of Christian rule and the rise of the Islamic Ottoman Empire.

Named Byzantium by the ancient Greeks, Constantinople lay on the edge of the narrow waterway separating Europe and Asia Minor (present-day Turkey). Constantine the Great, the first Christian emperor of Rome, made the city his capital in the 300s. Renamed Constantinople in his honor, it became one of the greatest and most magnificent cities of the Middle Ages. After the western part of the Roman Empire collapsed, the city remained the capital of the eastern Byzantine Empire.

In the 1300s the Ottoman Turks emerged as a major power in eastern Europe. In 1394 the Ottoman sultan Bayezid I began an eight-year blockade of Constantinople. The blockade ended only after the Mongol* ruler Tamerlane defeated and captured the sultan. In 1422 another Ottoman sultan, Murad II, led an unsuccessful siege* of the city.

Determined to capture Constantinople, Murad's son, Mehmed II, raised an army of more than 100,000 men and a naval force of more

than 100 ships. By this time, the great Byzantine Empire had dwindled to a minor state. The emperor, Constantine XI, had fewer than 7,000 soldiers. Christian leaders in the West tried to send aid, but it arrived too late. Mehmed began a siege of Constantinople on April 6, 1453. The city held out for nearly two months, but on May 29 Mehmed launched a full-scale attack and captured Constantinople.

For several decades, Christians called for a new crusade to take Constantinople back from the Turks. But efforts to organize a crusade failed. Instead, the Ottomans continued on the offensive, seizing several territories in Greece and Italy. The fall of Constantinople ushered in a 250-year period during which the Ottomans threatened to overrun central Europe. (*See also* **Christianity; Greek Émigrés.**)

Constitutionalism

The term *constitution* first appeared during the 1700s in connection with the written constitutions of the United States and France. However, the idea of constitutionalism, a philosophy of government based on the rule of law, can be traced back to ancient Greece and the writings of ARISTOTLE. A constitutional government can be democratic or under the rule of a monarch, but everyone involved is bound by certain basic principles and procedures. This type of government stands in opposition to tyranny, in which a single person holds absolute power.

Historians have noted that tyrants were generally on the rise in Renaissance Italy. However, some Italian cities, including Florence and Venice, maintained constitutional regimes*. Florence had the Ordinances of Justice drawn up in the 1290s. The Ordinances barred the nobility from the city's ruling councils and established what was called a government of the people—although it did not really include all the people. Amended from time to time, the Ordinances served as a kind of constitution in Florence for about 300 years. Leonardo BRUNI, in his *Eulogy of Florence* (1405), praised the city's form of government. He called it a republic, using a term drawn from ancient Rome.

* **regime** government in power at a particular time

In 1434 the MEDICI family came to power in Florence. Although these rulers preserved the forms of the republic, some Florentines viewed them as tyrants. The people of Florence overthrew the Medici in 1494 and restored the republic. With a Grand Council of 1,500 citizens, the new republic gave more Florentines a voice in government than any previous regime. However, it lacked the military strength to fight off invading troops from Spain.

Niccolò MACHIAVELLI, a statesman and political thinker from Florence, analyzed the weakness of the city's constitution in his book *The Prince* (1513). Machiavelli believed that a lasting government could only be established through the actions of a powerful leader. Once founded, the state could develop a constitution. Several other Italian writers of the early 1500s devoted thought to the question of the ideal constitution. Their views helped shape the democratic political ideas that emerged in the United States and France in the 1700s.

The first hints of constitutionalism arose in France during a troubled period in the 1500s. The Protestant reformer John CALVIN observed that

people had a duty to obey their king, but that governing bodies also had a duty to resist kings who become tyrants. Political writer Jean BODIN disagreed, arguing that power must rest completely in the monarch. Some groups in France found justification for the monarchy in the Fundamental Laws, an unwritten constitution that had helped preserve the state through a series of wars with England in the 1300s and 1400s. The exact content of the Fundamental Laws was a matter of dispute, but most people agreed on one law: that the throne should always be passed down through male heirs.

The Netherlands developed a constitutional regime more or less by accident. Between 1568 and 1648, while seeking independence from Spain, the nation was ruled by a representative body called the States General. At first, its members opposed a republican form of government. They wanted to bring in a ruler from Germany, France, or England who would recognize the traditional privileges of the States General. However, when an acceptable ruler was not found, the Netherlands settled for a republican form of government in which the noble House of Orange played a leading role. (*See also* **Florence; France; Government, Forms of; Monarchy; Netherlands; Political Thought; Venice; Wars of Italy.**)

Conversos

The Spanish word *converso* originally referred to anyone who had converted to Christianity. By the late Middle Ages, the Spanish and Portuguese had begun using the term to identify Jews who had been baptized as Catholics—either willingly or by force. The term also applied to the descendants of the original converts, even those born as Christians several generations later. Some people also used the term *conversos* to refer to MORISCOS, forced converts from Islam.

* **Iberia** large peninsula in western Europe occupied by present-day Spain and Portugal

The roots of the *conversos* in Iberia* date from 1391, when riots broke out against Jews in the Spanish kingdoms of Castile and Aragon. The rioters accused Jews of hating Christianity and swindling Christians. Thousands of Jews died in the riots, and thousands more converted to Christianity to save their lives. Although the kings of Castile and Aragon opposed forced conversions, they demanded that *conversos* honor the sacred rite of baptism and remain loyal to the Christian faith.

* **anti-Semitic** referring to prejudice against Jews

Throughout the next century, anti-Semitic* attitudes and attacks created a mood of despair among Jews and prompted many to convert to Christianity. The temptation was perhaps greatest among wealthy Jews, since conversion opened doors to social and economic advancement. Many *conversos,* however, were true believers and supporters of their new faith. *Conversos* blended into Christian society, but they also developed their own social and cultural identity. They concentrated in certain neighborhoods and practiced traditional Jewish professions, such as banking and medicine. Most rabbis condemned *conversos,* but many practicing Jews maintained close contact with them through family ties and old friends. Jews also assisted many *conversos* in keeping Jewish customs and traditions, usually in secret.

In the mid-1400s, hostility arose toward *conversos,* especially in Castile. Christians accused them of secret loyalty to Judaism and of denying basic Christian beliefs. In the Castilian city of Toledo, many *conversos* were executed. Authorities there also passed a law denying *conversos* any official function or position of authority in the city. This was the first "purity of blood" law in Iberia. Similar laws soon became common in both Spain and Portugal. The laws barred people of both Jewish and Muslim origin from institutions such as city councils, religious and military orders, and universities.

* **Spanish Inquisition** court established by the Spanish monarchs that investigated Christians accused of straying from the official doctrine of the Roman Catholic Church, particularly during the period 1480–1530

The problems faced by *conversos* took a new turn when ISABELLA OF CASTILE and FERDINAND OF ARAGON established the Spanish Inquisition*. Trials held under the Inquisition supported the idea that *conversos* must be separated from Jews, who were blamed for keeping Jewish beliefs strong among the converted. Under pressure from the Inquisition, the Jews were expelled from southern Spain in 1483 and from the rest of the country in 1492. This order led to a new wave of conversions. Many Jews fled to Portugal, but in 1496 the king of Portugal expelled the Jews from that country as well. However, he changed his mind a few months later and instead ordered all Jews in Portugal to convert to Christianity.

* **theology** study of the nature of God and of religion

Among the *conversos* who remained in Spain and Portugal, certain Jewish beliefs and practices survived. For example, many *conversos* kept some Jewish holidays and rituals. Some learned Jewish prayers or refrained from eating pork and other foods banned by Jewish law. Over time, however, the religion of the *conversos* drifted farther and farther from its Jewish origins. *Conversos* blended various Christian symbols with Jewish beliefs, creating a unique theology*.

* **mystic** believer in the idea of a direct, personal union with the divine

Throughout the Renaissance, *conversos* trickled into Spanish and Portuguese communities in North Africa, the OTTOMAN EMPIRE, Italy, and Palestine. Some established communities of their own in Italian cities such as Venice, Pisa, and Ferrara. In the 1600s and 1700s, some *conversos* returned openly to Judaism and founded communities in western Europe and the Americas. Meanwhile, those *conversos* who remained in Iberia developed their own form of Christianity. Many prominent mystics* in Spain were *conversos.* (*See also* **Anti-Semitism; Jews; Teresa of Ávila.**)

Copernicus, Nicolaus

1473–1543
Polish astronomer

In the early 1500s, astronomer Nicolaus Copernicus challenged the ancient Greek model of the universe. This long-accepted view stated that Earth was at the center of the universe and the Sun and planets revolved around it. Copernicus developed a new system with the Sun at the center of the universe. Though not widely accepted during his time, Copernicus's new vision of the universe laid the foundations of modern astronomy.

Life and Scholarship. Born in Torun, Poland, Copernicus lost both his parents by age 12. His uncle, a priest who later became a bishop, cared for the boy and gave him an education. Copernicus attended a church school and later studied at the University of Cracow. Through

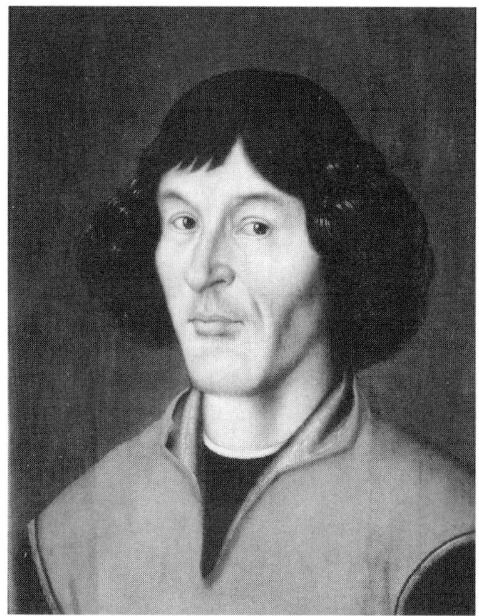

Renaissance astronomer Nicolaus Copernicus challenged the long-accepted theory that Earth stood at the center of the universe. Though his ideas met with little support during his time, modern scholars rely on his model for the solar system.

his uncle's influence, Copernicus gained a lifetime position at the cathedral of Frauenberg (present-day Frombork) in Poland. The administrators of the cathedral sent him to Italy to study church law. Copernicus also studied astronomy in Italy. His first recorded observation, in March 1497, was of the Moon passing in front of the star Aldebaran.

Between 1499 and 1501 Copernicus gave a few lectures on astronomy and mathematics in Rome, observing a lunar eclipse while he was there. He received his degree in church law in 1503 and also became a licensed physician. He then returned to Frauenberg, where he spent the rest of his life serving in his church and making important astronomical discoveries.

Though he is best known for his work in astronomy, Copernicus also contributed to several other fields of scholarship. In his position as a church administrator, he produced several works on money and the economy. He also standardized the weights and measures in his region. In 1509, he published a translation of a Greek literary work. Copernicus's knowledge of Greek enabled him to read a work by the ancient Greek astronomer PTOLEMY, which was not then available in Latin.

Astronomical Works. In 1513 Copernicus built a roofless tower for observing the sky and tracking the positions of the Sun, Moon, and stars. A year later he had written the first draft of *Little Commentary,* his first description of a theory that would revolutionize astronomy.

For nearly 2,000 years, scholars had based their view of the universe on the works of Ptolemy. According to Ptolemy, Earth stood in the center of the universe, and the Sun, Moon, and planets revolved around it in large circles. Ptolemy's model of the universe showed the Moon circling nearest Earth, followed by Mercury, Venus, the Sun, Mars, Jupiter, and Saturn.

Copernicus proposed a new model in which the Sun held the central position and the planets revolved around it. Earth occupied the fourth position from the center, where the Sun had been in Ptolemy's model. Copernicus stated outright that objects in the heavens do not revolve around Earth. They only appear to do so because Earth itself is moving, spinning once on its axis every day and revolving once around the Sun every year.

Copernicus was concerned about the consequences of creating a new model of the universe. One reason was that the Roman Catholic Church, of which he was a loyal member, strongly supported the Greek model. He pondered his findings for 26 years before making them available to the public. Finally, at the urging of several friends and colleagues, Copernicus allowed the young scholar Georg Rheticus to write a summary of his manuscripts. In 1540 Rheticus published his "First Report" of Copernicus's new system.

A full mathematical explanation of Copernicus's sun-centered system appeared in 1543. The six-part work, titled *On the Revolutions of the Heavenly Spheres,* did not raise controversy at first. Its editor added a preface by a theologian* who described the system as merely a tool for

* **theologian** person who studies religion and the nature of God

calculating the positions of heavenly bodies, rather than a factual view of the universe. Over time, however, the sun-centered view began to attract support from astronomers such as Galileo Galilei. In 1616 the Catholic Church placed *On the Revolutions of the Heavenly Spheres* on its list of forbidden books, where it remained until 1758.

Most scholars agree that Copernicus greatly simplified the study of the solar system. In order for Ptolemy's theory to fit their observations, astronomers had burdened the system with 55 special calculations and adjustments. Copernicus's system, while not perfect, reduced that number to 34. It also laid the groundwork for later scientists, such as Galileo and Johannes Kepler, to develop more useful theories of the universe. (*See also* **Astronomy; Index of Prohibited Books; Science.**)

Correggio

1489–1534
Italian painter

Antonio Allegri, known as Correggio after the town where he lived, was one of the most influential artists of his generation. His dramatic paintings of religious and mythical themes appeal powerfully to the senses. His style played a significant role in the development of Baroque* art.

* **Baroque** artistic style of the 1600s characterized by movement, drama, and grandness of scale

Little is known of Correggio's early life and career. However, his work reflects the styles that first developed in northern Italy in the late 1400s and the influence of such Italian Renaissance artists as Andrea Mantegna, Leonardo da Vinci, Raphael, and Michelangelo.

Art historians believe that Correggio spent some of his early career in the Italian city of Mantua, decorating church walls with frescoes*. Only two of Correggio's works from this period survive. Both are altarpieces* the artist created for churches in his hometown between 1514 and 1517. The delicate quality of the facial expressions in these pieces and the painter's careful use of color hint at the style of his later work.

* **fresco** mural painted on a plaster wall

* **altarpiece** work of art that decorates the altar of a church

Correggio moved to Parma, Italy, around 1518. One of his first projects in Parma was a series of frescoes for the monastery of San Paolo. The paintings in the private chamber of the abbess* are masterful illusions, transforming the space into a lifelike scene out of ancient mythology. He also painted frescoes in the church of San Giovanni Evangelista and the cathedral of Parma. These works focus on important events and figures in Christianity, such as the deaths of saints and the Virgin Mary's entry into heaven.

* **abbess** female head of an abbey or convent

Correggio spent more than a decade in Parma. His paintings from this period are vivid and dramatic. One hallmark of his style is the use of foreshortening, a technique that involves changing the body proportions of figures to make them appear as though they are projecting upward into space. Correggio's figures are often powerfully built, their gestures are bold, and their faces express great emotion. In *Adoration of the Shepherds,* an altarpiece he created for a church in Dresden, a servant turns away in awe from the glory of the infant Christ, while a donkey strains eagerly toward the holy child.

Around 1530 Correggio left Parma and returned to his hometown. His late works deal largely with mythical subjects, and they focus less on spiritual joy and more on physical pleasure. The masterpiece of these

years was a series of four paintings called the *Loves of Jupiter,* created for the duke of Mantua. Powerfully sexual, they mirror Correggio's earlier works in appealing directly to the senses. Correggio's emotional style, complex arrangement of objects, and vivid use of color all contributed to the Baroque style of the 1600s. (*See also* **Art in Italy.**)

Cortés, Hernán

1485–1547
Spanish conqueror

* **conquistador** military explorer and conqueror

Spanish conquistador* Hernán Cortés sought adventure, fame, and fortune in the Americas and found all three. He conquered the Aztec empire in Mexico, bringing vast expanses of territory in the New World under Spanish control. He also gained personal wealth and power. Acting like a businessman, Cortés financed trading ventures and established a sugar plantation in Mexico.

Born in Medellín, Spain, Cortés studied for a while at the University of Salamanca. In the early 1500s he joined a voyage to Santo Domingo, Spain's colony on the Caribbean island of Hispaniola. There he fought local Indians and was rewarded with land and Indian workers. In 1511 Cortés left Santo Domingo with Diego Velázquez to take part in a campaign to conquer Cuba. After seizing the island, Velázquez became its governor and named Cortés mayor of the new colony's capital. When Velázquez heard about the rich Aztec civilization of Mexico, he chose Cortés to lead an expedition to open trade with it. Cortés, however, wanted to conquer the Aztecs.

Cortés arrived in Mexico in 1519 with about 500 soldiers. In some provinces within the Aztec empire, he found Indian allies who helped in the long fight against the Aztecs. The Spanish had the advantage of metal weapons and horses, both unknown to the Aztecs, and they soon learned that killing an Aztec commander usually resulted in his army giving up the fight.

Cortés employed a variety of strategies in the conquest. He captured the Aztec ruler Montezuma and ruled through him for a time. He also built a fleet of small ships to control the lake that surrounded the Aztec capital of Tenochtitlán. In 1521 the Spanish destroyed Tenochtitlán, gaining control of all of central Mexico. Cortés was appointed governor of the colony of New Spain. He went back to Spain in 1540 and never returned to the lands he had conquered. (*See also* **Americas; Exploration; Spain.**)

Councils

Over the course of the Renaissance, the Roman Catholic Church held several councils. At these meetings, church leaders gathered together to discuss issues and resolve disputes within the church. Since the Middle Ages, some people had argued that these councils should be the supreme authority of the church, superior even to the pope. This belief, called conciliarism, rose and fell over the course of the Renaissance. Some councils held during the Renaissance challenged the authority of the pope, while others supported it.

The Question of Authority. In 1378 the election of competing popes in France and Italy caused a split within the Catholic Church. A council called in Pisa in 1409 deposed* both sitting popes but confused matters by electing a third pope. With three popes claiming power, another council was called five years later in Constance. This meeting, which lasted four years, accepted the resignation of one pope and deposed the other two. It then elected a new pope, Martin V.

* **depose** to remove from high office, often by force

To prevent a similar problem from arising again, the members of the council tried to establish councils as a permanent church institution. They demanded that the pope hold future councils at regular periods. Martin V honored the council's wishes, but he made it clear that he did not consider himself bound by them. He declared that the council had authority only during the split within the church, and that now that the split had ended, the pope once again held supreme power.

Supporters of conciliarism challenged this idea at the Council of Basel (1431–1449). In 1438 the pope attempted to move this council from Basel to the Italian city of Ferrara. Some of the council members made the move, but the majority stayed behind and took action against the pope. First the council declared that it was superior to the pope, that the pope could not dissolve or move the council, and that denying these beliefs was heresy*. Then it deposed the pope and elected a new one.

* **heresy** belief that is contrary to the doctrine of an established church

Most Catholics did not respect the council's decision. The ruling pope remained in power, and conciliarism lost much of its influence. In fact, papal* authority grew even stronger after the Council of Trent, which met three times between 1545 and 1563. This council declared the pope responsible for enacting all the reforms it ordered.

* **papal** referring to the office and authority of the pope

Other Issues. Papal authority was only one of many issues raised by church councils during the Renaissance. One longstanding goal of the councils was to reunite the Roman Catholic Church with the Orthodox Church, which had split off from it many centuries earlier. This issue became the focus of the Council of Florence (1438–1445). This council was the same group that had originally met in Ferrara after breaking away from the council of Basel. At Florence, Catholic and Orthodox church leaders came to agreement on certain aspects of theology* about which the churches had long disagreed. Several branches of the Orthodox Church agreed to reunite with the Catholic Church. However, many Orthodox Church leaders later rejected this decision, and the churches remained separate.

* **theology** study of the nature of God and of religion

Other councils focused on responding to the threats the Catholic Church faced from Protestants and from Muslims. The Council of Constance (1414–1418), for example, condemned the teachings of the English religious reformer John Wycliffe and his followers. Two of these followers were sentenced to death and burned at the stake for their beliefs. The Fifth Lateran Council (1512–1517) and the Council of Trent both called for crusades to recapture the Holy Land from Muslim forces. The Council of Florence pledged to aid the Byzantine Empire* against Turkish invaders, but the papacy proved unable to provide effective assistance.

* **Byzantine Empire** Eastern Christian Empire based in Constantinople (A.D. 476–1453)

Many councils also focused on internal church reform, especially after the Protestant Reformation*. The Council of Trent, in particular, attempted to reform church offices. For instance, the council limited bishops to holding one office at a time and required them to live in their dioceses*. The council also worked to improve the training of priests. (*See also* **Catholic Reformation and Counter-Reformation; Christianity; Popes and Papacy; Protestant Reformation; Trent, Council of.**)

* **Protestant Reformation** religious movement that began in the 1500s as a protest against certain practices of the Roman Catholic Church and eventually led to the establishment of a variety of Protestant churches

* **diocese** geographical area under the authority of a bishop

Counter-Reformation

See *Catholic Reformation and Counter-Reformation.*

Every Renaissance ruler maintained a court. More than just an established residence, the court provided a visible symbol of the ruler's power and splendor. A court was a world within the larger society, governed by its own ceremonies and rules of etiquette, where everyone from the ruler to the servants sought to advance his or her own interests. As settings for the display of wealth and culture, courts were among the most important and colorful centers of Renaissance life.

The court was also a part of the government. The prince might use his courtiers to express his wishes to members of the administration, and courtiers could also bring advice from government leaders to the prince. Some members of the court also served in the administration, making the distinction between court and government unclear.

The Structure of the Court. At the center of each court was a ruler, such as a king, queen, pope, emperor, duke, or duchess. This central figure was commonly identified as a *prince.* Surrounding the prince was a vast assortment of other individuals, including family members, servants, advisers, government ministers, nobles, artists, writers, entertainers such as jesters and dwarfs, and others seeking patronage*. Members of the court constantly struggled to gain the prince's favor and increase their influence. Many courtiers were female, and the court was one of few places in Renaissance society where women had a real influence in government and politics.

* **patronage** support or financial sponsorship

The inner circle of the court consisted of the prince's household—a group of officials, headed by a chamberlain, who tended to the ruler's personal needs. Within the household, the prince could enjoy protection and some degree of privacy. In many cases the consort, or spouse, of the prince maintained a separate household. The extended court formed a much larger group, containing all the councillors and officials under the ruler's direct supervision. This larger court formed the setting for the prince's contact with government officials, citizens, and visiting princes or their representatives. A steward or majordomo saw to the management of the extended court.

Renaissance Courts. During the Renaissance, courts grew more elab-

The courts of the Renaissance served to display the power and splendor of their rulers. This painting by artist Andrea Mantegna, dating from the late 1400s, shows the court of Ludovico Gonzaga, who ruled the Italian city-state of Mantua.

orate. In several countries new dynasties, such as the Tudor royal family in England, came to power. These new rulers created splendid courts to draw attention away from their origins. The rise of diplomacy* also contributed to the growth of courts. Princes treated visiting rulers and their agents to magnificent spectacles that underlined the host's power and wealth. Occasions such as the arrival of a visiting prince or a bride for the ruler became lavish ceremonies that brought together artists, architects, musicians, actors, courtiers, and the entire population (as viewers) in a celebration of the state or ruling dynasty. Such spectacles dazzled the common folk and allowed the prince to dictate the behavior of the nobles—an important means of control at a time when central authority was still weak.

* **diplomacy** formal relations between nations or states

The most splendid court of the mid-1400s was that of the duke of BURGUNDY. Because the duchy* was a scattered patchwork of lands, the court provided a way to bind together groups of unrelated nobles. Elaborate ceremonies ruled every aspect of court life. By 1474 more than 1,000 officeholders, most of whom had their own servants, lived at court at the duke's expense. An English writer compared this glorious setting to the court of the legendary King Arthur.

* **duchy** territory ruled by a duke or duchess

The most magnificent court in Italy was that of the pope, followed by those of Milan and Naples. Italian courts became centers of artistic patronage, helping many artists gain status and freedom from the control of craft guilds*. Humanist* scholars also found places at court as teachers to young princes and their companions. The small but elegant court of the dukes of URBINO holds a lasting place in history as the subject of Baldassare CASTIGLIONE's *Book of the Courtier,* published in 1528. This book outlined the ideal of courtliness, which included good manners, high morals, and a fine intellect.

* **guild** association of craft and trade owners and workers that set standards for and represented the interests of its members

* **humanist** referring to a Renaissance cultural movement promoting the study of the humanities (the languages, literature, and history of ancient Greece and Rome) as a guide to living

Court Life. A complex set of rules, called protocol, governed life at court. They not only dictated the proper behavior for courtiers, but also

emphasized differences in rank. For example, most people were required to stand in the presence of the prince. Being allowed to sit was a sign of high favor, jealously observed by others. Throughout Europe, courts set standards for manners. Nobles sent their sons to court as pages* to learn the rules of behavior that set courtiers apart from the rest of society.

* **page** boy or young man who served as an attendant to a noble

Courtiers spent most of their time trying to advance their position with the prince. Every detail of court life had meaning for them. The setting of a guest's reception, the location and quality of assigned lodgings, the seating at banquets—all served as signs of the prince's favor or disfavor. Princes made a point of limiting their personal contact with others to make their favors seem more significant. A private interview in the prince's bedroom or study was the greatest honor.

Maintaining a court was tremendously expensive. Princes constantly tried to hold down their expenses and reduce the number of courtiers entitled to free meals. Many nobles, under pressure to put on grand displays to catch and hold the prince's favor, fell deeply into debt. Low-ranking courtiers endured shared rooms, bad food, and the insults of others in return for the chance to advance. The English courtier Sir Walter Raleigh expressed his disgust with the struggle of court life in his poem "The Lie": "Say to the court it glows and shines like rotten wood." Although Renaissance courts dazzled and delighted with their splendor, they also corrupted many with the lure of power. (*See also* **Monarchy; Patronage; Princes and Princedoms.**)

Crafts

See *Decorative Arts.*

Cranach, Lucas

1472–1553
German painter

See color plate 12, vol. 1

Lucas Cranach, known as "the Elder," was a painter and illustrator who dominated the art of northern and eastern Germany during the first half of the 1500s. He produced more portraits than any other painter in Renaissance Germany. He also introduced an expressive style of painting that influenced many other artists.

Born Lucas Maler in Kronach, Germany, Cranach changed his name to resemble that of his birthplace. There is little information about his life in Kronach, except that the work of German artist Albrecht DÜRER influenced him. In 1502 Cranach moved to Vienna, where he joined a humanist* group led by the poet Conrad CELTIS. He created emotional religious paintings in which he used contrasting colors to set off agitated figures and landscapes. These works of Cranach, especially the way he represented nature, influenced other artists of the time. He later created nonreligious works in which outlines of nudes were displayed against a dark background.

* **humanist** referring to a Renaissance cultural movement promoting the study of the humanities (the languages, literature, and history of ancient Greece and Rome) as a guide to living

In 1505 Cranach moved to Wittenberg, Germany, where he painted for the royal court of SAXONY. For nearly 50 years he created portraits for three successive Saxon rulers. In addition, Cranach was associated with Martin LUTHER and the Protestant Reformation*, working on religious

* **Protestant Reformation** religious movement that began in the 1500s as a protest against certain practices of the Roman Catholic Church and eventually led to the establishment of a variety of Protestant churches

pamphlets and Bible translations. His portraits of Protestant reformers projected their cause far beyond Wittenberg. However, he also accepted commissions from Catholic patrons*. (*See also* **Art in Germany; Bible; Protestant Reformation.**)

* **patron** supporter or financial sponsor of an artist or writer

Cranmer, Thomas

1489–1556
Archbishop of Canterbury

Thomas Cranmer served as Archbishop of Canterbury, the highest church official in England, during the reign of HENRY VIII. In this position, he presided over the nation's break with the Roman Catholic Church and the formation of the new Anglican* Church.

* **Anglican** referring to the Church of England

Cranmer began his career teaching religious studies in Cambridge, England. In 1520 he became a priest, and soon afterward he received an appointment as part of a diplomatic mission to Spain. On his return to England, he met Henry VIII, who invited him to join a team of religious scholars working to obtain an annulment* of the king's marriage to CATHERINE OF ARAGON. Henry wanted to end the marriage so that he could remarry, but the pope had denied his request. Cranmer and the other scholars developed an argument to justify it.

* **annulment** formal declaration that a marriage is legally invalid

Cranmer strongly favored reforms within the Catholic Church, such as allowing priests to marry. He showed his support for this idea by taking a wife in 1532, but a year later he had to hide his unlawful marriage when he was unexpectedly named Archbishop of Canterbury. Soon after that, King Henry decided to break away from the Roman Catholic Church. He established a new Church of England with Cranmer as the top religious official. In that role, Cranmer worked closely with the king's minister, Thomas CROMWELL, to build the Anglican Church on new lines, moving it farther from Catholic views. He drew up the document called the Forty-Two Articles of Faith, which laid out the beliefs of the Church of England. (The church later reduced his list to 39.) Many of Cranmer's theological* views were close to those of the Lutheran Church, particularly those relating to the ritual of communion.

* **theological** relating to theology, the study of the nature of God and of religion

Cranmer also promoted translations of the Bible and other sacred works into English. He created a version of the prayer service in English, much of which still survives in the modern Book of Common Prayer. He also produced two English prayer books. Cranmer's writings included many words borrowed from Greek and Latin, which had a lasting impact not only on the church service but also on the English language itself.

In 1553 Cranmer cooperated with an unsuccessful plot to place Jane GREY on the throne. The new queen, MARY I, returned the nation to Catholicism. Her government arrested Cranmer and convicted him of treason and heresy*. In prison he signed a series of statements denying his Protestant beliefs, but he was still condemned to burn at the stake. At the ceremony before his execution, he rejected the statements he had signed in prison and restated his Protestant faith. (*See also* **Bible; Christianity; England; Protestant Reformation.**)

* **heresy** belief that is contrary to the doctrine of an established church

Crime and Punishment

Ideas about what was a crime and how crimes should be punished changed considerably during the Renaissance. As many countries adopted ancient Roman legal codes, the task of defining crime shifted from the community and the church to the monarch. Roman law also provided new methods for investigating crimes. Those found guilty faced punishments ranging from fines to execution.

Defining Crime. During the Middle Ages, each community had its own set of legal standards. The definition of a crime depended on local standards of behavior. The only exceptions were crimes of morality, or sins, which depended on the laws of the church. However, in the late Middle Ages, these standards began to change. First Italy, then most other parts of western Europe, adopted some aspects of ancient Roman law, which gave the monarch the power to outlaw acts. Therefore, during the Renaissance, the state had complete authority to define crimes, even crimes of morality.

The justice system divided unlawful acts into two categories: crimes against people and crimes against property. Crimes against people, the more common type, ranged from verbal insults to rape and murder. Insults were considered a form of violence in a society where words often led to blows. Acts of violence almost always involved some kind of weapon. Most men who were not members of the clergy carried a weapon, if only a heavy stick. The law treated crimes of violence as more serious if they led to a flare-up in a vendetta, an ongoing feud between families. Crimes against monarchs, such as attempted assassinations, carried the most severe punishments of all.

Crimes against property, though less common than those against people, increased during the 1500s. The most common property crime was theft, which ranged from stealing a loaf of bread at a market to failing to repay a debt. The crime of highway robbery posed a special problem in the countryside because, unlike theft in the city, it always involved the use of deadly weapons. Roving gangs of brigands, or bandits, presented an even more serious threat. The size and number of these lawless bands required special armed forces to hunt them down, at considerable cost. Another type of property crime involved hunting, fishing, or grazing sheep on another person's property—or the state's property—without a permit.

Trying Crime. Two different methods of trying crime existed side by side during the Renaissance. The accusatorial method, a carryover from the Middle Ages, gradually gave way to the newer inquisitorial method, based on Roman law. In the accusatorial procedure, the plaintiff—the person who brought a charge to court—had to investigate and prove the case against the accused. A plaintiff who failed to prove the case had to suffer the same punishment the accused would have received if convicted. In addition, the unsuccessful plaintiff had to pay court costs. This form of prosecution gave little power to judges.

Italian towns first adopted the inquisitorial method in the 1100s. By 1500, it had spread to most of western Europe. In this method, government-appointed judges investigated the case, attempting to sort out the truth. The quality of judges varied throughout Europe. In England, Germany, and some parts of Italy, many judges had no legal training. France and other areas of Italy, by contrast, placed trained legal experts on the bench.

A person accused of a crime had either to pay bail—which most people could not afford—or to await trial in jail. By law, prisoners had to pay for their own upkeep in jail, but most could not afford this either. As a result, the government had to support the prisoners, and it often underfed them to save money. Suspected criminals were frequently tortured to obtain confessions and reduce the amount of time they spent in jail. A confession was usually the only evidence the system could produce against an accused person.

If people accused of a crime could not provide bail money, they had to await their trial in jail. Conditions in Renaissance jails were poor, food was scarce, and often the accused would be tortured to obtain confessions.

Punishing Crime. Renaissance societies had a variety of possible punishments for crime. Although penalties depended largely on the nature of the crime, several other factors played a role. The law dealt differently with commoners and nobles, foreigners and natives, men and women. The status of both criminal and victim influenced the level of punishment. For instance, crimes against royalty resulted in more severe punishment than similar crimes against other people. By contrast, crimes committed by royalty and other members of the aristocracy* often went unpunished.

* **aristocracy** privileged upper classes of society; nobles or the nobility

The typical punishment for a minor violation was a fine. For insults that led to violence, the law laid out a carefully calculated scale of fines, based on how much damage the insult had caused. However, the law seldom imposed fines on poor people. Instead, it imposed penalties such as confinement—requiring a person to remain within a specific area in the state for a fixed period of time. In the 1500s, the town of Florence relied heavily on confinement as a punishment for both rich and poor. This form of punishment affected people of different classes more equally than fines, which imposed a much heavier burden on the poor.

Exile and imprisonment were penalties for serious crimes, such as a violent crime within the family. The state reserved execution for the most dangerous criminals, such as murderers, brigands, and career criminals. Those involved in an attack on the monarch also might face execution. (*See also* **Law; Piracy; Social Status; Sports.**)

Croatia and Dalmatia

Located on the Adriatic Sea across from Italy, Croatia has come under the control of many foreign powers in the course of its history. During the Renaissance, the powerful republic of VENICE ruled the southern region of Croatia known as Dalmatia. Venice had a profound influence on Croatian culture, especially in the cities of Split, Zadar, and DUBROVNIK. It also played an important role in the formation of Croatian humanism*.

* **humanism** Renaissance cultural movement promoting the study of the humanities (the languages, literature, and history of ancient Greece and Rome) as a guide to living

Italian Influence. Venice affected the development of Croatian humanism in a number of ways, such as the influence of Venetian rule

on the Dalmatian nobility and the literary connections between Venice and Dalmatia. But the most important factor was Italian education. The Croatians who studied in Italy brought back to their homeland both their knowledge of and passion for humanist ideas.

After studying in the Venetian city of Padua, Juraj Sizgoric wrote the first book of Croatian poems to be printed (1477). Ivan Cesmicki studied church law in Italy and spent much of his life at the court of king Matthias Corvinus of Hungary. Cesmicki is best known for his short witty poems. Another important poet, Marko Marulic, also studied in Padua. When he returned home to Split, he assembled a large group of Dalmatian humanists. They had all been educated by Italian teachers and remained in contact with Italy and its humanistic movement.

Major Italian writers such as Dante and PETRARCH had a significant impact on Dalmatian writers, both in style and literary themes. The works of Petrarch were first introduced to Dalmatia in the 1380s. Some of his Dalmatian admirers wrote most of their own poetry in Italian. Others translated Petrarch's works into Croatian. The influence of Petrarch can be seen in the works of Marin Drzic, who wrote comedies.

Dalmatian humanists preferred to write in Latin to make themselves more "European." They often used Latin when dealing with historical matters. One important author was Vinko Pribojevic, whose history of the Slavs was published in Venice in 1532. Although many Dalmatian humanists wrote in Latin, some also worked in the vernacular* of Croatia. Because many works from Dalmatia were published in Venice, Venetians played an important role in discovering the works of Dalmatian humanists.

* **vernacular** native language or dialect of a region or country

Croatian Patriotism. Although Dalmatian humanists owed a great debt to Italy, they also developed their own Croatian style of expression. Many showed their patriotic pride by adding the name of their birthplace to their Latin names to identify their origin. In addition, their works portray the background and tradition of their native lands. For example, in his epic* *Judith* (1521), poet Marko Marulic refers to medieval* Croatian literature and Dalmatian folk poetry. Marulic combines Latin literary forms in the tradition of ancient Rome with images inspired by the sea breezes and storms of his native Split. Many other poets also depicted the Dalmatian landscape in their work, including Petar Zoranic, whose work *Mountains* (1569) was the first Croatian novel.

* **epic** long poem about the adventures of a hero

* **medieval** referring to the Middle Ages, a period that began around A.D. 400 and ended around 1400 in Italy and 1500 in the rest of Europe

Croatians believed that they were part of a wider group of Slavic peoples. They felt a common bond with Czechs, Poles, Russians, and other Slavs. *On the Origins of the Slavs and the Events Among Them* (1532), by Vinko Pribojevic, was the first work to express an overall sense of Slavic unity and identity. At times, Croatian patriotism took the form of criticism directed at Venice and its policies. In *Slavic Fairy,* the author Juraj Barakovic expresses sorrow and regret over the changes that occurred in the town of Zadar after its takeover by the Venetians.

Art in Croatia and Dalmatia. During the Renaissance, Croatian

lands were divided between Venice (Dalmatia, Istria, and Kvarner) and Hungary and Austria (northern Istria, Croatia, and Slavonia). Only the Republic of Dubrovnik remained free and independent. The historic division between northern and southern Croatia was reflected in the contrasting cultural heritage of the two regions. Works of Renaissance style were produced in Dalmatia, but the Turks occupied the region of Slavonia and constantly threatened to invade the rest of northern Croatia. While both religious and secular* architecture flourished in southern Croatia, military architecture dominated in the northwestern regions.

* **secular** nonreligious; connected with everyday life

The greatest achievements in art and architecture in southern Croatia occurred in the 1400s and 1500s. This region, which included Dubrovnik, chose freely between various artistic models—such as the styles of Florence and Venice—and combined them in creative ways with the ancient heritage of Dalmatia. The early Renaissance appeared in southern Croatia before the mid-1400s. Renaissance-style palaces and houses, churches, bell towers, and city halls were added to cities of the Adriatic coast and islands. New walls with rounded towers and strongholds went up around many cities, including Dubrovnik, where the impressive walls and towers still remain.

Most of the monuments of the 1400s and 1500s in Croatia are in Renaissance style. Yet several architectural works of that period stand out because of their originality and their contribution to the European Renaissance. For example, the Sibenik Cathedral, designed in the 1440s by Juraj Dalmatinac, marks the first appearance of the early Renaissance in Dalmatian architecture and sculpture. Constructed entirely of stone, without the use of mortar*, the cathedral incorporated large tiles, pilasters*, sculptural elements, and other features that reflect early Renaissance style.

* **mortar** bonding agent between bricks or stones

* **pilaster** ornamental column or pillar set partially into a wall

Another significant monument, the Trogir Chapel by Nikola Firentinac (1468), uses the forms of early Renaissance style typical of Florence. However, its stonework and the harmony of architecture and sculpture reflect Dalmatian tradition. The third great building of the period is Sorkocevicev's summer palace (1521) in Dubrovnik. Its unique organization of interior space reflects both Renaissance and Dalmatian styles. A number of monuments in Croatia also provide outstanding examples of Renaissance art of the 1500s. Among these are the facade* of Hvar Cathedral, St. Mary's Church in Zadar, and various villas in Dubrovnik and Hvar.

* **facade** front of a building; outward appearance

While many Croatian artists worked in their native land, many also went to Italy (where they were identified as *Schiavoni,* or Slavs) and created masterpieces there. Among the most notable of these are the architects Juraj Dalmatinac and Luciano Laurana, the sculptor Giovanni Dalmata (Duknovic), and the painter Andrea Meldolla (Medulic). Among the painters who remained in Croatia, one of the most significant was Nikola Bozidarevic in Dubrovnik. (*See also* **Architecture; Art; Humanism; Literature; Palaces and Townhouses; Poetry.**)

Cromwell, Thomas

ca. 1485–1540
Chief minister to English king

Thomas Cromwell, faithful adviser to Henry VIII, played a significant role in the development of modern England. His policies on religion, relations with foreign powers, and government organization strengthened the king's authority. Cromwell's most far-reaching action involved the restructuring of the English church.

Born into a working-class family in London, Cromwell left England at an early age to fight in Italy. Upon his return home, he practiced law and came in contact with friends of the statesman Thomas More. Around 1514 Cromwell entered the service of Cardinal Thomas Wolsey. He handled most of Wolsey's legal affairs and supervised the closing of several monasteries. Funds from the sale of monastery lands helped found a grammar school and a college that later became part of Oxford University.

In 1529 Cromwell entered Parliament. While there, he attracted the attention of Henry VIII and soon became an adviser to the crown. Over the next three years, Cromwell played a leading role in arranging the king's break with the pope and the Catholic Church. He wrote some crucial legislation, such as the Act in Restraint of Appeals (1533), which declared England an empire, free to do as it wished in both church and secular* matters. Over time Cromwell accumulated official positions, which allowed him to centralize some government functions. He also took an interest in social and economic reform.

* **secular** nonreligious; connected with everyday life

Cromwell made his greatest mark on the English church, which he reorganized beginning with the creation of the Act of Supremacy in 1534. This act named Henry VIII head of the Church of England. Cromwell oversaw the king's religious affairs and strictly enforced the new royal supremacy over the church. Cromwell generally encouraged religious reform—most notably through an English translation of the Bible—and worked closely with Archbishop Thomas Cranmer, who shared common goals.

Cromwell's relationship with the king soured in the late 1530s with his eagerness to forge an alliance between England and a German Protestant prince. Cromwell arranged a marriage for Henry and the prince's sister, Anne of Cleves. However, Henry found Anne unpleasant and unattractive. In addition, England's alliance with the Protestant prince was likely to increase its isolation from European powers.

Archbishop Cranmer annulled* the marriage, but Cromwell's mistake gave his enemies ammunition against him. They convinced Henry that Cromwell was a traitor, leading to Cromwell's arrest in 1540. He was stripped of his offices and executed without a trial. Henry VIII quickly regretted his loss, mourning Cromwell as "the most faithful servant" he had ever had. (*See also* **England; Popes and Papacy; Protestant Reformation.**)

Index

Note: Volume numbers precede each page number, separated by a colon. Page numbers in boldface type refer to main discussions of a topic.

C

F

G

H

M

T

W

X

Y

Z